Also by Melissa Fay Greene

Praying for Sheetrock

The Temple Bombing

Last Man Out

*There Is No Me Without You: One Woman's Odyssey
to Rescue Her Country's Children*

NO
BIKING
IN THE
HOUSE
WITHOUT A HELMET

NO
BIKING
IN THE
HOUSE
WITHOUT A HELMET

Melissa Fay Greene

Sarah Crichton Books
Farrar, Straus and Giroux   New York

SARAH CRICHTON BOOKS
Farrar, Straus and Giroux
18 West 18th Street, New York 10011

Copyright © 2011 by Melissa Fay Greene
All rights reserved
Distributed in Canada by D&M Publishers, Inc.
Printed in the United States of America
First edition, 2011

Library of Congress Control Number: 2011922709
ISBN: 978-0-374-22306-9

Designed by Abby Kagan

www.fsgbooks.com

1   3   5   7   9   10   8   6   4   2

To David Black,
Melissa Glass,
and Mitchell Black

Contents

Introduction: Still Here, After All These Years   3

1. Room for One More?   13
2. Nine Hundred and Eighty Thousand Websites   19
3. Foreign Film Festival   24
4. Motherhood vs. the Career   29
5. Chrissy   35
6. First Trip to Bulgaria   39
7. Just a Weekend Getaway   46
8. The Decision   53
9. Return to Bulgaria   60
10. Post-Adoption Panic   66
11. Love at Second Sight   72
12. The Art of Playing   78
13. Crash and Burn   83
14. Monkey *icka* Lion   90
15. *Sing, Goddess . . .*   95
16. Enormous Families, Group Homes   99
17. Dogs We Have Loved   105
18. The ABCs of Preliteracy   111
19. A Continent of Orphans   117

Contents

20. First Trip to Ethiopia   122
21. Old Friends   131
22. Helen in America   137
23. Questions of Heaven   144
24. Why This Is Not a Cookbook   151
25. Married to the Defense   156
26. A Boy Moves Out, a New Boy Heads Our Way   163
27. Meeting Fisseha   168
28. Searching for Grandmother   173
29. Tsehai   178
30. The Labyrinth of Nightmare   185
31. The Professor Gives Birth   188
32. The Young Hunter-Gatherer   192
33. Identity   197
34. Sandlot Ball   203
35. Squirrels We Have Known, Also Insects   209
36. A Wonderful Number of Children   215
37. An Orphanage League   225
38. Room for Two More?   233
39. Their Histories   241
40. Homeland Tour   246
41. Class Differences   252
42. Swim Party   257
43. Reunion   261
44. A Family Feast   265
45. Daniel and Yosef in America   273
46. Strife   280
47. Fighting Words   284
48. A Haunted Night   289
49. The Silent Treatment   293
50. Everything You Always Wanted to Know About Sex, but Couldn't Spell   304
51. Songs of a Summer Night   312
52. Another Mother   320
53. The Jewish Guide to Raising Star Athletes   324
54. Gurage   333
55. Ten Things I Love About You   341
56. DNA   347
    Acknowledgments   353

NO
BIKING
IN THE
HOUSE
WITHOUT A HELMET

Introduction: Still Here, After All These Years

This is my twenty-first year in elementary school. For twenty-one consecutive years I have carried in cupcakes, enclosed checks, and provided emergency phone numbers. I have staple-gunned and hot-glued. I have rented band instruments. I have given standing ovations, volunteered at the school library, and stood in the cafeteria line as the servers dropped balls of Thanksgiving-flavored foods from ice-cream scoops onto my wet tray. My husband and I have clapped with pride at a child's graduation in May and returned in August with a different child for registration day in the "cafetorium." Where else can you find a deal like a PTA membership? For five dollars, you're in, and urged to accept the presidency. Where else are adults so thrilled to see your children? "Did you have a great summer!?" cry the beaming teachers, and your child shyly leans into your side and confesses that yes, it was a great one.

The friends with whom we raised our oldest three (now in their twenties) are enjoying their empty-nest years. They have warm memories of long-ago kindergartners dressed as puppies, swinging their arms and dancing onstage in winter musicals. They recall the night the fourth-grade band attacked "Au Clair de La Lune" with shiny cheap instruments for the first time, honking and bleating like a pen of panicked farm animals. They remember the gift-wrap sale and the Fun Run. For them, as for most of our generation (we're in our fifties), it happened a long time ago.

My husband, Don Samuel—a gray-bearded criminal defense attorney—and I have lingered here longer than most. We pushed beyond our biologically reproductive years into adoption. To our children by birth—Molly, Seth, Lee, and Lily (born in 1981, '84, '88, and '92)—we added five school-age children, four from Ethiopia and one from Bulgaria: Fisseha, Daniel, Jesse, Helen, and Yosef (born in 1994, '94, '95, '96, and '97). While the parents our age have graduated, Donny and I—like the big, dim-witted students of yore who hunched over small desks at the rear of the classroom—have been held back, forced to repeat grades with people a lot younger.

There is a gravitational pull around a grade school in autumn. Donny and I have not yet broken free of the annual rotation. Like outmoded satellites, we still circle, rattling in close again each rusty fall. For us, the annual fund-raising gift-wrap sale is going on *right now*; the Fun Run is coming up; and last night I fitted Yosef in my satin quilted vest and my widest belt to make him into a courtier for the school musical, *Cinderella*.

All this lends a knowledgeable perspective.

For example: I can state with some confidence that the school musicals repeat once every five years.

Because this is our fourth *Cinderella*.

And only one of our nine children ever got a speaking part.

Donny's courtroom skills and constitutional knowledge have earned wide respect among judges and attorneys. He spends his days with accused drug dealers, gunrunners, murderers, tax evaders, heroes of the NFL (Ray Lewis, Jamal Lewis, Ben Roethlisberger), or hip-hop superstars (DJ Drama, T.I.). At night he puts his children to bed by practicing his closing arguments. This began years ago as a stratagem to avoid reading Berenstain Bears books aloud. We owned the whole skinny paperback collection: *The Berenstain Bears and Too Much TV*, *The Berenstain Bears and Too Much Junk Food*, *The Berenstain Bears and Too Much Birthday*, etc. Donny said the books were "boring," but I think he didn't like Mama Bear being the fount of wisdom, catching and scolding Papa Bear when he crept downstairs late at night to watch TV during No TV

Week. Donny may have felt that Papa Bear's transgressions struck a little too close to home. And he doesn't like to see people like Papa Bear get in trouble, even though he has spent his entire career with people who are in deep, deep, deep trouble.

"May it please the court, ladies and gentlemen of the jury . . ." he boomed as the children snuggled happily under their covers. Seth, on the top bunk, got knocked out instantly, but Molly, on the bottom bunk, tried to hang on, sucking the middle fingers of her right hand and watching wide-eyed as Daddy patiently explained the actions of the accused arsonist, drug dealer, or kidnapper. After Molly conked out, Donny turned to a jury consisting of Raggedy Ann, Neal the Bear, Pluto, and a stuffed eagle, their button eyes luminous in the glow of the Jack and Jill night-light. A pleading note entered the counselor's voice when Raggedy Ann (clearly the jury foreman) refused to make eye contact, always a negative indicator of the jury's state of mind toward the defense.

When Molly was six, Donny invited her to attend the trial of a man accused of training his pit bulls to attack and fight. Molly got dressed up and we drove to the DeKalb County Courthouse. She sat up alert and curious through the testimony of witnesses and the prosecutor's closing argument. Finally the great moment arrived: it was Daddy's turn! *Daddy*, in a suit and tie, stepped to the front of the courtroom. "May it please the court, ladies and gentlemen of the jury," he began. Molly slid her two fingers into her mouth, sucked hard, and toppled against me into a deep sleep.

When Lee was little, he'd answer the phone and yell, "Daddy, it's for you! I think it's a criminal!"

At the start of the adoptions, when the presence of Bulgarian Romani and Ethiopian children still felt a little surprising, Donny referred to their end of the upstairs hall as "the international concourse." If one child was complaining and another one piped up, Donny said, "Oh, great. Another country heard from."

Now our family is so diverse that our cousin Julian Haynes suggests that I call this book *Why Our Babysitters Are Entitled to Peace Corps Credit*.

Our son Seth proposes *We're Not a Youth Group, Dammit*.

Or *The Phylogeny of My Progeny*.

My friend Andrea Sarvady, who is aware that, to our surprise, we ended up raising sports stars, nominates *The Jewish Guide to Raising Star Athletes.*

Julian returns with *Leveraging Love: How to Choose Your Favorite Child During These Hard Economic Times.*

In July 2007 the eleven of us flew on a plane together for the first time (because two Ethiopian brothers, Daniel and Yosef, thirteen and ten, had joined the family two weeks earlier). At the Delta check-in desk, eight minutes into our first public appearance, a stranger approached and said, "Excuse me? Miss? I think one of your students dropped a mitten."

Mitten? I thought. *In July in Atlanta? Are you kidding me?*

Later it hit me: *One of your students.*

In flight, a middle-aged African American businessman leaned across the aisle to ask our son Lee, "What's the name of your organization?"

Lee said, "Um . . . the Greene-Samuel family?"

Disembarking from the plane, the businessman tapped Donny on the shoulder and said, "I'd like to shake your hand."

At baggage claim in Santa Fe, a frail, elderly white couple from our flight made their way toward me on walkers. "May we ask you a question?" said the old woman in a quavering voice. "Are you a scout leader? Because we were always *very* involved in scouting."

I'm raising two generations of children. With mothers my own age, I breast-fed my babies and wore them in inward-facing pouched slings. They slept in the Family Bed and played with handwoven dolls made of one hundred percent organic Egyptian cotton and with smooth, colorless wooden blocks that left everything to the imagination.

Now, in the vineyards of parenting with mothers and fathers ten or twenty years younger, I note that three-year-olds are entitled to computer time and second-graders need cell phones. *Then* we spoke of Attachment Parenting, in warm tones of praise, with subscriptions to *Mothering* magazine and memberships in La Leche League; *now* people blog or Twitter about Helicopter Parenting with sarcasm. Over three decades with nine children, Donny and I have covered most of the milestones of child rearing, including quite a few we would have preferred to skip.

Some lessons we mastered in the 1980s and '90s have stood us in good stead; others have grown more complicated. Sixteen-year-old Lily was HORRIFIED, SCANDALIZED, when I joined Facebook. She had to shriek, "MOTHER! ARE YOU KIDDING ME?! DON'T EVEN *THINK* ABOUT FRIENDING ME!" She had to get on her cell phone and wail the news to all her friends. She had to get on her Facebook page and type madly away, fingers flying, about this violation of social-networking cyberspace by the elderly. I agreed with her! I hadn't wanted to join, but friends said it was a good way to keep up with one's children. Stung, I said, "I didn't even want to be your Facebook friend!" When Molly, Seth, and Lee were teenagers, there was no Facebook; this was a new parenting question, very twenty-first century.

I've learned over the years that not all standoffs end in parental victory. Sometimes the epiphany is: *this* is one battle I'm going to lose. "It's okay, I have lots of Facebook friends," I told Lily.

"Yeah, how many?"

"Thirteen."

And I've learned that sometimes the act of throwing in the towel yields surprising results. One morning I logged on to Facebook and saw that an invitation to be someone's new friend awaited me. It was from Lily.

This book is the story of the creation of a family. It began in the usual way: a woman, a man, some babies. But then it took off in a modern direction, roping in a few older children from distant countries. In retrospect, I see that Donny and I have steered by the light of what brings us joy, what makes us laugh, and what feels right and true. Those instincts have served us well. In shaky times, I've thought, *Did we do a wrong thing? Did we take on too many? Are we at risk of capsizing? What do the experts say?* But we and the children all seem to be thriving; it seems we were right to trust love, laughter, and happiness.

The story will be told in the roughly chronological order of the children's arrivals. The older four joined the family at conception and birth, while the younger five arrived at older ages and not in birth order: Jesse at four and a half in 1999; Helen (a year younger than Jesse) at five and a half in 2002; Fisseha (a year older than Jesse) at age ten in 2004; Daniel and Yosef (a year older and two years younger than Jesse) at thirteen and ten in 2007. This book is about the joy of living with these children: learning to ride the wake of wrong turns, near collisions, stalls, rivalries, and self-doubts without despairing or ever giving up on a child; and about the thrill of hanging on for the ride when first one, then another, then another happens upon the spark of something great that may give shape and meaning to the rest of his or her life. With us, the bonds of love and commitment coexist with the bonds of DNA. Middle-aged parents and their young-adult children can still play in a backyard never-never land of ongoing childhood.

Everyone wants a happy family, but some parents fear they don't have the knack for it. We tilt anxiously above our children, examining them from every angle, consulting experts, and reading how-to books about increasing their popularity and enhancing their odds of getting into the expensive university of their choice. We're afraid to steer by the light of what makes us laugh, of what makes us feel good. Yet most of today's adults grew up happily enough while our parents were otherwise engaged. Concerned with work and mortgages, our mothers and fathers didn't know the word "parenting," didn't give a damn if we had "self-esteem," and didn't regard us, their offspring, as their most important achievements. They mainly wanted a little peace and quiet.

Like many modern parents, I have invested a lot of energy in non-emergencies over the years; I tried to fix problems when it was a child's right to try to set things straight by himself or herself. I dashed onto the field when I should have stood on the sidelines. I overempathized with transient disappointments when I should have invoked the big picture, the bright future. I validated when I should have pooh-poohed. For example, when Seth was seven, he woke me one night by suddenly appearing at my bedside, wide-eyed and pale. "What if I'm buried alive?" he whispered.

I should have asked, *What on earth were you reading last night?*

I should have said, *Don't be ridiculous. Go back to bed.*

I might have said, *If you ever wake me up again with anything this moronic, you're grounded.*

Instead, ever the empathetic mother, I propped myself on one elbow and—thinking of Edgar Allan Poe—nodded and sagely replied, "That's a very important consideration. Some very famous writers have wrestled with that issue."

When I looked back at Seth by the light of the digital numbers on my clock radio, the look on his face was now that of the character in the Edvard Munch painting *The Scream*. Many nights over the next few weeks he startled me awake at a god-awful hour to elaborate upon his concerns while I groggily invented, and swore to install, safeguards, including an in-casket walkie-talkie, an underground TV camera, an all-glass casket, and an Eject! button. Donny was out of town for a trial and Seth was wearing me out. As I heard him creep down the hall toward me one night, I sensed that my empathy had ended. He leaned over in the dark, to make sure I was awake, and then whispered, "What if the dirt they shovel onto the coffin clogs up the walkie-talkie?"

That was it. No more attachment-parenting nurturing mothering murmurs were coming from THIS mother, not at this hour of the night. It was time to react more like my father would have reacted.

"FOR THE LOVE OF GOD!" I shrieked. "Can't you ever have a HAPPY thought?!!"

Startled, my skinny, curly-topped little boy turned and trotted away confusedly.

He returned a few minutes later with a trembling smile.

"WHAT?" I snarled.

"I had a happy thought," he timidly offered.

"WHAT IS IT??"

"Why would anyone want to bury me alive? I'm just a little kid."

And that was the end of it.

Like many modern parents, I've helped too much with homework. I've engaged with science fair projects as if they were assigned to *me*. "Oh no, another *science fair project*??" I groan when the teacher's memo comes home, glancing at my calendar to see when I'll have time to get it done.

Lee, in sixth grade, brought home an assignment so far over his head that I sent him to bed and took over. The teacher, wanting to offer accelerated work to top students, had gotten hold of somebody's old college exam. Essays by two French eighteenth-century Enlightenment philosophers were presented, excerpted from Montesquieu's "Persian Letters" and Voltaire's "Letters on England." The questions included:

"Summarize Montesquieu's critique of Louis XIV."

"Which aspects of the English political regime appealed to Voltaire?"

"Discuss Voltaire's characterization of the mercantile character of English society vs. the feudal character of French society."

I sat up well into the night, working on my answers and fielding calls from Lee's friends. "Hi, Josh," I said, picking up the phone around 11:30. "No, Lee's asleep. But what did you get for, 'How does Montesquieu show that self-interest can overawe justice in human affairs?'"

A few days later Lee came running down the hill from school, waving his graded homework. "Mom!" he yelled from the stop sign across the street. "You got a seventy-four!"

And I have worried too much. I've worried about the right things and I've worried about stupid things. When Seth was sixteen, there was a party, a bad party, the kind of party you remember fondly from your youth and begin to dread the moment your first baby is born: parents out of town, underage drinking, pot smoking, music blasting, drunk boys hooting at passing cars, and neighbors calling the police. The scandal swept the tenth grade.

Seth missed it. He had been upstairs in his room that Saturday night, reading science fiction and playing trombone. As the news of the party tore through the high school community, I, like all the tenth-grade parents, felt very concerned. I wanted to get to the bottom of it. I didn't want to get to the bottom of why these young people were already experimenting with substance abuse. I wanted to get to the bottom of why, while young men of his generation courted arrest, my child was upstairs reading and practicing his instrument. "So, did you hear the police came to Scott's party Saturday night?" I asked.

"Yeah, well, that was obvious. I knew that would happen. That's why I didn't go," he said.

"You were *invited*?" I asked happily, my chief concern laid to rest.

Donny and I feel most alive, most thickly in the cumbersome richness of life, with children underfoot. The things we like to do, we would just as soon do with children. Is travel really worth undertaking if it involves fewer than two taxis to the airport, three airport luggage carts with children riding and waving on top of them, a rental van, and a hall's length of motel rooms? Can sleep be as sweet as when it is wrested from those who would interrupt it? I love the Atlanta Symphony, but it's a sixth-grade band that moves me to tears when the children play the C scale together for the first time.

Of course we have careers, friends, functions to attend, holiday parties to dress up for. But by the mid-1980s, we noticed that our favorite part of social events was dressing up for them while small children bounded in and out of the room in excitement. I remembered, from my childhood, the sense of anticipation kindled by shower steam wafting into the parents' bedroom at night, mixing with the golden scent of aftershave and the astringent odor of black shoe polish, while a mother sits on the bed in satin underthings, pulling on sheer stockings, and the father requires a small girl's help to insert his gold cuff links. Compared to this buildup, this breathless anticipation of the exclusive and bejeweled affair the children *think* we're going to, the actual party feels a little anticlimactic. When we reach our destination—at the summit of the long brick walkway across an expensively maintained green lawn—and the massive door opens to us and we're swept into the champagne-colored candlelit rooms, no one gasps, "You both look so *beautiful*!" We circulate, chuckle with friends, nibble canapés, remember a funny thing that happened years ago, and return home before the children are all asleep so we can be greeted like celebrities returning from a successful foreign tour. The children peek down from the top of the stairs—"Are they really *home*? Is it really *them*?"—and then slide and leap into our arms while I remove from my purse the chocolate meringue puffs and Key lime shortbread cookies I've wrapped in cocktail napkins and smuggled out of the party for them.

Donny and I loved these times and wanted them to continue. When the clock started to run down on the home team, we brought in ringers. We figured out how to stay in the game.

1

Room for One More?

Lee, at ten, was the first in the family to mention adoption. He tore out of a friend's backyard at dusk when I honked from the driveway and clattered in cleats into the backseat, rosy and dirty under his baseball cap. "I have a surprise for you!" I said as he buckled in.

"Are you pregnant?" he happily cried.

"*What?!*" I stopped and turned around to look at him in amazement. It was 1998. I was forty-five. "Lee, no."

"Oh!" he said with disappointment, but then offered knowingly, "But did you find someone really, really sweet to adopt?"

I pulled into traffic and silently swung my arm over the seat to deliver a paper bag containing a brand-new bike lamp that had suddenly lost most of its sparkle.

It was uncanny that he'd asked this. A few years earlier I had struggled with the question of whether I was too old to give birth to a fifth child, and as it turned out, Donny and I were but a few months away from wondering if we might *adopt* a fifth child.

I'd been surprised, as I turned forty-one, by a sudden onset of longing and nostalgia. The older children were thirteen, ten, and six. Lily was only two. But she'd moved to her "big girl bed," and the crib stood—now and forever?—empty. Why did I hesitate at this moment to leap across the great divide—from childbearing years to non-childbearing years? Sometimes, standing at the kitchen sink, looking out the window into the front yard and the shade of the massive tulip poplar where the children lay in the deep grass, chewing on weed stalks, I wanted it never to end. If our home were a houseboat, we'd started to throw off the ropes and rumble away from the dock, but what if one last child were racing down to the pier, hoping to leap onto the deck?

On my mother's side, I have one female first cousin, Judy: she gave birth to her fourth child at forty-two. That long-ago baby had been greeted by merriment and snickering among the medium and upper branches of the family tree. As I turned forty-one, I knew that having a last baby at forty-two was within the bounds of physiological possibility and ancestral sanction. At forty-one and a half I pressed myself to make a now-or-never decision.

Donny was surprised.

"I kind of feel we're set up to handle a larger population here," I said. To assist, he wordlessly extracted from a closet shelf an explicit wooden figurine he'd lugged home from a summer trip to Europe twenty-four years earlier. Shops offering African jewelry, sculpture, and dashikis weren't then ubiquitous in American shopping malls, and this item had struck the shaggy backpacking seventeen-year-old as a real find. A foot and a half tall, the rough-hewn fertility man-woman had sharp, pointy breasts, a pregnant belly, and an erect male genital. Young Donny, back at home in suburban White Plains, had glued tangles of black thread to key locales to serve as the statue's pubic hair. Now he brought it down from behind his sweaters (I'd forgotten the thing existed) and stood it up on his night table beside the clock radio.

Having his/her sharp parts all aimed at me felt threatening rather than encouraging. And I felt deeply undecided.

Other than Donny, I could find no one who thought it was a good idea to try for a fifth child at forty-one. The months scrolled by, narrowing my window of opportunity. Then I turned forty-two. Then I was forty-two years and one month old. I made my first-ever appointment with a psychologist. "I need help deciding whether to get pregnant again," I told her. "I have two months left to decide." But she wanted to talk about every sort of unrelated thing! She wanted to hear about my marriage. She said, "You know, I used to be afraid of empty nest, too, but it can be an absolutely wonderful time for you and your husband to find each other again."

"I haven't lost my husband," I said. "We're very close. Can you just tell me yes or no here?"

"Many women find that once their children are raised, they have a chance to discover their own gifts and to pursue their own career aspirations."

"Yes or no?" asked Donny that night.

"She's not telling me until next week. Meanwhile, could you please turn that thing to face the wall? I don't like the way it's looking at me."

The following week the therapist wanted to explore my relationships with my parents. "You're not going to give me a yes-or-no answer, are you?" Honestly, I knew this wasn't how therapy worked; still, I'd hoped for just a slender clue about which path to take.

"The empty-nest years can be a very fulfilling time of life for a woman," she replied.

"The answer is NO," I told Donny that night.

Of course I didn't have to listen to the therapist, but in the light of her disapproval I began to picture myself as an old, gaunt mother struggling to shove a stroller up the sidewalk while the professional achievements and the season symphony tickets enjoyed by my friends remained out of reach for decades. By April 1994 it was too late to conceive a baby to whom I could give birth at forty-two. With gratitude to the universe for our four glorious children, I moved on. Donny stuffed the wooden fertility figure back on the closet shelf so it could return to the business of poking holes in his sweaters.

Four years later—a couple of months after Lee asked his question about whether I'd just adopted somebody very sweet and I handed him a bike lamp instead—I stood in front of an audience, giving a talk, when I suddenly wondered what had become of my menstrual cycle. Was this menopause? On the way home I detoured to CVS to pick up a pregnancy test that would rule out the unlikeliest scenario. A pregnancy test is an embarrassing item to show a drugstore cashier at any age, but especially at forty-five. "You will not *believe* what I just bought," I called laughingly to Donny as I came in and jogged upstairs to rule out the ludicrous possibility that . . . *oh my God I'm pregnant.* The timeline that came with the package estimated that I would give birth seven months hence, at the age of forty-six.

Four times before, Donny and I had rejoiced at such news; we're not dancing people (*he's* not), so our only spontaneous pas de deux have occurred at these moments with a brief turn about the bedroom. But now I exited the bathroom and threw myself stiffly facedown on our bed. As every previous time, Donny was amazed and thrilled, his eyebrows raised in happiness, his round cheeks red beneath the beard, his lips parted for a great laugh. Seeing my woodenness, he froze. "I want whatever you want," he offered quickly.

"Can we even handle this?" I moaned into the bedspread. "Financially, I mean?"

"A baby?" he roared with happiness. "Of course we can afford a baby!"

Case closed! as we say in this family in which the father is a litigator.

My elderly obstetrician, retired, agreed to meet with me for old times' sake. Creeping into his long-ago desk chair, he confirmed the physical toll and genetic risks foretold by the data. "I don't know if I can do this again," I told Donny that night. "It's not healthy for me or for the baby. It's a high-risk pregnancy in every way." I thought, but didn't say, *What would I even wear?* Sentimentally, I had saved my favorite maternity T-shirt, billowing white and dotted with small pink storks. It was a seventeen-year-old shirt, older than Molly. I got it out and looked at it but didn't try it on. While elbow-deep in memorabilia, I pulled out Lee's baby book. Here he was moments after birth, full of soft-lipped, plump-cheeked sweetness and the round-eyed promise of good humor. Just looking at the picture reminded me of the sucking, slobbery, exhaustive needs of newborns. Donny looked at the photo and drew a different conclusion. "There's our answer!" he yelled. "*SO CUTE!*"

We took a moment to banter about names, always one of our favorite parts. "Finally we can name a child Gideon!" I said. "Giddie! Such a great nickname!"

"Forget it."

"You think Gideon Samuel sounds too Jewish," I accused, and he declined to comment.

"I still like Kenny," I mused.

"Too plain."

"I still like Miranda for a girl."

I said this only as a prompt for his reminder: "A criminal defense attorney cannot name his daughter Miranda."

But I was worried. This child was so much younger than the others that he would be an only child by middle school. (I felt it was a boy.) Instead of food fights at dinnertime in the noisy kitchen, there'd be a poorly lit dining room heavy with the silence of impeccable manners. Instead of raucous Hanukkahs and crowds of mittened friends stomping into the front hall, there would be long winter weekends during which the pale fellow wandered quietly from room to room, turning the cold pages of coffee table art books while his elderly mother upstairs took a three-hour nap.

"I'm not sure this is a good idea," I said the next day. "I'm not sure I can do this again. I can't really picture this kid's childhood."

Donny, taken aback, nodded somberly, tactfully.

It was a weekend of hard rain and high wind. I sat at the kitchen table anguished by confusion and fear. The children were mystified by my sorrow. "Look! Look at Dad!" yelled Seth, fourteen. Below the kitchen bay window, on the brick patio behind the house, Donny, in the downpour, was wrestling with contraptions and wire.

"What on earth?" I said. "Run, help him. What is he trying to do?"

Eager to cheer me up, Donny had driven to a garden store and purchased a bird feeder. Now he was jerry-rigging it so that he could hoist it by wire ten feet above the patio to swing in midair beside the bay window where I miserably sat. Engineering is not one of Donny's strong points, nor is he happy when wet. I watched him struggle in the rain, drenched, calling out instructions to Seth as if they were sailors trying to turn a boat in a gale. It was the most loving gift, the most romantic thing I have ever seen.

The next day, I started to lose the pregnancy. I hurried to bed and elevated my feet. I called the doctor's office. I drank herbal teas and hugged a hot-water bottle. As I was losing the baby, I suddenly realized how much I wanted it, how much I wanted *him*. Far from a goofy and embarrassing situation to have conceived a child in my mid-forties, it now seemed brilliant, miraculous, one in a million. Gideon! I held my belly. "I'm sorry I said this would be too hard. Really I wanted you. I *do* want you. Please stay." But it was over.

I was overcome with grief and remorse. Why had I not welcomed the new life wholeheartedly from the first second of its delicate touching down? I'd been offered a gift beyond measure, and instead of rejoicing, I'd whined. I'd made wisecracks. Now I blamed myself. Five was a marvelous number of children to have! It was a prime number, too, and prime numbers were Seth's favorites! What had I thought was more important? What "data" had I thought it was urgent to collect, to weigh what kind of decision? Now it was too late.

Life was short—for the little zygote, life had been six weeks long. Life was short, and our family capacity was big: both Donny and I had started to make room for a fifth child. Again he longed to cheer me up, but he doubted that another bird feeder would do the trick. "Listen," he said one night as he punched socks into his overstuffed dresser drawer and I lay mournfully on my side in bed, my stack of books untouched, my lamp turned off. "If we really want another child, why don't we adopt one?"

2

Nine Hundred and Eighty Thousand Websites

"Oh, right," I said listlessly.

Neither of us knew anything about adoption.

The next morning, after the children went to school, I slumped half-heartedly at my computer and began logging on. The Pentium II Gateway took a long time to gear up. It hissed, vibrated, and did some heavy breathing in its attempt to make contact with the invisible filaments looping the earth. I used it for word processing. I sought out the Internet gingerly and hastily, as if an expensive resource was being wasted during those static-filled minutes. The computer rumbled and swayed on its haunches, trying to launch its signal through the roof and into the magnetic poles and electronic latitudes of cyberspace. Finally the clouds parted and interstellar contact was established. I found a search engine and typed in the word "adoption." When I touched the Return button, 980,000 links rippled into visibility. For the first time in a week, I stopped grieving and leaned forward, beguiled.

If you are not planning to adopt a child, it's safest to avoid typing the word "adoption" into a search engine; 980,000 links are more than a person can visit in a lifetime, and that was ten years ago. Today, in "0.16 seconds," you get "85,800,000 results," which is a good thing, I think, in case you can't find a child to adopt in the first forty to fifty million websites. Hundreds of the websites displayed pictures of children languishing in foreign orphanages or in American foster care. Once I started to look at their faces, I found it hard to turn away.

The news that you could pursue a thumbnail photograph into the computer screen and out the other side struck me first as unbelievable, then as alarming. The computer was the threshold to an alternate universe! In response to certain light taps on the keyboard, like the dialing of a secret combination in a spy thriller, invisible doors opened through which a handsome young boy from India, a smiling baby girl from South Korea, or a shy pair of foster care sisters from St. Louis could show up and move into your house. Some adoption agencies offered "delivery." You could adopt without leaving your desk! "I'd better be careful not to accidentally hit Send," I told Donny. "We could open the door one day and find some little kid standing there with a suitcase."

I began to detour frequently into our home office, where I pushed the buttons and moved the levers to fire up the computer. The computer did its squat thrusts. A blast of static announced to the family that I was logging on again. I closed the door. Our fifth child was only a click away.

Pastel-tinted angels, cherubs, storks, fairies, rainbows, hearts, kittens, and puppies festooned the websites of many adoption agencies. So much cuteness gave me pause. There were names like Adopt an Angel, Loving Stork, All God's Children, and Little Miracles. Many websites anonymously quoted the nineteenth-century Scottish novelist George Macdonald: *"Where did you come from, baby dear? Out of the everywhere, into here."* One was lulled to a soft-focus dreaminess by this fantasia: our family's perfect child was out there! He was without family history, trauma, ethnic affiliation, or congenital issues. He waited for us on a fluffy cloud!

Donny was immune. He had no taste for fairies, cherubs, or leprechauns. "Yes, very cute," he agreed if I asked him to look at a photograph.

I had a book to write, but I got deeply distracted. Adoption had led me to the information superhighway, and I bought a faster computer to keep up. E-mails pulsed into my in-box. I frequently clicked on the major photo-listing sites to see if any new adoptable children had been added. The children didn't smile in their photos. They weren't promoting anything, not even themselves. They just floated in the pixilated world of the computer monitor. As months passed and the pictures weren't updated, I began to wonder: Is the Ukrainian toddler still two years old? For how long has he circulated through cyberspace as a two-year-old?

The photos were sweet, but the captions were terrifying. Intended to sway the hearts of browsing parents, the promotional prose made light of serious issues: words like "this little cutie" were interspersed with words like "blind." "Liam is a special little boy in need of very special parents!" wrote agency staffers who had never met the children. "This sweetie has a cleft right hand and heart murmur. We are told that she is at high risk for developmental delays. She loves to push up from her tummy!" Like unfinished poetry, the captions hinted at unknowable mysteries and strange futures. Some were written in the imagined voices of the children: "Hi there, my name is Brawney! I am a twenty-one-month-old boy with big brown eyes and the cutest little face! I am deaf and have developmental delays. I am ready for my forever family to find me!"

The write-ups sounded like the *SkyMall* catalog. Were the agencies trying to inform or to deceive? *Hi Forever Mommy and Daddy! My name is Vladimir! I am a sociopath with big blue eyes who loves teddy bears, herring, and arson!* We prospective adoptive parents (I'd begun to include myself among them) couldn't know if we were face-to-face with an angel child beyond all angel children, or if we were peering down a chute that was going to cost a hundred thousand dollars in medical or psychiatric care.

To begin, parents filled out an agency questionnaire. First it asked if you wanted to adopt from American foster care or from one of the top five donor countries: Russia, China, South Korea, Guatemala, Vietnam. (India, Romania, Colombia, the Philippines, Ukraine, Mexico, Bulgaria, the Dominican Republic, Haiti, and Brazil sent smaller numbers of children.)

Then you had the fun of checking the box for Boy or Girl.

Then you had the fun of checking whether you preferred an infant or an older child. "Older child" was someone older than two. This was a fairly new option; for most of the twentieth century, the goal of American adoption agencies was to place healthy newborns with childless young couples of the same race, religion, and ethnicity, and then to throw tarps of secrecy over the transaction. But the widening availability of contraception and abortion and the growing social acceptance of unwed motherhood meant that there were fewer healthy white American babies in need of adoption. Starting with postwar South Korean orphans, white Americans began to adopt babies from abroad. They began to search in ever-widening circles that included African American babies; babies from China; babies from elsewhere in Asia and from Central and South America; and then older children, young teenagers, sibling groups, children from Eastern Europe and Africa, and children with physical or cognitive challenges.

On the questionnaire, the fun was over. Because now you scanned the list of what special needs you would accept, with the dawning impression—as you skipped over children with spina bifida, Down syndrome, and dwarfism without checking their boxes—that you weren't such a nice person after all. If not those, then how did you feel about children with cleft palate or limb differences? Fetal alcohol syndrome or epilepsy? Albinism, deafness, blindness, cerebral palsy, or hepatitis B?

Scarier still were the possibilities that didn't appear on the questionnaire, that couldn't be detected in the photos and that you knew about only if you'd done your homework: fetal alcohol effect, autism spectrum disorder, complications of extreme prematurity, drug addiction at birth, failure to thrive, and—scariest of all—the extreme forms of attachment disorder. Children who started life in institutions, or with neglectful or abusive birth parents, might reach the safe haven of a loving adoptive family but find it impossible to respond to kindness and affection. For a child accustomed to indifference, abuse, or neglect, the warm welcome offered by new parents could look false, temporary, or dangerous.

"Love will cure all!" the agencies implied, but—as children were rescued from prisonlike foreign orphanages and from maltreatment in birth or foster families in the United States or abroad—new truths dawned in the adoption community: the human child is not a blank slate to be wiped clean by a new mommy and daddy. What happens in utero and in the early part of a child's life makes indelible imprints.

A body of literature began to be written by adoptive parents and psychologists involved in the struggle of wounded children to adapt to family life. The titles were terrifying: *When Love Is Not Enough. Damaged. Parenting the Hurt Child. The Forever Child: A Tale of Anger and Fear. Dandelion on My Pillow, Butcher Knife Beneath.*

Of course every child is entitled to a home and happiness! Every child is capable of enriching a family and of making breathtaking advances when showered with love. But it was hard to know what you were letting yourself in for. The risks were high. When blithe and naïve parents took in traumatized, neglected, or seriously sick children, the rainbows and teddy bears evaporated. The agencies often disappeared then, too. And yet . . . beautiful connections *were* created through the midwifery of adoption agencies. If I abandoned this search, we wouldn't have our fifth child and this intriguing path to happiness would be unexplored. Sometimes, at the end of a pixilated rainbow, your heart's own child waited.

I clicked through the endless mazes of the photo listings while agencies blew commercially produced magic dust into my eyes.

3

Foreign Film Festival

Strange packages arrived by mail. Padded manila envelopes contained videotapes recorded in Russia, Bulgaria, and Romania. Adoption agencies sent them to enlarge my acquaintance with children displayed in the photo listings. The first child I asked about was a pale, huge-eyed, somber boy in a Russian orphanage. Five-year-old Tomas's caption said only "He might be Armenian." I couldn't wait for Tomas's video to arrive. When I was out of the house, I drove home feeling destiny as cool and real in my hands as the steering wheel. I returned one day to find a padded manila envelope propped beside the front door.

The video began with a professionally made commercial about the adoption agency. Two blond, rosy-cheeked children skipped into the waiting room of an airport after their flight. They looked Austrian. They glowed with sunlit vigor, as if they'd just returned from an Alpine ski vacation, and they dashed straight into the arms of the middle-aged white couple kneeling on the carpet. I understood the message: *Adoption is easy and fun! Pull into the nearest airport and pick up a couple of cute blond kids, but better make sure you've got a roof rack for their snow skis!*

The trailer ended, and the real footage—black-and-white, dimly lit, shakily handheld—began. I was stunned to see Tomas. The huge, melancholy eyes and the big, pale face sat atop a shrunken body; he did not look normal; he was awkwardly propped on a chair. I couldn't tell if he was two years old or four or six; he was stunted. He couldn't seem to help himself to sit up straighter in his seat. He looked like a hand puppet whose painted plaster head is the most significant part. Before I could send out motherly feelers toward him, his screen time ended and a terrified girl, nearly unbalanced by the gigantic hair bow someone had pressed upon her thin hair, stood trembling before the camera, silent in a dark office, as all the children on the video were silent and scared in the gloom.

I rewound and watched again: first the Tyrolean child actors, then the listless unloved Russian orphans. These mini-documentaries, one to three minutes devoted to each child, ingeniously, almost brilliantly, foiled any attempt to learn something real. When I rewound a third time to Tomas, imprisoned in an Armenia of orphanhood, my heart leaped out to him, but the rough hand of fear yanked it back. Who was to say he wasn't a beautiful child accidentally misplaced from the vibrant outside world? If Donny and I were childless, we could love this boy and set him up with a full-service American childhood. But I would not risk unbalancing my family for this mystery child. I slid the videotape back into the envelope and returned it. What I learned from that videotape—aside from what I had already guessed about some adoption agencies, and aside from nothing about Tomas—was that I'd better not plunge any deeper without professional guidance.

A few groundbreaking American doctors had launched the new subspecialty of "international adoption medicine." They treated orphans abroad, noting the extreme obstacles to normal development; and they also saw, as their patients, post-institutionalized (PI) children who'd been adopted into American families.

I pitched a story to *The New Yorker* about international adoption medicine, and it was commissioned. By phone and in person I interviewed the doctors. I did not conceal my personal interest in the story.

In a tall, narrow Greenwich Village apartment crammed with lithographs, teacups, picture frames, and overstuffed bookshelves, a doctor sat watching videos until well past midnight. Four or five a night, twenty a week, a thousand a year, the doctor snapped the videocassettes in and out of the living-room VCR and made notes on a legal pad. Prospective adoptive parents had mailed the videos to Dr. Jane Aronson, a pediatrician and infectious disease specialist. Lanky and angular, wearing a loose-knit sweater, khakis, and boots, her unruly salt-and-pepper hair released from the ponytail she wore at work, Aronson was having a frustrating night at the movies. In the first video, a baby girl on her back in a crib began to cry, so her tape instantly ended. Was she going to be inconsolable or easily comforted? Would she hold her head up with nice muscle tone or be floppy? Would she be latching onto a caregiver she loved or twisting away from one of ten strangers in her life? There was no way for the doctor to tell. In the next video a little boy was seated at a child-sized table and invited to place big, colorful plastic rings in order of size onto their base. With great caution he chose the wrong ring. The thick, bare arm of the caregiver reached across the table, snatched the ring away, and shoved the correct ring into the child's hand. He lifted it onto the base. Then he very slowly reached for another ring, also the wrong pick. Here came the arm of the caregiver again: she gathered the correct ring and placed it on the base herself, then another and another, until the task was efficiently completed and the small boy silently, and without facial expression, sat. End of tape. "Good God," Aronson said.

From each film and accompanying medical report Dr. Aronson hoped to gather enough clues to be able to comment on a child's fine motor and gross motor skills and personal-social development. She hoped to see close-ups of the face in order to rule out fetal alcohol syndrome. She hoped to have enough "growth points" in the medical report to be able to chart a child's height, weight, and head circumference.

Children institutionalized at birth were at greatest risk of long-term effects; the longer a child lived in an orphanage, the more catch-up time would be required to restore elements of ordinary life. Children lost roughly one month of linear growth—length or height—for every three months living in an orphanage. When Aronson phoned prospective parents with her impressions, she did not recommend that they adopt or not adopt a particular child (though that's what the parents hoped she would do): instead she arranged her findings into categories of "average risk," "moderate risk," and "severe risk."

In the adoption of PI children, there was no category of "no risk."

The international adoption doctors had front-row seats for an unprecedented social experiment: the gathering of thousands of deprived and traumatized children out of institutions into homes of loving plenty. For each set of parents and child, there were two big questions: What are the odds of this child being able to lead a fairly normal life? And will these parents be equal to the challenges presented by this child? The doctors hated to recommend against a child's chance of rescue by loving parents, but if the child's needs overwhelmed the parents, the adoption—and even the marriage—could fail.

I sat in Dr. Aronson's Manhattan office as she phoned prospective parents about their videos. Some understood the risks; others had fallen in love with the child in the video and begged for her stamp of approval. Some feared they were "baby-shopping" and asked what would happen to the child if they declined the referral. Some *were* baby-shopping, trying to make so guarded a choice that they had solicited six or eight referral videos from as many different agencies and shipped them out to half a dozen adoption doctors.

I understood them all. Few parents commenced an adoption journey with the plan to transform their homes into therapeutic placements for damaged children (though some heroic adults did just that). Most hoped, by whatever stratagem, to reach a simple outcome: a loving child, a happy family.

At her desk in her midtown office, Aronson used both hands to curl into place the wire earpieces of a pair of rimless eyeglasses, took a long look at the medical summary accompanying a videotape of a pretty Russian baby girl she'd watched the night before, and got the first set of parents on the speakerphone. "Mrs. Murphy? Dr. Aronson," she said in a brusque Brooklyn voice.

"Oh! Let me get my husband on the extension."

"Dr. Aronson, good morning!" The husband was on the line.

Though her low voice sometimes resonated with fervor, Jane Aronson reined it in, became a conveyor of facts—a not unsympathetic deliverer of unvarnished truth. "Her height and weight are on the curve, but the head is below the fifth percentile," she said. "There's an unknown here in terms of her potential. There's no such statement as 'a small head equals mental retardation,' but the small head circumference suggests she did not have the kind of brain growth normal for a healthy youngster."

"But her height is good," said the mother.

"Yes, the height is normal."

"And her weight is normal," said the mother.

"Yes, her weight is normal," said Dr. Aronson.

"Did you see how she looked at the caregiver?" asked the father.

"Nice eye contact with the caregiver. She turned when her name was called."

"Is there any piece of information we could get that would tell us it's going to be okay?" he asked.

"I think that's going to be a tall order. I think a premature baby from Russia is a risky referral. A baby who's delivered with a small head has had some sort of insult to the brain. This is just tough, this is a difficult one."

"Maybe we could ask the orphanage to double-check the head measurements," said the father.

"Yes, you could ask," said Aronson.

It was a delaying tactic. Maybe they would get better news. If not, maybe in the extra time they would find the courage to say, "We will adopt her, come what may." But they hung up reluctantly, having been unable to dispel the clouds of uncertainty and fear.

"She could be one of those smashing babies," Aronson told me, "but how the hell do I know what's going on inside her spirit? I see these videos and I want to be there, holding these tiny creatures who are not growing, learning, or really living. I cry when I think of how few of these lives we touch."

One researcher described PI children as falling into three broad categories: "Challenged Children" could require extensive and perhaps lifelong therapy to try to achieve normal life; "Wounded Wonders" would make good strides toward recovery when given a chance; and "Resilient Rascals" inexplicably seemed to defy the odds stacked against them, emerging from their dire institutions fundamentally intact.

Could I find a "Resilient Rascal" peeking out from the photo listings? How would I spot him?

4

Motherhood vs. the Career

Rather than wondering, *How will I spot a resilient rascal?* I might better have asked: *Do I really want to do this to myself again?* My four children were all in school, and here I was poised to hurl myself back into the trenches of full-time motherhood. Hadn't I complained, practically since day one, about how hard it was to combine motherhood with a career?

Well, day one, Molly's birth, October 11, 1981, was the happiest day of our lives. "She looks like a little Eskimo baby," someone said, with her bright, round dark eyes and her fringe of black hair peeking out of the hooded, tightly wrapped hospital blanket. A nurse came on duty and said, "Oh! They told me an incredibly beautiful baby was born this morning!" I was sailing around the earth with happiness, Donny beside me.

We brought the baby home to our rental house in Rome, Georgia. Two doors down lived a couple with eight children, and they came right over to meet Molly. While Sharon showed me how to bathe the baby, John said in a strong North Georgia country voice, "The hardest year, I swear to God, is when you go from six kids to seven."

Now, if an astronaut wants to explain to you the best way to approach a moon crater, you're going to nod politely and thank him for his good counsel while knowing that in your own life it's absolutely never going to come up. In this spirit we thanked John for his warning. But I had more pressing concerns than keeping an eye out for that tricky transitional year of going from six to seven children; going from zero to one child was unhinging me entirely.

I was getting no sleep, no showers, and little to eat. I couldn't figure out where to put the baby while inserting my contact lenses (Was I supposed to just lay her on the floor of the bathroom?—*that* didn't seem healthy), so I wasn't seeing clearly. I was mis-buttoned, braless, sore, haggard, and bewildered. I had taken maternity leave from my job with Legal Aid, and I couldn't begin to figure out how to push ahead with the writing career I'd been trying to launch in after-work hours. If the baby was awake, I was holding her. When the baby slept, I collapsed nearby.

For a few minutes every night, I wrote thank-you notes for our baby gifts. Small hinged note cards—with covers displaying happy bluebirds grasping baby rattles or grinning clowns holding balloons that spelled out T-H-A-N-K-S—I crammed with densely worded tightly spaced paragraphs that employed subjectivism, fragmentation, paradox, irony, black humor, and other postmodernist techniques. One friend assured me that I certainly would publish a book someday and it would be entitled *Melissa Fay Greene: The Collected Thank-you Notes.*

At six months of age, the rosy-cheeked baby propped herself up into a slump on my bed one afternoon, reached across the bedspread to my notebook, ripped out a page of an essay I was writing, and ate it. It hung out of her mouth like the legs of a public television documentary frog swallowed alive by a public television documentary snake. I took a picture of Molly at that moment as she slobbered and devoured my prose. It was an important visual representation of the direction my life had taken. And of who was winning.

We moved from Rome to Atlanta when Molly was eight months old. I spent the first few weeks scraping wallpaper and painting the interior of the old house we bought, while the baby happily rolled around in her walker nearby, fiddling with her beloved set of plastic nesting cups. A neighbor rang the doorbell to welcome us to the neighborhood. Plastered with paint, squinting through paint-covered eyeglasses, with a paintbrush in my hand, I opened the door. "Sorry to disturb you!" she said. "Looks like you're hard at work!"

Through paint-crusted lips I replied, "I haven't published a lot lately, between the baby and the move, but I'm really hoping that once we get settled in, I'll be able to start freelancing for some of the major national magazines."

But Missy was already backing away. "I just meant . . . well, you seem to be painting."

The anxiety that I'd never have a career deepened alongside the parallel vocation that *was* taking off nicely for me: motherhood. Seth was born in 1984, Lee in 1988, and Lily in 1992. Still clinging to the notion of becoming a writer, I shoved, with Donny's help, a long Formica-topped desk between the wall and the bed in our upstairs bedroom and called it my home office.

There are many benefits to working at home: no commute, no dress code, no office politics, and your children understand what you do for a living. "*My* mommy sits at home all day!" they announce at preschool, or "*My* mommy doesn't have a job!"

There's really only one disadvantage to working at home, but it's a big one, and that is: sometimes your children are home.

In 1986, when Molly was five and Seth was two, my workweek followed the preschool schedule called Two-Day Twos, which should have been called Let's See You Try to Get Anything Done, Much Less Have a Career, in Six Hours a Week. I researched articles, composed them longhand, typed them up, and mailed them to magazines based in New York and Boston. Acceptances came by phone, but rejections came by mail. I was having trouble moving my articles up and out of the house. They were like the modern so-called failure-to-launch young adults, each making one feeble effort to get a job in New York before moving back home.

I developed a close and melancholy relationship with the mailbox. Before opening it, I drummed lightly on its aluminum flank. If it replied with a deep, hollow *pong*, that was good news—it was empty! No rejections today! But if it gave back a higher, duller note, that meant that a thick manila envelope leaned in the dim interior. One package came back so fast from New York City that I stood at the curb studying the postmark to determine whether the mailman had ever actually picked it up. But then a three-page proposal I sent to *The Atlantic* about new trends in zoo design did not come winging back to me. On a life-changing day in January 1987, William Whitworth, editor in chief of *The Atlantic*, called from Boston to commission the story.

Pinned in the narrow space between my desk and the bed, I had nowhere to go but up. I stepped onto the bed and continued the conversation from close to the ceiling, while inhaling deeply and looking out the window into the distance. It had taken me twelve years to reach this day. Mr. Whitworth and I agreed on the important points. Enthusiasm was expressed on both sides. After we said goodbye, I got down, pulled out my address book, and called everyone I'd ever known, beginning with Donny, my parents and his parents, my brother and his brothers, and extending through my neighbors, old friends, and some people I sort of knew across town. At midnight I thought I might have to stop, but then I remembered that my freshman college roommate, Sue Kaufman, lived in Portland, Oregon. It was only 9:00 p.m. in Portland, Oregon!

The underlying theme, no matter what I gave as the impetus for the phone call, was: I'm going to have a career after all.

I had twenty-six hours of joy, and then Mr. Whitworth called back. It seemed there were concerns, second thoughts. He wondered whether the new approach in zoo design was really so new after all. I was caught completely off guard. Rejection loomed. I needed to drop everything and spontaneously and eloquently defend my thesis. And today was not one of two-year-old Seth's Two-Day Twos.

"More beans!" called Seth. My little curly-haired fellow sat on a stool at the breakfast counter enjoying a dish of baked beans while waiting for his hamburger.

"Mr. Whitworth!" I enthused. "You know what?" I said, as if he'd caught me in the outer office at the receptionist's desk. "Let me quickly change phones."

I jogged out of the kitchen, across the living room, and up the stairs, leaped onto my bed, grabbing the phone as I flew past, and said "Now then" into it.

"More beans?" came a lonely little voice through the other end of the phone. The downstairs phone lay off the hook on the breakfast counter beside Seth.

"One moment again, please," I said in a sort of elevator attendant's voice, masking the beginning of tremendous anxiety.

I sprinted out of the bedroom, hopped down the stairs four at a time, darted into the kitchen, slid across the linoleum sideways in my socks. "More beans?" asked Seth, brightening when he saw me. I hung up the phone, tore back across the house, clawed my way up the stairs, picked up the upstairs phone, and panted for breath into it.

"Is this a convenient time?" asked Mr. Whitworth.

"Oh yes," I gasped. "Marvelous time! Perfect time!"

"BEANS!" came the piercing little voice, beginning to despair, up through the floorboards of the bedroom.

"Well, we have some issues to hammer out," said Whitworth, and I was forced to deliver a lengthy and intelligent monologue, a credo, a soliloquy, invented on the spot, in defense of my proposed story, while a toddler downstairs alternately wept and shrieked for baked beans.

"Hold on one moment, won't you?" I gently inquired, and then vaulted down the entire flight of stairs, fortunately not breaking both legs on impact, hobbled into the kitchen, ripped open the cabinet, seized a can of baked beans, all but ripped the top off with my teeth, dumped the beans into a bowl, slammed the bowl into the microwave, watched thirty seconds take an hour and a half to tick by, spun the bowl and a spoon across the counter to my tearstained but cheered-up son, and worked my way up the stairs rapidly while crawling. I picked up the phone and huffed loudly into it and heard from downstairs, before I could begin to speak, a full little mouth yelling "JUICE!!"

The Atlantic did ultimately commission the story, but not as a result of that conversation.

And yet I loved working in a house full of young life! On the wood-planked floor of the playroom, the children sat and manipulated their Playmobil people and Construx sets and LEGO kits. When they were engrossed in their projects, the house was quiet except for the pleasant light clicking noises of small pieces of plastic coming together nicely. The brightly colored Playmobil people with the frozen smiles and shel-lacked yellow or black hairstyles clicked when they mounted a horse or when they were bent and inserted stiff-legged onto a throne. They clicked when a sword or a flagpole was pushed into their mittenlike hands.

When I sat and wrote on a good morning, when the house was quiet and the children were at school, it seemed to me that my words snapped together with the same deft, clever clicking noises that came from the playroom in the afternoons. I placed a hat on a character's head, I seated a nonfiction personage at a desk, I added shutters to a house, I snapped a bird onto a tree branch, and the words felt like shiny bits of plastic. I heard in my mind's ear that most pleasant sound: *click! click!*

Meanwhile, Molly, in high school, showed a flair for writing. She considered becoming a journalist or a writer. Maybe someday, I thought, she'll have finished a nice piece of writing and will look up to find *her* baby ripping, munching, and drooling over her beautiful pages. At that moment, I knew, she wouldn't want to trade that baby for all the empty mailboxes in the country.

5

Chrissy

Back in Atlanta, better educated as a result of my visits with international adoption doctors—or educated just enough to get into serious trouble—I clicked through the photo listings again. In the Bulgarian orphanages most of the children were Romanies (a.k.a. "Gypsies," a name based on the mistaken assumption that the people originated in Egypt, like the misnomer "Indians" for the indigenous people of the Americas). These children were the youngest victims of the bitter poverty and social exclusion of their people. The Romani people emigrated westward out of northwest India a thousand years ago, beginning a historic wandering. Linked by language, religion, and customs to India's Punjab region, they were a distinct minority who encountered, in Europe, discrimination, violence, enslavement, and genocide—and not only at the hands of the Nazis.

To us, those kids were especially cute, with the black eyes and dark hair Donny and I had come to expect from our children. A famous introduction to the *Tzigane Tarot* (*Tarot of the Romanies*), written in 1984 by Tchalai, begins: "They had eyes dark as night, my brothers, / As if cut in black diamond. / They had moon-woven hair, my brothers, / Glistening blue in endless mist . . ."

There was a four-year-old boy named Christian who posed, unlike most of the frightened children in the photo listings, with a snaggle-toothed smile. He'd been delivered to orphanage care, according to the write-up, at seventeen months; and on the slender evidence of this possibly average start in life (he'd not been "institutionalized at birth"), I contacted his adoption agency and asked for a video.

With lowered expectations this time, without the tilting sensation that the globe was about to lurch forward on its axis, I bounced the padded envelope lightly between my hands when it arrived, slid the tape into the VCR, and stood back skeptically. Then I went to toast a Pop-Tart, as if to signal that I wasn't a prisoner of the videotape, and I returned to stand behind the sofa while the film got under way. For starters, there was no artifice—no professionally staged arrival of well-fed Austrian youngsters. This was a different agency. The video opened on-site in the director's office in a Bulgarian orphanage. Two women—a trim, dark-haired, businesslike director and a stout, bleached-blond caregiver—cooed over a little boy: "Chreesie! Chreesie!"

He was seated at an adult table in the director's office; his round eyes peeked out just above the table's edge. The director removed a small stuffed bunny rabbit from a shelf. She danced it in front of the boy. He cried *"Kuche!"* (*koo*-chay) in a breaking happy voice and reached for it; the staff women laughed because (I later learned) *kuche* means "dog." Then the women urged him to sing a nursery rhyme. He compliantly whispered a small song in Bulgarian. I knew that the international adoption doctors were always happy to hear any sound at all from an institutionalized child, as many orphans become effectively mute under the regimen of group care. The two ladies in the office clapped and laughed. The director gave the little boy a muffin as a reward.

He looked startled and gratified to find the dark-grain glossy muffin in his hand. It might have been his first muffin. But the women didn't tell him to eat it, so he didn't. He sniffed it, though. He eyeballed it from several angles and he brushed his lips across it and then he licked his lips to discern a flavor, but he didn't bite into his muffin. He sighed and lowered it to the table and waited for further instructions. The heavyset caregiver left the office and the director turned her back and suddenly Chrissy felt himself alone, alone with the muffin, though whoever held the video camera continued to silently film him from across the room.

In my den at home, I spun the wooden rocking chair around to face the television and sat down. Chrissy glanced over his shoulder to make sure the director was not watching, opened his mouth *wide* for a decisive and delicious chomp, but then he stopped again. The baked good hovered in midair. Then the small boy did an amazing thing: he returned the muffin to the table. He looked at it sadly. He was waiting for permission.

I was seeing a real thing, a true scene. Not a pale Russian urchin frozen in fear in a dimly lit office, but a real flesh-and-blood boy and, beyond that, a moment of his actual life, a glimpse of how he acted when he thought no one was watching. He was acting with restraint; he was trying hard to behave. There was something deeply intact, seriously okay about this boy. I knew that the international adoption doctors considered a prospective parent's intuition about a child to be a valuable piece of information. For the longest time that's all I had: the intuition that Chrissy was a nice, regular little boy.

That night, watching the video, Donny pronounced Chrissy very cute; the kids said he was very cute; the verdict was unanimous: Let's have a new brother! This will be great! Go get him!

Bulgarian adoption required two trips: a get-acquainted first visit, during which the authorities appraised you and your interaction with the child, and then, if you were approved, a second visit during which the adoption was finalized and you could leave with the child.

This was the moment I'd been waiting for, the culmination of months of obsessive irrational investigation and global Internet searching for our fifth child!

Why, then, surrounded by big smiles and encouraging nods from all sides of the family, was I mentally flailing backward? *Don't push me!* I wanted to say. *You're rushing me!* But who among them had urged upon me the sleepless Internet-browsing nights? No one! Had Donny suggested that I lay aside the book I was writing in order to have more time to click on the before-and-after pictures on the websites of adoptive families? He had not. It had all been me me me, addicted to my first strange brush with virtual reality.

Like a child shakily learning to ride a two-wheeler, I had learned to maneuver around cyberspace, pedaling from one orphanage to another and staring through their windows. The simulated journey had been as absorbing as a great novel, but now it threatened to lap over into my real life. The computer monitor, like a tin basin of water, brimmed and began to spill onto the wood floor of my office. My family now expected me to buy a plane ticket to Bulgaria! "When is he coming?" asked the kids. Donny had become one of them. "Will he know how to Rollerblade?" he asked one night as we monitored a school skating party. He was savoring, in advance, the variety of new things it would be fun to teach Chrissy.

"Of course he won't know how to Rollerblade!" I snapped. "He lives in an *orphanage*. In *Bulgaria.*" (*Where*, I was thinking fiercely, *you're expecting me to* go. *And where the* hell *is Bulgaria?*)

I felt backed into a corner. But how could I tell my children—regarding the long-lashed orphan, lisping his nursery rhyme, postponing his muffin—that I'd decided after all *not* to adopt anyone? And furthermore, that I wanted to swap my humming, intergalactic new computer for the old rattling one? The old one, doing its serviceable word processing and infrequent asthmatic e-mailing, had kept me confined to my office, while the new one flung open windows into the private lives of orphans abroad.

Telling myself that I was basically traveling to research the magazine article about the international adoption doctors, I bought a plane ticket to the land of *Homo sapiens'* first footfalls in Europe: the site of a seventh-century B.C. Thracian encampment; ruled in the fourth century B.C. by Philip of Macedon and his son Alexander the Great; bordered by Romania, Serbia, Greece, Turkey, the Republic of Macedonia, and the Black Sea; freed from forty-four years of Soviet domination just nine years earlier: the Balkan nation of Bulgaria.

6

First Trip to Bulgaria

March 1999

Cellophane—some kind of plastic sheeting—was stretched and taped across the outside of the bedroom window in an Eastern European version of a storm window. Intended to muffle the cold, it mottled the sunlight instead, while a brisk wind rattled the plastic sheeting like grade school offstage thunder. It was a bright winter day, but I was shut off from it, trapped in this freezing bedroom with delicate displays of cut-glass perfume bottles on the mirror-backed laminate shelves of a massive headboard that took up most of the room. The bottles were the prized collectibles of the apartment owner, who'd given up her bedroom to me for the four days of my stay in this midsized Bulgarian city of Pleven.

She—middle-aged, large-boned, with stiff yellow hair coarsened by cheap dye and eyebrows thinly plucked into two thin, high arches—was napping on a bench in the kitchen, barefoot and wearing a cotton housecoat. With those eyebrows, even asleep she looked startled. Violeta was the stout, chalky-skinned caregiver I'd seen in the videotape. Beside her, wide awake underneath her arm, lay the handsome four-year-old boy plucked from the rural orphanage, an hour's drive away, where Violeta worked; he'd been brought here—no matter how nicely we phrased it—

for my closer inspection. If I approved of him, he could become my son. The orphanage director and a Bulgarian lawyer awaited my assent to set the adoption paperwork in motion; then, half a year from now, with all procedures complete, I would be invited to return to Bulgaria, claim the child, and take him back to America. But I'd said nothing to anyone yet about future intentions. I insisted, at least in my own mind, upon the fact that this was the *first* of the two visits required by Bulgarian law and I had not yet committed to anything. I asked that our joint appearance in this apartment be presented to the boy as a mini-vacation, a long weekend getaway from his crowded orphanage. Couldn't we pretend to be—weren't we really—just two weekend guests of our hosts? I spelled out that no one should tell Chrissy that I might become his mother. I didn't want him to feel he was auditioning for me, and I didn't want to be forced to sign any paperwork that obligated me to return for the second trip.

Over lunch today—a china platter of cold cuts, sliced tomatoes, feta cheese, and olives carried in from the balcony, which served as the icebox—I'd asked if I could take a walk after we finished eating. The little boy, seated across the metal-legged table from me, laughed with baby teeth whenever I spoke. The macadam road, the humped 1950s-looking automobiles, and the post-Soviet apartment block sparkled with ice and bright wind beyond the balcony.

"No good!" yelled Violeta. She had a gold eyetooth. "No safe! Where you must go? What you need? He will get for you what is need."

Her surprisingly good-looking husband, Mihail, a bulky mechanic with grease-stained fingers, a kindly, lined face, and a cowlick, looked worried. "I drive you," he said, rolling the *r*, pushing back from his lunch. "Now. We go."

"No, that's okay, never mind," I said, realizing that the concept of a walk was as foreign to them as I was, and I was extremely foreign: a white American woman, married to a lawyer, who'd flown around the world to adopt a Romani orphanage child even though I had four children at home.

They were polite about my mission—even enthusiastic: "No racism in America! Wonderful! *Wonderful!*" Mihail exclaimed over lunch, marveling that a white family like ours would accept a Romani boy, and that all Americans would accept him. Seeing myself through their eyes made me forget completely what had inspired me to do this. Not because of race—but because . . . weren't four children enough? And what did I know about this boy and how he would fit into our rich American house?

After lunch Mihail returned to his job and Violeta took the child horizontal with her onto the kitchen bench and I sat alone in her bedroom in the cloudy intermittent bedroom light. I tiptoed down the cold hall once and peeked into the kitchen. Pinned under Violeta's ample arm, Chrissy saw me. His eyes lit up and he grinned. I ducked away and sped back to the bedroom, where I sat and listened to the racket of the plastic storm window in mounting claustrophobia and fright.

I'd met him the day before at the orphanage in a village an hour away. I'd been picked up from the Sofia airport by the adoption agency's driver and translator, a man of about thirty named Petko. He and I waited in the office of the orphanage director, a woman I will call Madame Gancheva. She was well educated, sharply dressed, and in her sixties. She spoke no English and I no Bulgarian, so we conversed in French. She congratulated me on being an American who knew a foreign language. Then a four-year-old boy came willingly, shyly, bravely, with a small swagger, into the office holding Violeta's hand. He was very small and very cute, black-haired and bright-eyed.

He stopped in front of me.

"Christian!" I said admiringly. "I'm so happy to meet you!" With a sweet smile, he allowed me to hug him.

"He's adorable! So sweet! He's a Romani, right?" I asked Madame. I meant this as a compliment. His dark skin had not come across on the referral video. He was incredibly handsome.

"Romani? Gypsy?" asked the director in concern, pursing her lips. "No, no, I do not think it."

"No, no Gypsy!" shouted Violeta. "Very nice boy!"

"But . . ." I said innocently. "He looks . . ."

"Let me looking," said the director, while rapid-fire Bulgarian words snapped between her and her staff person. "*Voilà*," she said, pointing to an open file on her desk. "Here, mother might be half Gypsy, *one half*, father unknown, maybe Bulgarian."

"Bulgarian" or "ethnic Bulgarian" meant white.

Drawn to the small boy, who stood at attention beside me facing the director's desk, I'd begun unconsciously to stroke his warm head. Though engaged in conversation, I felt his short hair tingling under my touch. Petko filmed us. Later my mother would watch this video in her bedroom in Dayton, Ohio. She'd been completely mystified by my desire to adopt, but when she saw me smoothing Chrissy's head, she felt a surge of pity for him. When I looked at the video later, back in Atlanta, I saw in my movements, in my unconscious petting, something of the way I'd instinctively smoothed the heads of my confused, wet newborns when each lay upon my chest for the first time.

Sitting on a low sofa across from the director's desk, I recognized instantly that Madame Gancheva was lying: Chrissy was of course a Romani child, a full-blooded beauty, black-eyed and black-haired, son of a thousand-year-old diaspora that began in India and possessor (we would discover) of many of the arts and gifts of his people. Madame Gancheva and Violeta feared that I was about to reject him and demand my money back immediately unless they produced a white child.

"He's darling," I said, continuing to stroke his hair.

"Yes? You like?" asked Madame very happily.

Violeta shouted again, "Very nice boy! No Gypsy!"

Chrissy had a square-shouldered, wide-legged stance. He was round-eyed and ready. He was dressed in a worn gray sweat suit and cotton slippers. He didn't know why he'd been called to the director's office, but he clearly expected the best.

"What's your name?" I asked him, wondering if he'd been taught any English.

Violeta repeated the question in Bulgarian: *"Kak se kazvash?"*

Now the little boy froze, with an expression of worry.

"Kak se kazvash!" she repeated sternly.

This was a hard question. He looked from one to another of us with his glittery black eyes, hopeful but also anxious. Everyone seemed to be waiting for his pronouncement. Finally he ventured, almost inaudibly, "Tian?"

He was four years of age and unsure of his own name. At the time, I thought it was stage fright; over the following hours and days I realized—by watching the confusion among Bulgarian adults who tried to communicate with him—that he possessed only tatters of language, shards of gibberish that had fallen carelessly from the lips of hired care-givers and were passed around and shared among the semi-feral com-munity of neglected children that lived under this roof. Christian hadn't been spoken to very often by adults, not often enough to be certain which sound was his name and not someone else's name or a collective name for the tumult of unwanted children.

Violeta rooted around in a box and fished out a pair of old Velcro sneakers for the child they enjoyed calling "Chreesie." The shoes were too small but would have to do. The nameless boy stuffed his feet into them eagerly, unaware that there was any quality of "fitting" that applied to shoes. I zipped him into the American blue-jean jacket I'd brought for him, and we prepared to depart. As I gathered my purse and camera case, I suddenly realized that this was ground zero of the Muffin En-counter! Here were the table, the desk, the bookshelf, the orphanage director, and the caregiver. And Petko had been the cameraman of the video we'd watched at home so many times. The only thing missing was the muffin. The child must have eaten it!

The front door of the old two-story pink stucco orphanage opened onto a pebbled road and a grass field. Geese scuttled back and forth through puddles in the gravel path. Chrissy gave a high-pitched shriek of happi-ness when he saw the geese, and took off after them, but he didn't know the word for geese. He yelled *"Kuche!"*—the word he'd called the bunny rabbit in the referral video. We drove steeply uphill to an old national park that marked a point of Roman conquest. The park was full of mon-grels, hungrily stalking the landscape like wolves; Chrissy yelled *"Kuche!"* again and was eager to hug the mangy dogs. Petko swung Chrissy onto his shoulders.

At the park, we climbed over the ancient foundation stones, but Chrissy was mesmerized by a stream crackling and peeking out from beneath a blanket of mushy oatmeal-colored ice. I demonstrated for him that you could throw a rock into the ice for a black splash from beneath, and we threw pebbles and handfuls of sand and sticks for an hour. He was dazzled by it all—wind, sky, clouds, and the clatter of rocks into the water. In his gaiety he leaned so far over the stream, into the wind, that

I was hanging on to the back of his blue-jean jacket for the last ten minutes as he pockmarked the ice with his pebbles from a nearly horizontal position. He wanted to embrace the water, as he'd wanted to embrace the geese and the flea-bitten mutts; he fluttered his eyes shut to take in the sensations of the outdoor world.

We drove to a rusted post-Soviet playground. Hazardous pieces of metal protruded from the mud like shrapnel. Chrissy had no idea what to do  with the metal wreckage, so he walked gingerly among the pieces. A Bulgarian family arrived to try to extract some fun. I nodded to the father, but Petko led me and Chrissy away to an ice-hard field of mud and weeds. I had bought a green ball from a canvas-roofed kiosk at the side of the road; now Chrissy gamboled about with his new ball, hugging it. People strolled along the sidewalks, but Petko lured us farther out on hard, muddy ground. I sensed that he was trying to avoid the locals, but I didn't know why. Was there anti-Americanism here?

"Why do you do this?" I asked, and he struggled to explain: "I do not want . . . I fear that . . . someone can say ugly thing to you. About boy."

I understood: we had a Romani child with us against whom "ethnic Bulgarians" might mutter racist slurs.

Chrissy pursued his plastic ball into some tall grass, then tried to kick it back toward Petko. After several swings and misses he managed to nudge the ball out of the grass.

"He will be *futball* player, soccer player," offered Petko to lighten the mood.

"He'll play for the U.S. World Cup team!" I replied, since the only thing I knew about soccer was that it involved a World Cup.

"Oh, no," said Petko, his mood darkening again. "You see, he is very small now. He have not good food. Not energy. But when he have good food, he will grow and be strong. When strong, he play for *Bulgarian team!*"

And *this* I understood to mean *Please do not insult excellent child from Bulgaria by implying that he will play for inferior U.S. national team instead of returning to our country to play for superior Bulgarian national team that finished fourth in the 1994 World Cup, which fact we Bulgarians intend to insert into every conversation we have with foreigners.*

7

Just a Weekend Getaway

Petko dropped us off at the orphanage for an hour. We walked down the dark linoleum hallway, through a back door, and onto a fenced-in yard of cracked concrete and dirt. It teemed with small, unwashed children, many of them crying. On a sagging wooden bench, a row of two-year-olds sat in wet pants, wailing.

Chrissy yelled in delight, "Tanya!" and ran to embrace his caregiver, a young peasant woman of forty, with missing teeth. The children all slowed their activity to look at me in astonishment. Suddenly the word "Mama!" was spoken and flew from mouth to mouth. A mama had come! A mama was here! A mob of small children surrounded me as if I were a movie star and they were teenage girls. "Mama! Mama!" they screamed, jumping up and down deliriously and waving their arms to catch my attention. I had become the desperate focus of forty preschoolers now; their small hands patted me, stroked me, tried to hold my hands, slipped in and out of my pockets, and tried to relieve me of my purse and camera bag. "Mama! Mama! Mama!" The two-year-olds against the wall slipped off their bench and staggered toward me, still wailing.

There was an old swing set and a rusty, peeling slide, but nothing else to play with. There was a broken handle from a spade and some pebbles and a few scraps of cellophane, and these rare and special items were passed hand to hand among the children. Children brought them to me, too, and I caught the rhythm: that I was to examine it, praise it to the skies—"This is a very fine piece of packaging you have here"—and hand it back.

A caregiver clapped that it was time for lunch. The children ran to line up. It was like day care twenty-four hours a day, seven days a week, or like a poorly equipped preschool from which children were never picked up by parents idling in a long line of vans holding up placards with their car pool numbers.

Petko came back for us. Violeta, Chrissy, and I climbed into his Russian-made Lada for the drive to Violeta's apartment in Pleven. The small boy was in awe as we entered the apartment building and climbed stairs that stank of garbage. His eyes were huge when we stepped into a clean, sunny, and modern apartment, and his fingers twitched with eagerness. In the kitchen, he ran to touch all the drawers and cabinets. The drawers slid open and shut! Hinged wooden doors revealed cabinets! He stood on tiptoe to touch the light switch, and the overhead light went on. And off! And on! It was a hall of wonders! There was a crazed gleam in his eyes as he tried to look everywhere at once, overstimulated by colors and shining metal and sliding drawers. The room operated by magic, like the stirred-up self-cleaning nursery in the children's movie *Mary Poppins*, not that Chrissy had ever seen a children's movie. Now he capered down the hall awkwardly. He collided with the wall, righted himself, and kept going. In the master bedroom, he was frantic to explore my suitcase. He swayed from foot to foot in his eagerness to learn what he was permitted to touch. I taught him about zippers, and his breathing changed as he slowly, carefully, reverentially unzipped and zipped, unzipped and zipped every compartment on my suitcase, backpack, and camera bag. In a side pocket of the backpack he found a knot of baggies containing snacks I'd brought from a natural food store in Atlanta. He nibbled thoughtfully at the tip of a single whole raw cashew, as if it were to be eaten like a banana. He finished it and then paused, as if memorizing for all time the flavor. Then he returned to the unzipping. In an inner compartment of my suitcase he found a small drawstring velvet bag filled with earrings. I poured them out onto the bedspread for him. Now he was a rich man, like Aladdin in the cave, gold and silver reflecting off his cheeks. He rolled each earring between thumb and forefinger, then brought it up close to his eyes like a watchmaker. There were two of each style, he realized. He plucked one, and its twin, from the bedcover and showed me. "Yes, good! Good!" I said. The child worked in silent concentration, breathing slowly, until all the pairs were arranged.

As we finished, I remembered that I had a present for him in the suitcase, so I dug through it and extracted a dark brown teddy bear. Chrissy shrieked with fright, put up both hands to ward it off, and fell backward off the bed.

Violeta came for Chrissy then because it was his nap time. Now he lay awake on the kitchen bench, secured by her arm, and I was the one inwardly warding off something with both hands and falling backward in fear.

In the muddy park a few hours earlier, watching him wander enchanted through the decrepit equipment, I had thought, *If we're going to adopt, this is the child to adopt. The search is over.*

I had also thought, *But are we going to adopt?*

Now, forlorn in this room where even the white chenille bedspread stung like a patch of snow, I asked myself, *Whose idea was this anyway?*

I remembered: *Adoption was Donny's idea. He'd been trying to cheer me up. He should have stuck to bird feeders.*

I felt ill with homesickness. I sat on the edge of the bed and curled forward, bringing my head to my knees. It was three o'clock in the afternoon here, which meant 8:00 a.m. Saturday morning in Atlanta. But to place an overseas call from this city, you had to notify the post office, and the postmaster rang back within twenty-four hours to make the international connection. I'd reached home only once that week.

Six-year-old Lily had answered the phone and burst into tears at the sound of my voice. "Mommy, where *are* you? I'm scared!"

"You're scared? What's wrong?"

"The volcano!" she wept.

Donny had let her stay up late to watch a disaster movie with the family the night before, and now she thought Stone Mountain was about to blow. *Goddamn it, Donny!* I thought. "Sweetheart," I began, "Stone Mountain . . . ," at which point the phone connection dissolved. Was there ever a worse phone call home from a distant and lonely mother?

I stood, then sat, then stood again in Violeta's freezing bedroom, where mirrors magnified the cold air while the ice-blue wind pounded on the translucent insulation. The worst part was that Chrissy had started calling me Mama. I didn't know Bulgarian, but I understood that much. I didn't know if he thought that I was his first and missing mother who had returned for him or if he thought that all children endure a chilly, loveless, and institutional start in life while waiting for their mothers. But I sensed that a place had been carved out in his mind, in his soul, for a mother.

And she had finally shown up.

And it was me.

Of course all the children at the orphanage had shrieked "Mama!" at me, but that was like a pack of teenagers screaming "I love you!" at a movie star. This was no crowd scene. This was one small boy saying "Mama" with disbelieving happiness, gazing with love and amazement at every part of my face, circling round from my cheeks to my forehead to my hair and coming to rest on my eyes.

If I had thought this was a free look, a check-this-one-out, a no-risk trial with the possibility of a full refund, I was wrong. It is not permissible to dabble in that way in anyone's life—especially a child's.

A rickety wooden crib stood against one wall of Violeta's bedroom. When I picked up Chrissy and tried to insert him into it for sleep, he nearly backflipped out of my arms in protest, kicking soundlessly. It was like trying to insert a feral cat into a cardboard pet carrier. I transposed the windmilling child onto the double bed, and he calmed down instantly, all smiles. But in the night he woke up scared in the strange bed and room, and my gentle foreign words were of no comfort. He didn't know this room and he didn't know me, but he did know how to console himself. He rocked his torso back and forth, sitting up in bed. I felt as if I were looking into his past, at a long line of cribs in rooms to which caregivers didn't come when children cried in the night, cold rooms full of silently rocking abandoned children. He rocked faster and harder, staring forward into nothing, self-hypnotized. He threw himself down onto the pillow, rolled to his back, and rocked his head back and forth violently until he fell asleep.

He has no one. No one has rocked him, I thought.

I also thought, *People aren't lining up to adopt this boy. I may be his only chance for a mother.*

The next morning, Chrissy was awake before me and greeted me with laughing eyes and a huge smile, a smile made bigger by the fact that he was wearing many circles of tinted lip gloss. He had unzipped my suitcase and purse and cosmetic bag—like a series of Russian wooden nesting dolls—and opened the lipstick and used it just right, put it back into its case, into the bag, into the purse, into the suitcase, then zipped up everything and waited for me to wake up. What could I say? "Bravo, little boy."

I wondered what words Chrissy knew, since—compared with American four-year-olds—he spoke infrequently. "Does he know his colors?" I asked Violeta.

"Yes, he know colors!" she yelled. Her job title at the orphanage was, she informed me, "speech therapist."

"What color is this?" I asked Chrissy, pointing to my blue shirt.

"*Kakŭv tsvyat e?*" demanded Violeta of the child.

He looked abashed, and worried. He whispered, "*Sin?*" (blue).

"*Dobŭr!*" (Good!) Violeta clapped, and I echoed, "*Dobŭr!*"

"What color is this?" I asked, pointing to the yellow plate, and the little boy yelled, "*Sin!*"

Sin (blue) turned out to be the color of my black socks, the chipped green fruit bowl, and the red artificial carnations. *Sin* was the only color name he knew. But I was relieved to know that he possessed the mental category of color.

Chrissy had no idea how old he was. When I asked him, Violeta told him that the answer was *chetiri godini* (four years old). He nodded vigorously and shouted, "*Chetiri godini!*" Wondering if he knew his numbers, I held up seven fingers and asked, "How many?"

"*Chetiri godini!*" he shouted. Four years old!

"*Sedem,*" said Violeta.

I held up ten fingers.

"*Chetiri godini!*"

"*Deset,*" said Violeta, as if she were the one being tested.

Well, at least he also had the general concept of number. Then I remembered that he'd yelled "*Kuche!*" at the stuffed bunny rabbit in the video and the women had laughed; and that he'd yelled *"Kuche!"* at the geese *and* at the dogs; so clearly he had a concept for animal names. But I saw that my questioning of the boy was making Violeta uncomfortable. It reflected badly on her title of "speech therapist" that he knew next to nothing, and she may also have feared that I would refuse to adopt him if he failed these tests. So I stopped quizzing him.

After dinner the others left the kitchen and Chrissy and I moved to the cold linoleum floor. By then I was exhausted and shaken by misgiving and homesickness; I didn't want to prepare for bed yet, because I didn't want to be alone in Violeta and Mihail's cold bedroom with the child. Before going to bed, Violeta offered us a box of LEGOs from her small stash of toys. Chrissy sat cross-legged across the box from me, prepared to do whatever was required here.

His hair—damp from his bath—was parted and combed sideways; he looked handsome and mature. I pulled out a flat red LEGO platform, an eight-inch-by-eight-inch square upon which you could erect a building. I showed him that you could push a brick down on it, and it would stick. Chrissy took the platform and began pushing blocks onto it methodically, trying to fill up every centimeter of space. He thought that's what I wanted him to do. I wasn't up to teaching him how to raise walls and build a structure. I was counting down the hours until my dawn departure to the airport in Sofia; I was eager to consume those hours with sleep and be done with Bulgaria; I couldn't wait to take Lily in my arms and explain that Stone Mountain, a major Georgia tourist destination, was a solid hill of granite without lava. The little boy looked up at my face frequently, but I didn't have the energy to take in his milk-tooth smile and sparkling eye contact. Chin in hands, eyes downcast, I sat and watched his nimble fingers press the LEGOs down on the red square. He *was* doing it a bit cleverly, I noticed; with a tiny bit of innovation, he generated odd-sized openings that required not the basic six-pronged bricks to fill them, but an eight-pronged brick or a two-pronged brick or the rare one-pronged brick. Reluctantly I was drawn in. Seeing in advance the size block he would need, I got it ready; the next time his hand hesitated and his eyes narrowed to figure out the problem, I opened my palm, and miraculously, the correct LEGO was there. Our eyes met. Chrissy laughed. I looked down again and he went back to his work. He was probably exhausted, too, after his big day outside the institution. But he would do whatever it took to keep me nearby and to prolong the magical day. He stopped looking up at me, but tendrils of yearning emanated from the child toward me.

And I knew this sound so well—the skittering of a child's fingers through a shallow box of LEGOs in search of the missing piece. Seth spent years of his childhood on the hardwood floor of the playroom as rolling robots or winged dinosaurs or skyscraper masterpieces of his own invention kaleidoscoped out from his fingers. I happily sat on the sofa nearby, reading a book or magazine, while his fingers kicked and rustled through the piles of plastic bricks. So I recognized the light tumbling sound made by Chrissy's fingers as the music of home, a melody from the childhood of *my* children. The apartment was silent. Violeta and Mihail had gone to bed, and the city was quiet beyond the windows; the only noise in Eastern Europe at that moment was the scuffling of Chrissy's fingers through the LEGO blocks.

Even though we weren't looking at each other, I felt as if we were striking some sort of deal. *Take me home with you,* he seemed to offer, *and I'll play with LEGOs to your heart's content, just like your very own son.*

Early the next morning, a Monday, Petko came to pick me up for the drive to Sofia and the airport. I hugged the child goodbye. "Mama?" he asked in confusion. I settled myself in the backseat, waved, and leaned back for the long and jolting drive to the capital.

The Decision

Outside the airport, Petko handed me the videocassette he'd taped of our weekend. I planned to make copies and mail them to three of the top international adoption doctors. Then, without pressure or fright or loneliness, with input from experts, and without the pensive eyes of a motherless child gauging my every move, Donny and I could rationally discuss the next step: to adopt or not to adopt. Perhaps we would return to our normal life of great happiness with four remarkable children and adoption would be this thing we almost did one time.

But I forgot to factor in the four remarkable children. Adoption momentum was seized from me.

The moment I dragged my suitcase through the front door, the kids surrounded me and requested the videotape. Crowding around the television, they grew excited. Here was Chrissy in the park trying to kick his green ball, Chrissy waving at dogs and yelling *"Kuche!"* and Chrissy lurching around Violeta's apartment with spaced-out eyes. The children laughed with delight. For dinner they asked if we could go out to dinner to celebrate my return and the impending adoption. At a pizza place, the kids asked if we could pick out a new name for the little brother, since "Christian" is not the perfect moniker for a nice Jewish boy.

I got out in front with my traditional favorites: Aaron. Phineas. Kenny. Gideon.

The kids burst out laughing at every name as if I were joking. "But Giddie is such a nice nickname," I offered, not for the first time. They laughed harder. "I like Skip," I said, and they have never forgotten or forgiven me for suggesting it. "Skip is a dog's name!" they yelled. To this day they enjoy ribbing me about it: "Remember how you wanted to give him a *dog's* name?"

Unfortunately, I then produced Sky, as in Sky Masterson, Marlon Brando's character in *Guys and Dolls*, and Sky King, the 1950s TV adventure hero. "SKY?" shrieked the children. "What about *Sea*? What about *Tree*? How about *Plant*?"

"I've got it!" cried Seth. "No, really, I have the perfect name." We quieted down and looked at him, at which point he said, "Pocahontas."

Lily collapsed sideways in laughter. "Name him Meeko!" she choked out. "Name him Governor Ratcliffe!" It was rare that Lily, at six, could keep up with the rapid-fire conversations of her older siblings, but Disney's *Pocahontas* was in her wheelhouse. "Name him Grandmother Willow!" She glanced over at me in pink-cheeked pleasure as each of her suggestions produced a roar of laughter from Molly, Seth, and Lee.

"Sneezy!" called Molly. "Sneezy Samuel!"

The others took it up: "Dopey!" "Sleepy!" "Grumpy Samuel!" Gales of laughter. Donny's chest and shoulders went up and down in the eh-eh-eh-eh chortle the kids love to mimic. "Old Yeller!" called Molly. Lily was holding her side in pain from laughing so hard.

In a deep southern drawl Seth announced, "Billy Bo Bob. Mah name is Billy Bo Bob and you can jest call me Billy Bo Bob cause you mah friend."

"Your daddy is over to the jail," I drawled back.

"Yay-uh, and mah cat has one eye and mah mama has one eye."

A rainstorm spattered the front windows of the pizza place. Our cheeks were wet with tears of laughter as we dashed, in hysterics, through the rain to the van. I never got a chance to pose the question: *But are we going to adopt?*

The next morning I e-mailed a friend our goofy list of names, trying to hold on to the berserk joy. But she e-mailed back, "That makes me feel very sad for the little boy. It seems to me that you are making fun of him." Merriment departed, and fright crept back into my soul. Fear shivered through me like wind from Violeta's freezing bedroom. I felt homesick again, even though I was at home. That night I snuggled with the children after dinner on the sofa; we watched the musical *Grease* on TV. I drew Lily into my lap. I felt as if a force were prying me from them, as if a hard wind knocked at the front door that would blow me away from my children. No one mentioned the adoption for a couple of hours, so I didn't either. It was fun to pretend it wasn't happening.

I made three copies of the videotape and of Chrissy's medical report. I mailed one set to Dr. Jane Aronson in New York and another to Dr. Ron Federici in Washington. With the third set I drove, in the steeply angled white sunlight of March, to an international adoption medical practice in Atlanta. Dr. Amy Pakula and a few staff people ushered me into a meeting room. We sat around a boardroom table as an assistant wheeled in a television on a high cart.

The doctors and psychologists were accustomed to brief, dim, and soundless orphanage footage like the video I'd been sent of Tomas. They were astonished that I'd just spent a weekend with an orphanage child in Bulgaria! Adoption from Bulgaria was new, and the freedom to spend long hours with a child struck them as unprecedented. "Look how the child interacts with you," the staff marveled. "He's making eye contact with you. Look at him trying to play." "There is expressive language!"

"There is evidence of self-care," Dr. Pakula commented when Chrissy paused on the muddy field to put down his green ball and wipe his hands on his jacket.

"He really looks very, very good on this tape," everyone summarized. "Congratulations." "Yes, congratulations!" other staff people called as I left.

I felt more terrified on the drive home than I'd felt an hour earlier trying to find the office. My hands shook on the steering wheel. I was afraid of jerking the wheel left, into oncoming traffic, or right, onto the railroad tracks. The sun dropped rapidly; its parting rays gleamed briefly like cold silverware falling into a drawer. The hope I'd felt at the pizza place a few nights earlier, the confidence that my children could make *anything*—even *adoption*—okay and normal and fun, fled.

I was nearing the edge of the cliff; soon there would be no more reason to delay and I would have to jump. The late-afternoon sky was a heavy gray by the time I pulled up at home, and I was shivering.

Dr. Ron Federici phoned the next day from Washington, D.C. He zeroed in on the unusual fact that Chrissy had not been institutionalized at birth. "When I see in the records that Christian did not enter group care—that he was presumably with his birth family—until the age of seventeen months, this raises the possibility of a good outcome for him," he said.

On the third day, I heard from Dr. Jane Aronson: "The head circumference measurement is missing from his medical report." She really couldn't offer any general comments on the video or anything else until she received that information.

I promised to get the answer as soon as possible. I e-mailed the Bulgarian adoption attorney, a proper and sternly beautiful young woman named Milena, who favored tightly buttoned-up double-breasted suits and dark red lipstick, with her hair gathered into a smooth bun.

After one day, Milena replied to my e-mail: "I have phoned to Chrissy's orphanage and here is the number you ask: 45 cm."

I forwarded that e-mail to Jane Aronson and waited.

The next afternoon, she called from her office and said, without preamble, "His head is too small."

"*What?*" My heart began to violently pound. *I* was now the recipient of this news, like the couple I'd heard her call while doing the magazine story? I made my way to the daybed in my office and sat down, pulling a notebook into my lap. Jane was kind, but professional: "The growth of the head correlates with brain growth; it's the most important growth parameter. Chrissy has microcephaly. He has a small head."

I wrote all this down in overlarge and wildly shaky handwriting. She stopped talking, and it was evidently my turn to say something. "But he seemed *fine.* Did you watch the videotape?"

"I watched it. He seemed like a nice-looking boy and a lovely kid."

"He looked *normal!*" I said.

"We're finding that as many as forty percent of Eastern European orphans are not on the standard growth curve. Their heads are too small. We do see catch-up growth in very young children, but we don't yet know whether that correlates with cognitive advances. And a boy of four years is not going to see that kind of catch-up growth."

"What are you saying? He's not going to be normal?"

"It's impossible to predict. What we know is that his brain has suffered an insult and is not experiencing the normal growth of childhood. It can be from nutritional deficiency, from lack of stimulation, or from intrauterine exposure to alcohol, drugs, or toxins.

"I felt intuitively that he looked good, but having a head circumference not even on the border may mean we're looking at delays here. Still, a child can be delightful socially and enjoy daily activities while being limited intellectually."

She was not telling me to decline the referral.

"I know this is very hard. Decisions about adoption are so fraught with problems with regard to the objectivity piece; I'm not there examining him. But if we are to assume these measurements are correct, the referral becomes risky."

"How small is his head?" I whispered. I heard her turn a page.

"Chrissy is four years one month of age; we would expect to see a head circumference in the neighborhood of fifty centimeters. He's at forty-five centimeters. We're looking at three standard deviations below the mean. There has just been a tremendous insult to the child's brain. I'm sorry, Melissa."

"Should I ask the people at the orphanage to double-check the head measurement?"

"Yes, you could ask."

Where had I heard those words before?

Rage welled within me. I wasn't mad at the doctor but at a world that dumped little kids in Soviet-gulag-like orphanages and underfed them and neglected them and warped their development. I felt myself rising to the defense of the little boy. I sat on the daybed in my office where the phone call had pinned me, breathing in and out hard. I did not believe Chrissy was developmentally delayed, at least not yet, at least not beyond what could be explained by his narrow world. I would fight for him.

I e-mailed Milena, the Bulgarian lawyer: "Sorry to bother you again, but the doctor is confused by Chrissy's head measurement. Are you sure it's correct?"

Milena e-mailed back a few hours later with the worst possible news: "Yes, 45 centimeters is correct. Violeta made the measurement of Chrissy while I held on the phone with her."

Not yet ready to surrender, I replied: "The doctor says that the measuring tape must be placed across the very middle of the forehead, not too high and not too low. Do you think Violeta did it correctly?"

I stopped myself from dropping hints about whether "45 cm" was too high or too low to be normal. I didn't want to provoke a falsified result, although I kind of wanted to.

Two hours later another e-mail from Milena clicked into my in-box, and my heart stopped. "I will ask Violeta to take it again" was all it said.

We were on the verge of adopting a developmentally delayed child of limited potential. My self-congratulatory globe-trotting journalism-quality research into the risks and rewards of international adoption had brought my family to this point. Even with access to the smartest minds in international adoption medicine, I hadn't avoided a perilous result. But I was also nearing a point of deep moral revulsion. *Enough,* I thought. No matter what numbers Chrissy's head registered this time, we would *not* decline the adoption. Across the conquered lands of Eastern Europe, Nazi doctors had measured and charted the heads and noses of Jews and Romanies before exterminating them. There are chilling photographs of uniformed Nazis forcing Jewish and Romani men and women to sit very still while they take small metal rulers and other gadgets to their faces and jot down their findings. The victimized people tremble in their stillness; their dignity is breathtaking beside the barbarians in polished boots and pressed uniforms. The fact that I was asking, from rich America, for another measurement of an Eastern European Romani child's head felt unconscionable. It smacked of racial theory. No matter what the result, we *would* accept him. Besides, the sudden risk of losing Chrissy awakened my attachment to him. He was already my child.

Forty-eight hours passed without an e-mail from Bulgaria, an entire weekend without news. Donny got the picture, but as he'd done with the midlife pregnancy, he stood respectfully back, allowing me to navigate. He leaned toward giving the little boy a chance. I felt resolution, but not joy.

At close to midnight on Sunday night—early Monday morning in Bulgaria—I checked the computer once more before heading up to bed. An e-mail from Milena had arrived. To open it was to flip over the tarot card of our family's future. I tried to yell upstairs to Donny that there was news, but my throat had closed up. Alone, standing, I leaned over to read the message.

> Dear Melissa, I am sorry for these misunderstandings and incorrectness. When the orphanage staff person was dictating me the measurements of Christian, she first told me that the head circumference was 51 cm. I thought that this is too big circumference for very small child and ask her to take measurement once again. Then she has told me 50 cm. I suppose that from this interference of mine the misunderstanding has arisen. Excuse my inexperience. To me the circumference of 50 cm also seemed too big for such a little man. I encouraged her to measure again until she has found a better number.

Chrissy's head was fifty-one centimeters. I forwarded the e-mail to Jane Aronson. A night owl, she called instantly. "Children's heads are really big," she said. "Most adults don't realize how big. Chrissy is fine."

I tilted into bed in exhaustion. "I never want to hear the word 'circumference' again," I told Donny.

He said, "The next circumference we'll hear about is the circumference of the earth when Chrissy rounds it coming to America."

It was Monday morning in America when I sent the e-mail confirmation of our intent to adopt Chrissy. There was no rumble of thunder or blast of volcano to accompany this profoundly life-changing act. There was only a single plastic tap, not unlike the sound of one LEGO brick clicking onto another.

That, and the fact that Chrissy was born when I was forty-two.

9

Return to Bulgaria

October 1999

Lee, age eleven, was a great fan of airline comforts and conveniences.

He donned his slipper socks, plugged in his headphones, tucked his British Airways blanket around him, and closed his eyes with the gentle smile of a potentate. *I won't get homesick on this trip!* I thought. Molly and Seth could not miss a week of high school for the trip to Bulgaria, but Donny and the younger two were with me. Lily, now seven, lined up her Beanie Babies along the window for a view of clouds and ocean. She and I drew mazes and read stories; then we curled up together and slept. These were Lily's last hours as my youngest child, but neither of us realized the impending danger to our sweet intimacy.

In London, we downsized to Bulgaria Air and flew across Europe to Sofia. Petko met us at the airport and crammed us into his tin car with bald tires. We held our suitcases on our laps on the potholed road to Pleven, passing horse-drawn wagons and fields plowed by men walking behind oxen. It was dark when we arrived at the massive apartment block where Violeta lived. She and Chrissy stood on a cement stoop outside the building. As we pulled up, the little boy cried, with breaking voice, "Mama!" and leaped off the step into my arms. Lee later said that hearing the orphan's joyful greeting filled him with happiness. Donny lifted him up for a hug.

The children unpacked in Violeta's bedroom, where the five of us would sleep. Lee and Lily were without misgivings or foreboding. They trusted that they had landed in the right spot to meet the right boy. Lily sat cross-legged on the floor facing her suitcase; she carefully removed her things, tossed back her thick hair, then looked around innocently for a drawer. In my former Soviet-like arctic-cold outpost, the children spread a honeyed warmth. The light in the room was amber now, and the icy bedspread melted to a fluffy softness as Lee wrestled with his new brother on it. Donny and I were invited by Mihail and Violeta to join them at the kitchen table for cake, oranges, and vodka. We could hear the children laughing down the hall, bouncing on the bed and tickling each other. Chrissy, when I peeked in, had a look of almost demented happiness, as he'd had on our first afternoon together when he hectically ran down Violeta's hallway, bumping into the walls.

The next morning, we drove to the orphanage for the official removal of Chrissy from government care. Tanya noticed that Chrissy was sick. I saw that it was true: his face was hot and his eyes miserable. She picked him up, while I felt the sting of having failed at my first test as Chrissy's mother by missing his sudden illness. Morose, Chrissy laid his head on Tanya's shoulder and was carried to his little bed in an adjacent building. We followed. I took pictures of Lee and Lily trying out the bed, but Chrissy sat in misery, alone.

I didn't grasp until much later that Chrissy thought he was about to be abandoned again. He thought, despite his happy night of wrestling with Lee and snuggling with Lily, that he had failed to win us. He had been returned to the orphanage. He dully waited for us to leave without him as I'd done seven months earlier.

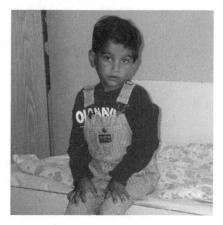

But of course we did not leave without him. I lifted him. He rested his arm across my back tenuously— not possessively—while we exited the building. We shook hands with the director on the gravel driveway. Tanya kissed Chrissy and wiped her eyes on her sleeve. We shared addresses. As we bounced in Petko's car west toward Sofia, Chrissy regained his good cheer. I pulled out some snacks, including a bag of raw cashews. He accepted one gingerly, nibbled the tip of it, and instantly recalled the flavor from my visit in March. He glanced up knowingly into my eyes to signal the secret we shared.

Our destination in the capital was a careworn 1930s hotel. We rattled to the fifth floor in an ornate antique elevator, dropped off our suitcases in a peeling, high-ceilinged room, and descended again to the lobby. As soon as we touched down, Chrissy took off at a sprint straight out the front door of the hotel and toward a busy street. Donny lunged and grabbed him. On the other side of the street was a small park. Donny carried him over and released him, and the child fled again, laughing devilishly whenever he looked back from farther and farther away. Lee and Lily, with their knack for inventing fun out of anything, chased him as if it were a game. Lee herded him back toward us and Donny swung Chrissy onto his shoulders. We returned to the hotel room for some rest.

We were jet-lagged, unwashed, and disoriented. The ceiling-high filthy windows were shot through with bright afternoon light. Chrissy hurled himself from one thing to the next, as he had in Violeta's kitchen. The lamps yielded and crashed, the television roared static, and the bathroom faucets ran hot. The toilet flushed again and again. Donny left with Petko in search of official permissions and visas, leaving me alone with the three children.

I drew back the thin bedspread, removed my shoes, and lay down as if I were free to take a nap. But Lee and Lily were too young to watch Chrissy, even with a mother napping nearby. "Mom!" yelled Lee. Chrissy was climbing onto the radiator to get a look out the unscreened fifth-floor window. I dragged out of bed with eyelids at half-mast and fiddled with the knob of the black-and-white television until I found *Tom and Jerry*. My two American children happily threw themselves on the floor to watch, chins cupped in their propped hands. Lily's head soon drooped onto her arms and she slept; Lee moved to the sofa and closed his eyes, too. My head was caving in from exhaustion, not just from jet lag and from driving all over Bulgaria, but from registering an emotional impact the equivalent of childbirth.

The little boy flew around the room like a bat smacking into the walls of an attic. I gazed across the room at my precious Lily and Lee, and I felt as if I were watching them from very far away, as if I were in Violeta's cold bedroom and they were asleep in Atlanta. I lay down again and closed my eyes. But water was pouring out of the toilet, and I ran to discover that Chrissy had dunked my 35 mm camera in the toilet basin.

The child had been utterly liberated. I tried to lure him to lie down next to me as he'd done on the bench with Violeta. He finally accepted my invitation to climb onto the bed, but only to jump on it, violently, with a look so defiantly happy his eyes might have been spinning in their orbs. I was the Sorcerer's Apprentice and he was the magically animated broom, spinning faster and faster and more destructively. I didn't know the secret words to defuse him.

Donny returned; we woke Lee and Lily and rode the rickety elevator to the hotel restaurant. Chrissy, in my arms, leaned over and punched every button, so that the elevator lurched and stopped, lurched and stopped at every floor. A group of Japanese businessmen bounced silently along with us.

Squeezed together in a booth, we studied the menu in bewilderment. "Minced meat baked in spiced sauerkraut juice" was the house specialty but didn't sound appealing, nor did "Turkish dish made with virgin soil." I chose a "soup prepared from the juice of cabbage pickles," but Chrissy hit the jackpot: he was served a huge yellow vegetable omelet. Sizzling with salt, it had crisp brown lace around the perimeter and flopped off the plate onto the table. He tore into it like a pup with a steak and gulped down half of it before sagging against the bench with an overfull tummy. Lily hated the unidentifiable gray-brown food she'd been given and she looked enviously at the leftover omelet.

Since Chrissy was finished eating, I cut a slice from the omelet and moved it to Lily's plate. As if he'd been shocked with an electrode, Chrissy startled upright, shook in a spasm, stiffened, and slid off the bench, landing under the table. He was having a seizure! On the dirty floor he shook, every bone in his body rattling. I dove under the table to rescue him. Suddenly I grasped that he shook not with a neurological impairment, but with fury. When he began to scream, everyone in the restaurant was alerted to the fact that an outrage had occurred at our table. We dragged him, crying, kicking, clawing, and screaming, out from under the table. Tears flew from his eyes; he shook and he bellowed. The waitress tried to interpret. "You . . . um . . . take his food? He . . . um . . . need his food?"

Before Lily could taste a morsel, I moved her slice of omelet back to Chrissy's plate and he calmed down. His chest heaved for a long time. We tried to sneak some tidbits to Lily, but she sadly declined, flinging her hair from side to side. She saw that the little brother, whom she'd welcomed wholeheartedly, didn't want her to have any of his food. It hurt her feelings. We led two melancholy children back to the hotel room, and even Lee drew apart from us.

We flew all night from Sofia to London and disembarked into the London Gatwick terminal not knowing if it was day or night. The terminal was rank with cigarette smoke and the aroma of bitter coffee. We felt dazed by the fluorescent lights and neon signs, the clicking of foreign destinations on the overhead charts, the expensive luxury-item shops, the wealthy men in Arab robes followed by women in burkas. We ate jelly beans and hard, cold breakfast rolls. Chrissy went berserk again and again; during one of his fits, as I pinioned him between my legs, he ripped my eyeglasses off my face and bent the earpiece; they couldn't sit straight on my face after that. Finally, we shuffled forward in the line to board the plane to America, and he threw another fit. He blocked everyone's path to the breezeway. Weary travelers detoured around us with tense disapproval.

"He thinks this is it. He thinks this is his new life, this is America," said Donny three hours into the flight. Chrissy, in his lap, raged and kicked the back of the seat of the despondent passenger in front of them. He had spent time rolling and screaming in the aisles; he had punched away the food tray; he spat out his chewed-up peanuts in fury. In a rare good mood, he took off down the aisle with the uninhibited snicker of liberation we'd seen in the park in Sofia. When a compassionate traveler took pity on us and tried to help by holding out his hands to slow Chrissy down and greet him, the child lunged into the man's lap, crushing his newspaper; and when we came to retrieve him, he clawed and kicked at us.

Lee and Lily occupied the two seats nearest the window; Donny, Chrissy, and I had the middle three seats across the aisle from them.

Again I looked at my two children with longing, as if from a great distance.

"Mommy, I'm *so tired*," moaned Lily five hours into the flight. She sat at the cold, smudged Plexiglas window on the far side of Lee, who was asleep. "And I'm *so bored*."

"I know, sweetheart!" I called over the head of the thrashing boy in my lap.

"I wish you could read to me," she whispered, feeling guilty for asking. She showed me a corner of *The Read-Aloud Treasury* from under the flap of her backpack.

"I wish I could, too."

She took the paw of a Beanie Baby tiger and waved to me with it. I had to turn away. My arms ached, my brain was splintering. I was beyond fatigue, beyond regret. Too late I remembered that the adoption doctors had said I might give him a dose of pediatric cough medicine to inspire sleep during the transatlantic crossing. He convulsed in my arms, trying to escape, as I attempted to pour a capful of Benadryl between his lips; he knocked the bottle against my chest. A gluey scarlet stain grew across my shirt and sank through to my skin.

As the plane tilted into the pale skies above Nova Scotia, Chrissy still tangled with us, snarling and scared. As we banked south down the eastern shoreline, he rocked in the aisle. As we began to descend the stairs of clouds into Atlanta's airspace, nine hours after departure, the Benadryl kicked in. We carried him snoozing off the plane and into Immigration, where we sat amid our piled-up luggage and waited for our names to be called. Chrissy threw himself onto the industrial carpeting to keep enjoying his delicious sleep. He was filthy, disheveled, and barefoot. I sat with a stiff pink stain of Benadryl on my chest, my glasses catawampus, and my stiff hair awry; Lee and Lily draped themselves in sleep over the suitcases; Donny leaned his head back against the white-tiled wall and wearily closed his eyes. We were all too tired and defeated to claim the waif snoring on the floor in the middle of the room as if he belonged to nobody.

10

Post-Adoption Panic

When I found myself weeping in our basement laundry room out of pity for my children's colorful old cotton sheets because I was about to spread them across the mattress of the small bed-wetting newcomer, I could tell I was in trouble.

Declining to take photos of the little guy (because it might mean that he was staying, because the photos might be used as evidence that he'd been here) also offered a clue. Refusing to let anyone else take a picture of the whole family (because his presence in the portrait would mar the effect) similarly sounded a warning note.

And there was the day, in the grocery store checkout line, when a cashier brightly asked, "Would you like to contribute a dollar for Thanksgiving dinners for the homeless?" and I snarled, with murderous anger, "I . . . HAVE . . . GIVEN . . . *ENOUGH.*"

Lying awake at night and plotting, *If I leave right now, drive all night, and check into a motel in southern Indiana, no one could find me,* also signaled that I was having some issues adjusting to the new presence in the family.

He was a cute and cocky kid, with dark brown eyes, a fringe of brown bangs, and a bounce in his step. We'd named him Jesse, a strong biblical name that rhymed with Chrissy. He took to his new name instantly, though he couldn't pronounce it. When people asked, "What's your name!" he pointed to himself and yelled, "Cha-chee!" He interacted eagerly with his new siblings. He grabbed Seth's or Lee's hand and smacked himself in the forehead with it, while making the sound "Ghee-ghee-ghee-ghee-ghee." His all-purpose word was *"Icka,"* as in *"Icka* hot dog!" and *"Icka* banana!" He loved hot dogs and bananas so much that Molly theorized he'd been deprived not of nutritious food in the orphanage, but of tube-shaped food. Standing on a chair at the kitchen sink, he washed and peeled his cooked hot dogs, laid them aside, and then washed and peeled his bananas. One day Seth found him on the deck, swinging a garden hoe over his head and bringing it down with a bang. He was slicing his hot dogs and bananas.

We assumed that *"icka"* was Bulgarian for "I want" or "Give me," but a local Bulgarian assured us that it was meaningless. She said Jesse had very little spoken language at all, just a few words of orphanage gibberish. Jesse's other all-purpose (non-Bulgarian) word was *"ne."* It was the universal preposition, as in—pointing to a playground playmate— "Cha-chee friend *ne* that." One day he had a bathroom mishap involving his swimsuit; he struggled toward us, dragging one leg and calling, "Penis *ne* stuck." The older kids hailed it as the greatest sentence ever coined in the Samuel family.

But I, a week after our return from Bulgaria, felt confused and weepy. I couldn't sleep. In the middle of the night I shook Donny awake so that he could agree with me that we'd irreparably altered our lives. I said, "It just doesn't feel like when we brought the other kids home from the hospital."

Donny answered softly, with some surprise, "To me it does."

I turned away and let the ridiculous man fall back asleep. I thrashed in the sheets and pummeled my pillow, in the grip of growing panic.

One night, scared and lonely at 3:00 a.m., I woke Donny and tried to take a different tack. "Okay, I think I figured something out. A *lot* of my friends are going through really hard times right now, like Claudia's family may lose their house to the bank and Patti just found out her husband's having an affair. So now I'm having a hard time, too!"

After a few minutes, Donny said, "I guess. But . . . this was supposed to be a *happy* thing."

I moaned. He rolled over and returned to sleep. When the clock radio blurted at 6:55 a.m., it sounded like any of a thousand mornings in my old life, but it heralded a life utterly changed. After the morning rush to get the older kids off to school, I trudged back upstairs in search of sleep, turned right down the hall, and shut myself in Seth's room. As my face touched his pillow, I felt that sleep would be found here in this sunny, book-lined room, with birds chattering under the eaves and the window blinds clicking lightly in the breeze coming through the autumn oaks. I felt as secluded as on a tropical isle. The breeze ruffled the pages of sheet music on Seth's desk. The skinny front leg of our American rat terrier, Franny, poked in under the door and waved around in search of me. I let her in, and the two of us lay down sighing and sinking contentedly. Then Donny yelled from the front door that he was leaving for work. I stood up, an automaton, exited the room, and descended the stairs robotically. A squealing boy in pajamas gleefully tackled me in the front hall.

I called my friend Judith Augustine and asked her to come over, and she did, eager to meet Jesse. I gestured wildly at him and asked, "Can you believe I've done this to myself?" He sat on the floor of the screened porch, facing a pile of colorful wooden blocks. He wore a red and white striped shirt under blue-jean bib overalls. He'd never seen blocks before and didn't know their purpose. He'd just confirmed that they weren't edible but was unsure what else to try.

"Can you remember why you *wanted* to adopt?" asked Judith kindly. The child looked fine to her; he looked very cute.

"No! I can't! It was another person; it wasn't me. I can't even remember that person. What was she thinking?!"

I knew what she had been thinking: she had been thinking, *Our children are so wonderful, our house is so full of love, we're good parents. Let's bring in another little kid from somewhere and we'll prolong the fun.*

Ha-ha. Instead of expanding the fun with my four children, I'd just carved a deep moat to separate us forever. If I tried to spend a minute alone with Molly, Seth, Lee, or Lily, Jesse frantically raced in circles in search of me. He was thrilled to have been given a mother, even a rumpled, disconsolate one. Perhaps he felt that he'd somehow lost his first mother but was not going to lose this one. "Mama!" he yelled, ordering that I watch him eat, or watch him fall asleep, or watch him dress. Dazed and weary, I obeyed. But one afternoon I refused to follow him into the small guest bathroom. Through hand gestures, he instructed that I should wait right there for him in the foyer. Instead, the instant he shut the door, I escaped! I dashed upstairs to visit Seth! Downstairs, Jesse washed his hands and emerged from the bathroom all smiles, only to confront the baffling and infuriating disappointment that the mama had run away again. *"MAMA!"* he screamed. He fell and thrashed in a seizure of rage like the one we'd seen under the table at the Bulgarian hotel restaurant. These rages were happening four or five times a day.

One morning, determined to salvage a single treasure from the wreckage of my former life, I asked Donny to stay home while I walked Lily to school. Lily and I used to walk to school together every day. Now I whispered to the second-grader, "I'll sneak out first, without Jesse noticing, and I'll wait in the front yard. You wait for a minute, then come out without him seeing you, and I'll walk you to school!"

But Jesse, hypervigilant, saw me escape. With a roar, he threw himself against the glass storm door. When Lily tried to get out, there was a scuffle at the glass door. The door closed on Lily's hand! Wailing in pain, she wrenched herself free, and we ran away together up the hill to school while Donny stood watch over a small boy convulsing in the front hall.

"I said he could come to our family," Lily sobbed, cradling her red hand, "but I didn't know he was going to *hurt* me." We staggered up the steep hill blinded by sorrow. I covered her with kisses at the school door and ran my fingers through her uncombed hair and noticed that she was wearing clothes that hadn't been laundered. Outside the school, I felt unable to go home. I made it to the street corner and stood there. Judith spotted me paralyzed on the sidewalk and pulled over. I got into her car and burst into tears. My spirits lifted faintly as we accelerated, and then they nose-dived when we pulled into my driveway thirty seconds later. I had hoped she was taking me somewhere new. Like Saskatchewan.

One day I called my friend Sue Fox for help, and she left work early to come sit with me. Jesse was happy to meet Mama's friend. He had new shoes from Mama he wanted to show her. "New one," he said about his little Velcro sneaker, pointing out his foot for Sue to admire it.

"Very nice shoe!" Sue laughed.

Then Jesse put that foot down and extended the other foot, explaining, "Two ones."

"Oh! Your mommy bought you two new shoes! Wow!" said Sue.

While she chatted with him, I pulled a telephone as far as the cord would reach from one room to the privacy of another. I shut the door and dialed the long-distance phone number of the adoption agency and whispered to the receptionist, "I'm not actually sure I can do this. What are you supposed to do if you're not sure you can really do this?"

"Well, gosh," chirruped a friendly voice. "Nobody's ever asked me that before! Let me find somebody to ask."

Undone to learn that I was the first, the very first, adoptive mother ever to ask that question, I hung up and doubled over in agony.

To escape the house during the long school hours, I buckled Jesse into the backseat of the van and drove aimlessly. The landscape had flattened; the houses, yards, and streets looked two-dimensional, like comic strips, and drained of color. I recognized everything, but couldn't remember how to insert myself into the scene. I'd slipped outside my own life.

As I drove, I tuned in to the NPR-affiliate radio station WABE's fall fund-raising drive. This year I listened not for the classical music, but for the studio chatter. I listened in the car; then I ran in and turned on the radio in the kitchen. I felt so frighteningly alone that the fund-raising pitches felt like conversation to me; the voices broadcast from the downtown studio felt like company.

One afternoon, running through the den, Jesse fell and cracked his face against the sharp corner of the brick fireplace; it looked like a serious blow, but he wouldn't let me examine it, and his dark bangs covered the point of impact. He didn't even whimper. He bounced off the brick and ran on. That night as he slept, I peeled back his fringe of hair and was stunned by the deep and clotted gash I found. He'd given himself a wound deep enough to require stitches. The fact that he hadn't cried in pain frightened me. I recalled having read that institutionalized children learn not to cry in response to pain, because nobody comes to their aid, but witnessing the phenomenon felt scary. And there were other classic orphanage behaviors: he rocked himself when distressed and at bedtime, and he sometimes clawed at the skin of his arm or his leg, plowing deep scratches till I restrained him.

I was moved to pity for the child, as trapped and solitary in his own strange world as I was in mine, but I didn't know who he was. I had no idea if he was going to turn out to be a regular little kid or if we were at the top of a staircase that would descend into years of confusion and difficulty and loneliness and chaos.

I'd never heard of "post-adoption depression syndrome." I knew nothing about depression of any kind. Later I would learn that this type of depression is common among parents adopting older post-institutionalized children. Adults are hardwired to attach to babies; trying to bond with a demanding, tantrum-throwing non-English-speaking four-year-old is much harder.

Adoption agency websites and literature brimmed with "love at first sight" epiphanies. Some parents felt love the moment they met their new child, others the first time they watched the referral video, and others as they caught the blurry black-and-white copy of a photograph buzzing out of their fax machine. It's possible that the promise of "love at first sight" set me up for a sense of failure when I didn't instantly feel it. Now I couldn't figure out how I would survive the coming eon that would fall on me in heavy blows of year after year after year. The little motherly tasks I'd done thousands of times—finding socks, tying shoes, wiping noses, zipping coats, slicing apples, taking temperatures, boiling noodles—seemed impossible to perform across the lifetime of a child I barely knew.

Because I hadn't heard of it, I wasn't thinking *post-adoption depression*. I was thinking I'd wrecked my dearest treasure, my family.

It wasn't Jesse's fault. When people asked me, "How are you all doing?" I said, "Oh, *he's* doing great, but someone ought to ship me back to Bulgaria."

11

Love at Second Sight

The preschool attended by Seth, Lee, and Lily was colorful and toasty, crammed into a few overheated classrooms and scuffed hallways of the Unitarian church. I had loved the free-haired hippie teachers in cotton skirts and Earth shoes. I had loved waiting in the car pool line and holding a paper plate out the window on which the number 19 had been written in black Magic Marker. I had loved the lumpy vases and mugs, the artwork and prose created in my honor for Mother's Day. Lee, at preschool, had authored a three-page biography of me:

Page 1: "My mommy is 30 years old."

Page 2: "My mommy is 30 feet tall."

Page 3: "My mommy weighs 30 pounds."

"I'm a perfect cube!" I rejoiced.

At least I was spared the Mother's Day Luncheon humiliation experienced by my friend Linda, who beheld, on the walls of her son Benjamin's preschool classroom, bright posters illustrating the concept "My Mommy Is Special Because . . ."

Benjamin had completed his illustrated poster to read "My Mommy Is Special Because She Has Hairy Arms."

———

Now I phoned our former preschool and told the director about Jesse. "Of course, bring him in!" she said warmly.

"I won't leave him with you," I promised. "But if we could just visit for an hour or two every day, we could work toward enrolling him. And I'll pay for the time!"

"Don't worry, don't worry!" she said. "Come on in, I'd love to meet Jesse."

I was thinking, *In the hours I spend at preschool, I won't be alone.* We got into the van with an actual destination. I tuned the radio to WABE's fund-raising drive and steered onto the beloved route. At the Unitarian church I took the little fellow by the hand and led him up the steps and down the hall to the classroom for four-year-olds. "You're going to like it here!" I promised. This almost felt like a scene from my real life! Sunlight shot through the tall, smudged windows, lighting up the guinea pig sawdust habitat, the costume corner, the beanbag chairs, and the wall of hooded jackets dangling from hooks. A Tom Chapin tape played in the background. It was four-year-old heaven! But not for Jesse. *"Pishka,"* he said anxiously, and I took him to the bathroom of miniaturized sinks and toilets. He finished, and I helped him climb the stool to wash his hands. The moment we returned to the classroom, he said *"Pishka"* again and pulled me toward the door. I tried to interest him in a soft slab of blue clay on the tabletop, and here was a bin of our old friends the LEGOs! And look, the teacher is reading *Lyle, Lyle, Crocodile*! . . . but he pulled on my pant leg and led me back to the bathroom. There he slid onto the tile floor and began to rock. It was the self-comforting movement of institutionalized children all over the world. I slid down against the wall next to him. In the hall I could hear the four-year-olds finding their partners for the march outside to the playground—they would board the painted plywood train pitched among the wood chips in the long, flickering shadows of the slash pines. They would run in happy circles and make their first best friends here. But Jesse, on the bathroom floor, rocked himself to a distant place, like a solitary rower on a dark lake.

A teacher I didn't know peeked into the bathroom, departed, did a double take, and returned. She looked from Jesse to me and back to Jesse, taking in the whole story. I shrugged and held out my hands helplessly—what could I do? I was stuck here.

"Good lu-u-u-uck." She laughed in an up-and-down sarcastic tune and then left us alone.

Now I was ready to start rocking.

In my own private hell, I failed to realize, *He thinks I've brought him to an orphanage.*

The director of the preschool, alerted to the fact that people had taken up residence in the bathroom, visited us next. I turned to her with pleading eyes. "Look at him," I said.

"I see him," she said kindly, lowering herself to the floor.

"Have you ever—" I choked up. "Do you think . . . can you tell if he'll be okay? Have you ever seen a kid come from this point, from this far away, into a normal life?"

"I think he'll do fine," she said, stroking his hair. "But I also think he's not quite ready for preschool."

Jesse was greatly cheered by our departure, to the point of making some small hops down the steps to the parking lot.

The next morning in the laundry room, awash in a feeling of pity for my children's old sheets, the thought crossed my mind for the first time: *You're crying over sheets. You're losing it.*

Followed by: *You'd better get help.*

Followed by: *If you succeed in convincing Donny that your lives are ruined, you'll never get out of this spot. There will be no one left to pull you out.*

I made a doctor's appointment. "Today. I need to see her today."

"Can you come tomorrow afternoon?"

"I guess so," I said in a small voice.

"People take something for this, don't they? Aren't there *drugs* for this kind of thing?" I asked the physician the next afternoon.

"You're completely exhausted," she said. "Are you sleeping?"

"No."

"I'm going to give you something to help you sleep."

I burst into tears. "I need something stronger! I'm crying over *sheets.*"

"Okay, okay," she said, and gave me a pharmaceutical sample. In my car in the parking lot, I ripped apart the package and swallowed the tablet whole, dry, without water. Instantly I began to feel better! The instructions said to allow four to six weeks for the medication to take effect, but the placebo effect kicked in during my drive home. Slightly calmed, I was able to reconsider the advice my friends had given. "You don't have to love him already," my friend Tema Silk said. "Just fake it. Jesse's in heaven. He's never been so mothered in his life. Your faking it is the sweetest thing that's ever happened to him."

I discovered that my body was okay with mothering him—my lips knew how to kiss him, my hands enjoyed stroking his hair. I tried to take a break from *thinking* and *feeling* and to follow, instead, the good-natured willingness of my body to mother the child.

Do I love him yet?

It's an awful thing we adoptive parents ask ourselves. *Do I love her yet? Do I love him yet?* Like the television ads for wireless phones: "Can you hear me now?" We don't pursue this line of questioning about the children to whom we gave birth. Yet here sat this little guy at the table, painstakingly peeling a hot dog, looking up with his sparkly eyes, and I asked myself, *Do I love him yet?*

Remarkably, Jesse was *not* having bonding issues with me. From the moment he shyly entered Madame Gancheva's previously forbidden office and stood bravely in front of me, he accepted me as his mama. "Good enough parenting" had become a popular catchphrase, and I began to feel that Jesse had been a recipient of it. The seventeen months of home-rearing someone had given him before taking him to the orphanage meant something, just as I'd hoped. Surely Jesse had not enjoyed the accoutrements of an upper-middle-class American infancy—crib mobiles, Beatrix Potter posters, Raffi tapes, a jogging stroller—but *someone* had cared for him. He knew about love. He accepted me instantly as his mother. He never seemed to wonder, *Why this mother and not another?* The closest he would ever come to appraising the odd events in his life was a remark he would make one day a year after his arrival: "I just didn't know that mamas have boingy hair." He was amused by my curly hair; his comment seemed to mean *I knew there were mothers in the world, sure; I just didn't know what mine was going to look like.*

He was happy. And *he* loved *me*. That steady, unwavering little beacon of love began to lure me.

One night within the first month of Jesse's arrival, sleepless again, I strayed from my bedroom and ended up resting on the daybed in my downstairs office. In the middle of the night Jesse, also a night wanderer, found me. He hadn't yet found me in my bedroom, because I kept that door closed all the time. He didn't know that room existed; it was my last bastion of privacy. Now, in my office, I opened the covers and he climbed in beside me. *Damn! He found me! I can't ever get a break!* I thought, feeling trapped and angry. Yet I was not insensitive to the sensation of the little boy curling and purring beside me; he nuzzled and snuggled like a kitten. At first light I sprang out of bed to put distance between us; when he got up, he found me in the kitchen and drew me by the hand back to the office. He pointed to the bed and said, in baby Bulgarian-English, *"Mama speesh; Cha-chee speesh."* (Mama sleep, Jesse sleep.) All day long he remembered, and reminded me, laughing, *"Mama speesh, Cha-chee speesh,"* pointing to himself to help me remember our great encounter, our wonderful secret. That night he tried to make it happen again, but I stayed in my own bedroom with the door closed. I heard him looking for me downstairs.

He was intoxicated with everything I did. One night as I dressed to go out somewhere, he sat high on my bed, swinging his legs, watching me. On went the stockings, on went the slip, on went the low heels; before I could finish buttoning the satin blouse, Jesse flew off the bed and into the closet to hug me. "Oh, MAMA!" he cried, utterly starstruck. He adored picking through my jewelry box to find pairs of earrings as he'd done in Bulgaria, and he took very seriously the responsibility of choosing a set for me to wear. It was as if he'd been starved not only for a mama but for all the accoutrements of a mama.

Under such an onslaught of tenderness, I began to soften.

I no longer assumed he was leaving; I assumed he was staying. He no longer assumed I was leaving; he began to trust that I was staying. He began to let me out of his sight for minutes on end. I was able to walk Lily to school in the morning, savoring every step, every breath of the fall air, as if heaven had been restored to me; and she returned to a feeling of normal life. I was able to listen to Molly practicing her upright bass and to Seth playing his trombone, and one day I pitched baseballs to Lee in the front yard.

One afternoon, feeling irascible and draggy, I gave in to Jesse's pleas of "Bagel, Mama? Bagel? Bagel?" and hacked so hard at a stale bagel that the knife glanced off the roll and slashed my finger. I ran upstairs to get cotton to stop the bleeding. Jesse followed in a panic. "Mama! Oh, Mama! Mama!" His eyes were huge and filling with tears. He stood beside me as I sat on the closed toilet trying to stanch the bleeding; he patted and patted my shoulder.

"Mama!" he announced. "Mama, nay bagel, Nay bagel, Mama." He was trying to help after the fact by unrequesting the bagel.

Downstairs, later, he stood on his tiptoes, reached into the kitchen drawer, extracted the big, guilty knife, and said, "Nay Mama this. Daddy. Nay Mama. Daddy." Meaning, *You should not use this knife anymore; let Daddy use it.*

Still later he had an updated announcement to make. He dashed into the kitchen, pointed to the knife, and said, "Nay Mama, nay Franny [the rat terrier]. Daddy." I didn't know if this policy statement was meant to protect the two individuals he most loved from the bad knife or if he now put me in the competence department with the dog.

Finally, toward the end of the day, he came to me with a plastic knife he'd found somewhere. He put it in my bandaged hand and said firmly, "Mama."

What was it I felt at that moment as I laughed and wept and accepted the plastic knife and hugged him? Was it, actually . . . could it be . . . Well, by then I was trying hard to stop grilling myself a dozen times daily with *Do you love him yet?* But if that wasn't the beginning of an old-fashioned sweet mother-son relationship—this repentant little boy handing me, so earnestly, a plastic knife—I don't know what it was.

I had made an appointment with a psychologist for the following day. After Jesse handed me that plastic knife, I phoned ahead to cancel it and made an appointment for a haircut instead. Jesse came with me. If he thought I was beautiful *before* the haircut, he really thought I was beautiful *after* the haircut. He thought the whole haircut experience was a glamorous, sparkling, and elegant affair, the air radiant with aerosol scents, nice ladies talking to him, a candy dish full of wrapped peppermints. On the drive home I glanced at him in the backseat, his cheek big with a peppermint. He gave me a huge, sticky smile. Did I love him yet? I was getting there.

12

The Art of Playing

"Find out if he's capable of imaginative play," a child psychologist had suggested to me before I flew to Bulgaria to meet Chrissy for the first time. It would tell us a lot about his cognitive and emotional well-being.

It hadn't occurred to me that children might not know how to play. Playing with my children, having access to the magic they casually fling around, has been the best part of motherhood. As little kids, each of my four spent time at the center of an imaginary universe.

When we drove to Disney World for the first time in 1994, everyone was excited. Two-and-a-half-year-old Lily's wildest expectations were realized when we pulled into a gas station along I-75 outside Valdosta, Georgia. A hard, warm wind was blowing; at the edge of the gravel driveway, there was a frayed pink plastic streamer nailed to the top of a stick, marking a spot for future road paving. Lily climbed down from her car seat and approached the streamer that snapped, fluttered, and contorted in the gritty wind. She stared at it wide-eyed, then pointed at it and began to laugh and hop. She clapped her hands. She turned around to make sure all of us saw this thing, this magical, frantic dancing pink Disney World Tinker Bell thing. She loved it so much, this piece of dirty plastic tossing its hair in the wind. Back in her car seat, she waved goodbye to it through the window. She sighed happily, deeply content with her visit to Disney World, and assumed we were now headed home.

(Not surprisingly, this was the same child who later saw the Tooth Fairy.)

Molly, at four, visited a petting zoo near Stone Mountain, and her empathy was captured by a three-legged fox, evidently rescued from a trap. By the time we left the zoo, Molly *was* the three-legged fox. From that day forward, she would, at random times, start hopping on one foot. "Is the three-legged fox here?" I whispered, and she nodded enthusiastically. The three-legged fox hopped into the kitchen for dinner and hopped up the stairs at bedtime. The three-legged fox hopped down the hall to preschool in the mornings. But then, one December night, Molly watched *The Nutcracker* on TV and was transformed into the Sugar Plum Fairy. I bought her a cassette of Tchaikovsky's ballet and a tutu. At night Donny and I heard the child upstairs in her bedroom, leaping, spinning, and landing like a ton of bricks. But she missed the three-legged fox! Not *being* the three-legged fox exacerbated her concerns about him. One night Donny and I were invited to a special performance in the living room. As we seated ourselves on the sofa, Molly turned on *The Nutcracker* and informed us that tonight the role of the Sugar Plum Fairy would be performed by the three-legged fox. And so it was, by a round-tummied little girl wearing a tutu and hopping on one foot.

I found a Superman costume at a garage sale once and brought it home to six-year-old Seth. He accepted it skeptically and went inside to try it on. He reemerged, a skinny, pale, nearsighted little sprite dressed as Superman. He scampered in joy across the yard to me and cried, "I look a *lot* more like Superman than I even *realized* I would!"

Lee was our baseball kid. He learned to read by sorting his baseball cards. He memorized statistics encyclopedically and, at a remarkably young age, was able to hold his own in baseball conversations with boys and men much older. Around a beach bonfire on the Outer Banks of North Carolina one Thanksgiving, Lee crept close to college guys throwing back beers and engaging in baseball trivia. They noticed the five-year-old's sparkling interest and tossed him an easy one. "Hey, buddy. You from Atlanta? You want a question? Okay, who's the all-time home run champion?"

"Oh!" cried Lee in delight. "I know this . . . oh, wait a minute, what's his name?" He tapped on his forehead to help the internal filing system spit out the correct player.

They scoffed at him, disappointed. "Rhymes with 'Bank'?" they prodded. "Rhymes with 'Baron'?"

"Oh, you're thinking of Hank Aaron, I know," said Lee. "But I was remembering Josh Gibson. He was a catcher in the Negro Leagues in the 1930s. He hit almost eight hundred home runs."

The older guys stared at Lee in shocked silence, then burst out laughing and invited him to be seated.

I sometimes worried whether the intensity of Lee's focus on baseball history and statistics came at the expense of his imagination, until I picked him up at T-ball practice one day. The little boys and girls were lined up at the plate, taking turns trying to knock a Wiffle ball off a plastic stand with a bat, after which each child ran to first base and then circled back to the dugout. There were no teams, there was no score, there was no game. As I approached the field, Lee yelled out over the crowd, "Mommy! We're *killing* 'em!"

At his T-ball game that weekend he paused at the plate and pointed with his yellow plastic bat toward imaginary stands. Only Donny and I knew that he was mirroring Babe Ruth's legendary gesture toward the center field bleachers in game three of the 1932 World Series. Lee *was* Babe Ruth.

Packing for my first trip to Bulgaria, I borrowed from Lily a diminutive rubber weasel with pricked-up ears, plastic whiskers, and a long, skinny tail, dressed in a cotton frock and sunbonnet. One afternoon as Chrissy and I sat on Violeta's kitchen floor, I pulled out the absurd creature and presented her to him. He gasped and fell back in horror. While I made the beady-eyed weasel dance, its toenails tapping the linoleum, Chrissy spun around the room, spotted a broom, took it by the straw end, and tried to beat Winona Weasel to death with the handle.

I was uncertain about the result of this experiment.

Now, in Atlanta, Jesse seemed lost as the older kids and their friends romped and chased through the house. I saw that childhood fun and make-believe were foreign to him. Though he'd spent the last three years in the nonstop company of other children, they hadn't been *playing*; they'd been trying to survive. Now Jesse, mystified, watched the lighthearted American kids at play. He could not make out the point of the trampoline in the backyard. He followed Lily and her girlfriends from a distance, like an anthropologist trying to decipher strange ways and customs.

Though Jesse was not acquainted with Maslow's hierarchy of needs, his body was. Every fiber of his being strained to meet the requirements for food and water. He woke up trembling in fear that there would not be enough breakfast for all. At every meal he looped his arms around his dish as he chewed, and lowered his head, and watched us guardedly out of the sides of his eyes. Water was precious, too. He accepted a plastic cup at mealtime as if it were a crystal goblet of 1787 Château Lafite. Once, he accidentally knocked over a cup of water and sprang up in fear and distress, assuming he would be punished. I bought a small canteen, filled it with fresh water, and draped the strap over Jesse's shoulder—his very own water! I showed him the drawers and cabinets in the kitchen where fruit, crackers, cheese, and cereals were available to him at all times, but he was afraid to take food without permission. Food was too precious and the risk of punishment too great.

Six months after Jesse's adoption I was forwarded a news item translated from a Bulgarian newspaper; it reported that a dozen desperately hungry children at Jesse's orphanage had been poisoned by digging out and eating roots from their dirt yard, and several children had died.

Given the intensity of his concern for food and water, imaginative play was a luxury that would have to wait.

Seth knew what was fun. One afternoon the fifteen-year-old pulled a deflated green balloon out of his pocket and gave it to Jesse. "Balloon," said Seth. Jesse was delighted. "*Icka* ba-oon! *Icka* ba-oon!" he cried, running to show me. I hadn't seen anyone so pleased with a deflated balloon since Eeyore accepted a popped balloon as a birthday gift from Winnie-the-Pooh. Seth steered Jesse into the bathroom, pulled over a stool, and helped Jesse fill the balloon with water. As the balloon expanded, the child's mouth rounded into an O. Seth tied it off, put the fat, jiggly thing in Jesse's hands, and led him through the house to the back deck. Jesse walked carefully and importantly, taking great care with the sloshing green bubble. Seth dragged a chair to the deck railing, helped Jesse step up on it, and then pantomimed that he should heave his beautiful green water balloon over the side. Jesse rolled it over the banister and watched the balloon drop. It exploded onto the driveway. He hung a long time over the railing, looking down.

I was surprised by Seth's strategy here: giving him a beautiful object, then showing him how to destroy it. I waited for Jesse to start crying. But he drew back and turned around with a look on his face that seemed to express *What a wonderful country.*

"Ba-oon! Ba-oon!" he cried to Seth. *Again! Again!* Seth indulgently spent the next hour repeating the procedure until his pockets were empty and the bottom of the driveway was a wet canvas of latex confetti. Jesse was playing!

Our friends the Foxes gave Jesse a two-foot-tall smoke-emitting plastic *Tyrannosaurus rex* that opened its mouth, roared, and moved forward on hidden wheels. He was beside himself with joy and terror. He pronounced it "the Noonocerous." He liked it by daylight, but he required that it sleep outside on the porch with the door locked during the night. It was real and yet not real. When it lurched forward, snorting and smoking, it inspired an imaginative sense of the fantastic.

One Saturday night, Lily and two friends draped blankets over the dining-room table and created a cave beneath it. They threw sleeping bags inside and taped strands of orange Halloween lights underneath the table. They invited Jesse to crawl into the dark cave. Once he was seated, Lily plugged in the lights. It took his breath away. In that instant, I thought, he got it. The magic of the place transmitted a message of childhood fun of such pure essence that even he couldn't miss it. He scooted out, ran upstairs for his pillow, returned, and made himself a nest, calling, "*Leka nosht!*" (Good night!) to everyone, as if he were in on a terrific joke. The smashing water balloons, the Noonocerous, the orange-lit cave, were the beginning.

13

Crash and Burn

"Have you seen Molly's new wall poster?" I asked Donny one night in 1995, during Molly's eighth-grade year. It showed a shaggy-haired British rock musician, in blurry close-up, offering an obscene hand gesture. "I think it needs to come down. It's nothing but a guy flicking you off."

"That doesn't strike me as such a big deal. I had vulgar posters in my room at her age."

"Like what?"

"I had a big one on my ceiling that said 'Fuck the War.'"

"Yeah? Well, at least that was *about* something. That was part of the antiwar movement. This one isn't about anything; it's just, like, 'Fuck you.'"

"Do you want to tell her it has to come down because there are younger kids in the house?"

"No, I want it to come down because I think it's demeaning for her to look at 'Fuck you' every day."

He shrugged, didn't agree, fondly recalled the First Amendment, and returned to his reading while I trudged upstairs for a confrontation of a type I'd never had with Molly.

What made it worse, in a way, was that to make room for this new poster, Molly had taken down a gorgeous poster of a white stallion heroically galloping across a flowery meadow at the foot of snowcapped mountains.

Molly had dedicated her childhood to horses. Glossy horse posters plastered her walls; books by Walter Farley and Marguerite Henry and the

Saddle Club series filled her shelves; and a plastic herd of Breyer model horses reared and grazed on her dresser. Her pet turtle was named Ruffian. Two or three times a week she pulled on long black riding boots, strapped on a helmet, and practiced English riding skills atop thundering mares in a musty indoor ring. She was slender and dark-eyed, with almost waist-long thick hair and a serious gaze. Her braided pigtails bounced against her straight back as she cantered. Over dinner, she described for us in great detail the personalities, friendships, and favorite snacks of the horses. *Black Stallion* was her favorite movie, and her favorite store was the tack shop. Then, one afternoon in her bedroom, at age thirteen and a half, she mentioned that she wanted to quit riding.

"What?"

"Can you cancel my lessons?"

"This week's lessons?"

"All the lessons. I don't want to ride anymore."

I sat down on her bed to absorb this unprecedented request. Finding access to horses had been a major component of being Molly's mother. I'd gone into labor with Lily at the horse barn during a riding exhibition. Now I reminded myself to stay calm and to hear her out; this was her beloved pursuit and her decision. I personally had no attachment to horses, I told myself; horses were the love of *her* life, not mine; and despite all those good reminders I burst out, "YOU DON'T LOVE HORSES ANYMORE?" and began to cry.

"I still love horses, Mom. I just need a break."

"I know. I'm sorry, I don't know why I'm crying," I said, crying harder because it felt like Molly's childhood had just ended.

She began to peel the shiny posters from her walls: stallions flying across meadows with windswept manes and arched tails; mares nuzzling their colts; Arabians pounding down a wild beach; Man o' War, Citation, Seattle Slew, Ruffian, Secretariat, Seabiscuit. Once the posters were down, Molly painted each of her walls a somber color: bloodred, forest green, midnight blue, and black. Instead of the horse pictures, she taped up gritty posters from the rock music scene known as punk.

In the mid-1970s the Sex Pistols and the Clash, in London, and the Ramones, in New York, were hailed as the vanguard of a new rock genre. The harsh-sounding, stripped-down songs inspired an antiauthoritarian underground and a strong DIY (do-it-yourself) ethic. Donny and I, at Oberlin College, missed it entirely. Devoted to Dylan and the Beatles, Laura Nyro and the Grateful Dead, neither of us encountered punk until it sprang up as posters on Molly's walls twenty years later.

"Moll, we need to talk," I said, letting myself into her bedroom. "I really don't think that new poster is appropriate. I want you to take it down."

Now it was her turn to be shocked. "Appropriate? It's not *appropriate*?"

"No, it's not. It needs to come down." I left the room, shaking. It was the most authoritarian thing I'd ever done. And I was completely missing the vanguard of the punk rock revolution as it came across the horizon of my life for the second time. She took down the poster, but her love of punk surged ahead, windswept, pounding down a wild beach.

That year, Molly's social studies fair project—"What Is the Real Meaning Behind the Georgia State Flag Controversy?" which explored continuing segregationist sentiment in the state—took first prize at the school level and then at the district level and then at the county level. For each successive competition Molly was obliged to dress up in a nice skirt, blouse, and sweater and to be interviewed by education officials and professors acting as judges. A huge poster of Kurt Cobain, lead singer of Nirvana, now hung from Molly's closet door. Every time I watched her drearily pull on tights and brush her long hair before another award-winning encounter with school officials, I suspected the question uppermost in her mind was *Would Kurt Cobain think this is cool?*

"I'm so proud of you!" I said, driving her home with another blue ribbon one afternoon. "I want to buy you something! Let's buy you a present."

"Really? Can I get a CD?"

"Definitely!" I said, and we detoured to a music store on the way home.

"You don't have to come in," she offered, so I handed her a twenty-dollar bill.

"You do have to come in," she said, reappearing moments later at my window.

"Why?"

"I don't know. They want you to buy it with me or something."

I gamely stood at the counter beside my dark-eyed, blue ribbon–winning daughter as she handed me the money and I handed it to the cashier.

"What's the name of the band whose CD you bought?" I asked cheerily that night as the family strolled to a neighborhood restaurant for dinner. I had hung back to accompany Molly and was just making conversation.

"Nine Inch Nails."

"Oh, that's interesting. And what kind of nails are they? Is it like long, manicured fingernails?"

"No, it's like hammer and nails."

"Oh! Why nine inches long?"

"Those are the nails they drove Jesus into the cross with."

"Okay then!" I said, and fled to catch up with Donny and the younger children.

A few weeks later I was driving Molly and her friend Andi home from the mall when Andi piped up from the backseat, "My parents won't let *me* have music by Nine Inch Nails."

"Shut up, Andi," said Molly.

"Why not?" I asked.

"My parents say it's too vulgar," said Andi.

"Shut up, Andi," said Molly.

"Oh, really? Like what?"

And Andi began to sing "Closer" from the hit 1994 industrial rock album *The Downward Spiral*: "*I wanna fuck you like an animal,*" it began, "*I wanna feel you from the inside.*" It went on to discuss violation, desecration, and penetration, by which time I had yanked the car into a steep right turn into the parking lot of some random apartment complex, hauled up the emergency brake, and whirled around in horror to look at the girls in the backseat.

"Does . . . does Molly own that music?"

Andi laughed. "Yeah! That's the album you bought her for winning the district social studies fair!"

Oh. So that's why she'd needed me to make the purchase.

What was I supposed to do now? Impound the CD? The music was out, it had been released into Molly's room and scorched into Molly's brain.

A few days later I found Molly studying her mirror image in my office bathroom. "What's up?" I asked.

"I'm thinking of shaving my head." Scissors and an electric razor lay on the counter.

"You're going to shave off all your hair?"

"Not all of it. I'm going to leave some in a kind of a pattern and dye it pink."

"Wow."

I left the bathroom to think.

I returned. "Moll . . . are there any *accessories* you'd like to have? Is there any jewelry that would go with . . ." My voice trailed off; I gestured toward her outfit, a kind of Punk Thrift Store Oversized Male Hunter Camouflage statement. *At least jewelry she could take off at night,* I was thinking.

"Well, there *is* something, but you wouldn't get it for me," she said.

"Yes I would."

"No, you wouldn't."

"Molly, I would, really."

"I know you wouldn't."

"Molly, is it a *crucifix?*"

"No."

"Fantastic! Let's go! I'm getting the car keys! Come on!"

In the car I asked, "Where are we going?"

"The store's called Crash and Burn."

"Of course it is. Do I need to come in this time?"

While I sat in the car, she chose two black leather wristbands with spikes. Soon afterward, for her birthday, I went back for the matching spiked belt. We were accessorizing! My fashion-conscious mother would be so proud! Instead of shaving her hair off, Molly tied it into many little braids she hoped would thicken into dreadlocks.

"Molly thinks punk is about music and fashion," I told Donny one night.

"And we think it's about sex and drugs," he replied.

We imposed new rules and stricter curfews. We tried to meet her new pack of friends. We wanted to know where she was going and with whom. Despite our regulations, she was a clever girl and tiptoed around the obstacles. She had found a great and powerful theme in her life, a raucous, rebellious sound that spoke to her (and scared us), and she wasn't giving it up.

"We need to pull Molly out of public school," I told Donny. He didn't disagree, but wasn't fully on board with what I proposed to do with her: transfer her to an Orthodox Jewish high school. She'd spent ten years in Jewish day schools and was no stranger to the dual English-Hebrew curriculum. Still, for a kid in love with an anarchic music scene, it would be a shock. And she was shocked. She was shocked at the news, and she came home shocked from her visit to the school as a prospective student. And yet she was never vulgar, rude, or hostile; nor were we. No one slammed doors. "I don't want to go. I didn't like it there," she said after her first visit.

"I know," I said.

What I felt was, *She feels driven to be radical, cutting-edge, plugged into a scene outside the conventional. At the public high school she's got a long way to go to reach the outer extremes; at the Jewish high school she's already there, on the risk-taking edge.*

On the morning of her first day at the religious school, still in shock, she donned the unattractive navy blue polyester calf-length pleated uniform skirt and the long-sleeve navy blue polo. Then she buckled on her spiked belt and wristbands and added fishnet stockings and steel-toed boots. Her hair was still twisted into dozens of future dreads. During the school day I waited for a phone call from an administrator, but none came and she returned home dressed the same way she'd left. Sensitively, the rabbis had said nothing. As long as she was modestly covered, one rabbi told me later, he was not concerned with her accessories, nor did he see the point of picking a fight with his newest student, who'd arrived, after all, with excellent grades, top test scores, Hebrew literacy, and an upright bass.

The student body was in awe. "Have you noticed the new student with the many braids, spiked wristbands, red fishnet stockings, and green Doc Martens in the halls this fall??" asked the student newspaper. "That's our *Feature Freshman for September*: Molly Samuel!"

She studied and made a few friends. One day I glanced into her bedroom and noticed that she had left behind her spiked jewelry; soon after that, the little braids came out and the silky dark hair fell again past her shoulders. She was adapting. And I was thrilled to have her in Jewish day school again! But she grew melancholy, passive, and lonely. We'd kept her safe, but we'd made her sad.

14

Monkey *icka* Lion

Seven-year-old Lily loved Disney's *Lion King* and invited Jesse to join her on the sofa one evening to watch it. It was his first movie. At first his eyes couldn't focus on the kaleidoscope of moving colors, but then a few shapes became clear to him: there was a lion! "See lion?" he asked Lily the next day after dinner. She consented and sat with him again. On the third evening the key event was revealed to him: not the murder of Mufasa, nor Simba and Nala falling in love, nor the death of Scar. For Jesse, the climax came when Rafiki the baboon hit Simba over the head with a stick.

"Monkey *icka* lion!" Jesse yelled to Lily, pointing and laughing.

Every night he asked her, "See lion?" Then he sat mutely for forty-five minutes until the great moment arrived. He jumped up and ran close to the screen to prepare for it. Here it came . . . "Monkey *icka* lion!"

Lily said, "He thinks this is a movie about a monkey hitting a lion over the head with a stick."

One night she slid in a new movie, Disney's *Hercules*. Jesse sprang up, distressed.

"He didn't know there was more than one movie in the world," Lily called to me.

"No Lily no Lily!" Jesse yelled, but she calmed him down.

I peeked in twenty minutes later. "How's it going?"

"He's waiting for a monkey to hit Hercules over the head with a stick," Lily said.

"Cha-chee not here," Jesse announced at dinner that night. He pointed to himself: "This Gercules." He'd evidently noticed important resemblances between himself and the hero: a handsome and strong off-spring of faraway gods, adopted by a humble peasant couple.

The next morning, Jesse ran into the kitchen after a sneeze, dripping and yelling, "Gercules need Kleenex!"

Donny said, "I believe that's the first time in history that the words 'Hercules' and 'Kleenex' have been used in the same sentence."

Jesse turned to Lily for wardrobe assistance. "This Gercules," he reminded her. He had come to the right place. Now he could study pretend-play at the feet of a master. At Jesse's age, Lily had been Pocahontas. Specifically, she had been Disney's Pocahontas at the moment the Native American princess peeks through high grasses, beholds John Smith, curls a strand of her long black hair behind her ear, and accepts Smith's extended hand of friendship. He is stunned by her beauty and they fall in love.

"Go, Mommy, start," Lily often whispered from behind the basketball pole in the driveway. My job was to be on the hunt for savages and to raise and aim my musket until a lovely young lady pushed aside tall grasses and stood before me, her long hair waving in the colors of the wind.

"Mommy, go!"

"Oh, it's a hot day here in Virginia!" I announced one buggy summer day in Georgia. "I better march around and see if I can find any savages! Oh, look, there's one!" I aimed a lacrosse stick like a rifle.

With a shy, downcast smile, Lily stepped from behind the basketball pole, pushing aside invisible tall grasses and weaving a long strand of hair behind her ear. She gazed softly at me. In awe at her beauty, I lowered my musket and offered my hand. We fell in love. Cut!

"Great! That was fun! Let's go in now!" I offered, since we'd performed this scene fifteen times already. Too late: the shy yet athletic Native American princess had stepped again behind the basketball pole. "Mommy! Start!"

"Oh, it's a helluva hot day here in Virginia! . . ."

Now, three years later, Lily dug through her costume basket and outfitted Jesse in a purple cape, a plastic knight's helmet, a belt, a toy sword, and a pair of sandals. He wasn't quite satisfied, though, because at that moment Lily and her girlfriends were painting their nails. He approached Lily with his fingers outstretched. The bevy of second-grade girls giggled, but Lily offered him his color choices from the Sassy Sparkle Collection. He studied the spectrum, then pointed to Poptastic Purple Sparkle. Lily shushed her friends, spread out a towel, and gently painted Jesse's nails.

He was still a little envious. With his shiny, wet fingernails, he pointed to the pile of Mardi Gras beads in the girls' possession, so Lily draped strands of gold and purple plastic beads around his neck, drawing from the color themes of Greek god and Sassy Sparkle Collection.

Now he was Gercules. You could hear him coming, what with the flap of overlarge sandals and the clicking of bead necklaces. The next afternoon, Jesse came along with us to Lily's soccer game. Gercules walked around the perimeter of the field, and I saw, from a distance, friendly parents from both sides bending over to compliment him on his getup. Jesse, not understanding all the English but definitely appreciating the admiration, spun in his cape, then revealed his sword, then lifted a sandaled foot, then lifted the other sandaled foot, and then held out both hands to show off his purple nail polish. From across the field I burst out laughing. The young Greek demigod swaggered off in search of adventures that would not chip his manicure.

Jesse had started preschool by now, four months after his arrival in America. As his English improved, I gleaned that some days he *was* Gercules and other days he was Cha-chee, Gercules's best friend. He learned about playdates at preschool and wanted to invite Gercules to our house. "Gercules play *ne* Cha-chee," he begged. "Mama, call Gercules' mama?" He was open to having the playdate either at our place or on Olympus, whichever was most convenient.

And he placed himself in charge of protecting our family from dragons. "You scared dragons, Mama," he reminded me one morning. "Chachee kill." But one night at bedtime he panicked—his plastic sword was lost! Only the magic sword from Lily could protect him! Defenseless against dragon attacks in the night, he began to weep. I ran downstairs and back up with forks and butter knives, but he shook his head no. I ran downstairs again, looked around, grabbed a fireplace poker, and sprang back up the stairs with it. He was flabbergasted. *"Mama,"* he said, awestruck. He stopped crying and got out of bed to accept Excalibur with knightly formality. "Cha-chee always fight dragons, Mama," he promised. He slid the fireplace poker under his bed and went to sleep content, a well-armed young Bulgarian-Romani dragon slayer.

Jesse often appeared at my bedside in the middle of the night after a bad dream, or after a good dream, or after waking up and thinking, *This could be better. I could be lying next to the mama.* That night, he came to wake me. I moved over and opened the covers. "Wait, Mama!" he yelled. He tore down the hall and then returned carrying the fireplace poker, which he slid under my bed. I humored him, of course. I loved seeing the dawn of his imagination. But I also knew this was one small boy who had known real-life evil and danger. He had survived abandonment, multiple orphanage placements, bullies, and the persecution and poverty of his people. My older children learned some dark lessons from Disney stories, stories of orphans and triumph, but Jesse had his own deep knowledge confirmed: in the life of a hero, there are always dragons.

One morning he bounded into the kitchen, dressed for school and wearing two freshly unwrapped sanitary napkins, one taped to each wrist, "like Gercules," he proudly announced. Seth and Lee fled from the room, choking with laughter. I said he really couldn't wear those to preschool.

"No?" he asked sadly. "Miss Pat saying no?"

"Mama saying no."

"Cha-chee too strong? Cha-chee scare *ne* children?"

"That's not really the problem."

"What? . . . What, Mama?"

"Because they're Mama's."

"Mama give *ne* Cha-chee?"

"No."

I took him out that very afternoon to a sports store and we bought two black Nike wristbands. "Strong," he said in a deep voice, admiring his own wrists. "Strong like Gercules."

Seth ushered Jesse into the world of live-action features by renting *Who Am I?* With Seth's help, Jesse watched Chan's entire filmography— English, Chinese, with subtitles, without subtitles, it didn't matter—one plot made no more sense to him than another, but he loved Jackie Chan. He was Jackie Chan's best helper! Thus empowered, he rewrote a painful memory.

"Bad spider, bad spider big spider *ne* bathroom," he'd told us as soon as he started speaking English. "I crying everyone crying I scared." The kind caregiver, Tanya, had helped the children. He acted out her swinging a broom. "Tanya HIT and HIT bad spider and kill!"

Now, half a year later, Jackie Chan's partner remembered the incident . . . differently. "One time very very bad spider come in our bathroom."

I started to say *Yeah, you told me this story*—but I stopped myself.

"A very scary spider. THREE very scary spiders. BIG ones! BIG like SHARKS! THREE ones!"

"Wow, what did Tanya do?" I asked.

"Tanya very scared all children very scared all children crying."

"That sounds so scary."

"I not scared! I know karate! I kill *three bad spiders!*" Here he demonstrated some jumps and kicks and slaps. Then he gave his downturned, proudest smile. "I save Tanya."

I thought: *You're saving yourself. The power of the human mind to repair itself is a remarkable thing.*

At bedtime that night, he told me, "When I get big, I going help Jackie Chan."

"Jess, that is a great career goal."

He lay back contentedly. But then something struck him and he sat up anxiously to ask, "When I help Jackie Chan, I still live here?"

"Of course you'll live here! You'll fly to Hong Kong every morning to help Jackie and fly home in time for dinner."

Reassured, he lay back to savor the good news. "Will my name be Jesse Chan when I'm big?" he mused.

"I'm sure that will make Jackie very proud."

Sighing happily, he asked, "Why does Jackie Chan *like* me so much?"

15

Sing, Goddess . . .

At eighteen Molly was very slender, not tall, with a fall of polished blue-black hair, deep brown eyes and dark eyebrows, and a hipster style—tight black jeans, a cut-up and restitched hoodie, Converse sneakers. She had a sharp sense of the absurd, with a cascading and bending-over laugh to go with it. At the end of her sophomore year in high school, we asked if she'd like to return to public school. She had grown so deeply resigned, it hadn't occurred to her to ask. She graduated from a magnet high school for high achievers. Punk rampaged on in her life, and now she was old enough to handle it.

In the fall of 2000 she left home for college. Donny said that driving the rental truck away from her, where she stood alone and brave on the curb outside her dorm at Oberlin, was the hardest thing he'd ever done in his life. She'd left for college with a few powerful aims, one of which was to read James Joyce's *Ulysses*. Since the twentieth-century novel was based on Homer's eighth-century B.C. epic poem, she planned to get a running start by first reading *The Iliad* and *The Odyssey*. She enrolled in Introduction to Ancient Greek Literature, assuming she'd soon return to the moderns.

But Homer, and Professor Tom Van Nortwick, had her at *"Sing, goddess, the anger of Peleus' son Achilleus / and its devastation, which put pains thousandfold upon the Achaians, / hurled in their multitudes to the house of Hades . . ."* and nothing would do but that she gain the ability to read the epic poem in the original. She chose Ancient Greek as her major and never found her way back to James Joyce.

At Oberlin, when not studying among the classics majors, she was blasting music in the indie rock scene, as the lead singer and electric bass player in a punk band called Red Tape Apocalypse. On a visit to Oberlin I was invited to hear a live performance in a sound studio at WOBC, the campus radio station where Molly hosted a weekly punk show. Molly led me up the stairs to the radio station for my first live experience of punk. The instant RTA started, the violent clamor tore through my brain like a fire alarm, like an emergency. Gusts of electrified, amplified fury blew over me. This music, I learned, was "straight-up Blatz-syle punk with two singers going full throttle." The singers two-fistedly strangled their microphones, and the drummer pummeled his equipment as if beating something to death with sticks. It was a savage joy, a riotous freedom. When, many songs later, the band stopped, the silence of my pulsing eardrums and pounding heart was as loud as a Manhattan traffic jam. Here they came toward me—dripping with sweat, their long hair plastered to their wet faces.

"How was it?" asked Molly, and they all looked over expectantly.

"I LOVED it! You all are fantastic!" I said.

"Really? I'm glad!" she said, and her friends seemed pleased, too.

Molly and her friends founded a record label, True Panther Sounds, and—in punk DIY style—they pulled all-nighters to photocopy, spray-paint, and glue the record covers together before mailing them to fans around the country. (True Panther was ultimately acquired by Matador Records. Molly's former bandmate, Dean Bein, manages the highly successful label from its Manhattan office today.)

After graduation Molly was offered the coveted position of arts intern for National Public Radio in Washington, D.C. NPR was evidently impressed by a job application reflecting dual mastery of Thucydides (in the original) and the Ramones (on vinyl). She later moved to San Francisco, where she and her friends created a new band: David Copperfuck. It made *The Onion*'s 2006 list of the Year's Worst Band Names. (Fellow honorees would include Honkytonk Homeslice, Sorry About Your Couch, Arsonists Get All the Girls, Here Comes Old Vodka Tits, and 16

Molly (center) performing with DC at a Seattle house party, 2007

Bitch Pile-Up.) In San Francisco she fell in love with Andy Reed (also Oberlin 2004) and became a public radio producer and arts and sciences reporter.

Had we overreacted years earlier in our handling of fourteen-year-old Molly? No. A young teen can take a bad turn, detouring into sex, drugs, alcohol, addictions, or dropping out. We were not wrong to try to shield her from dangers she didn't recognize, toward which she was sprinting.

But she wasn't wrong either. "It's worth noting that punk really isn't about sex and drugs," Molly tells me now. "A lot of things in high school could lead down that path, and an interest in punk could have. But that's not what any of our songs were ever about, and that's not finally what punk is about. There are a lot of dumb, loud bands with messy hair out there, but that doesn't make them punk. Punk means something more than guitar distortion and anger. It's about an antiauthoritarian attitude, subversive creativity, and independence.

"Even today, most of my friends come from the punk scene. If they're not from the punk world, they're from the journalism world, which has a pretty similar ethos."

Instead of crying the afternoon Molly asked to quit horseback lessons, I might, if I'd only known (though it wasn't possible to know), have celebrated the dawn of her finding another powerful inner drive, full of life and streaming with freedom.

The last time I visited Molly in her San Francisco apartment, I noticed a horse poster on her wall.

"It's a high-contrast black-and-white photocopied horse poster," she said. "I made it and assembled it myself. Kinda punk."

16

Enormous Families, Group Homes

Family-wise, as Jesse settled in happily, we should have been finished. Five children was a lot of children. But after Molly left for college, there were only four children at home again. And then Seth started musing about colleges, about conservatories of music. I did *not* like the way this was shaping up! But wouldn't I look insane if I adopted another child? How would I sell it this time? With Jesse, I'd implied, to family and friends, that I had met him while visiting Eastern European orphanages during a reporting trip. That was a narrative everyone understood and endorsed: the journalist's heart stolen by the dark-eyed orphan peeking out of the shadows of the grim institution. Of course she went back for him!

When people asked "Why'd you adopt?" Donny said, "We're backfilling! Every time one child leaves, we'll bring in another." Everyone laughed, as if Donny were joking. Many of our friends privately crossed off months and years in their minds on the trek toward empty nest. It just wasn't true for us. But I saw that I was slipping away from the norm. When I mentioned to a friend that I was starting to think about maybe adopting again, she said, "Who made *you* the Old Woman Who Lives in a Shoe?" Whispers of a sixth child threatened to place me, in the minds of friends and family, among the greats: the DeBolt family, the Kennedys, Mia Farrow, the McCaughey septuplets, the von Trapp family singers, and perhaps even Mrs. Feodor Vassilyev, who, according to the Guinness Book of World Records, gave birth to sixty-nine children in eighteenth-century Russia.

One day my *New York Times Magazine* editor phoned to ask if I had any stories up my sleeve. "What about a feature on enormous families?" I asked her. "Not parents of eight or ten kids, but parents raising fifteen, eighteen, or twenty-five." In online adoption groups I'd become aware of these "mega-families" in which parents added to their long-ago nuclei of birth children by adopting older children, special-needs children, and sibling groups. Outside of religiously observant communities, most supersized families in America included, for obvious biological reasons, adopted children. My editor had never heard of mega-families. (This was in 2000, before big-family reality shows appeared on cable television. That year, the Duggars had only ten children, Jon and Kate Gosselin were expecting twins, and Octomom was childless.) Amused, my editor commissioned the story, and I headed to Cincinnati to meet Nancy and Joe Kayes, parents of seventeen: three by birth and fourteen from Korea, India, Hong Kong, and Bulgaria, including many with physical challenges.

The Kayes family survives by two mottoes, Nancy told me soon after we met in the foyer of her two-story house in a nice subdivision. She was fifty-seven, friendly and relaxed, with soft, motherly skin, dark curls, and the sort of wonderful laugh that sounds as if she didn't mean to lose her composure at that moment but finds something irresistibly funny.

Their first motto: Better Dead Than Camping.

The second: If It Will Fit in an Aquarium, You Can Have It.

I had my own watchword to offer, though in the presence of a mother of seventeen, I felt like a bush leaguer. "My motto is: If They're Both Socks, It's a Pair," I offered hesitantly, and was instantly rewarded by Nancy's peal of laughter. She understood my shyness and told me that she had once met Dorothy DeBolt (the famous mother of twenty) and tried to apologize to her for having only nine.

"The trouble with my mother is that she thinks we're normal," said Nancy's oldest, Rebecca Kayes Boerner, thirty-three, who joined us for tea in the dining room. "My mother gets 'empty nest' whenever we drop down to about eight."

"I get that when we drop down to three!" I said.

Both curly-haired women nodded sympathetically.

Nancy said, "When only seven or eight of the kids are home for dinner, they look around and say, 'Hey! This must be what life is like in a small family!'"

For family road trips Nancy designed seating charts to minimize strife. "Once, there were two kids in the way back, fighting; they wouldn't stop, we were on the highway, and I yelled from the front seat, 'That's IT. I've HAD it. I'm coming back!'" She crawled and swam over the tops of her children's heads like a teenager in a mosh pit. She made it almost all the way to the back row when she got a paralyzing cramp in her leg. The kids in the middle rows of seats had to manipulate their mother hand over hand toward the front, but at least she had gotten the attention of the squabbling pair in the back, who shut up, awestruck, to watch.

"A bathroom stop for us takes forty-five minutes," called Mark from the kitchen, having just come in off the school bus. Born without arms, he was inserting pizza into the oven by foot for an after-school snack.

"You open the sliding door of the van, and half the stuff falls out," said Tom.

Kira said, "When we get out of the van, people ask us, 'Oh, are you a school group?' We say no, and they ask, 'Well, what kind of a group are you, then?'"

When Joe Kayes, a tall, gangly, graying mechanical engineer with a kind of Jimmy Stewart chuckle and affability, came home from work, Nancy handed him a typed sheet with his marching orders for the next morning—in this case, taking a couple of kids to the pediatrician.

"We have kept the university school of medicine busy for many years," Joe told me. "They were especially excited about malaria."

Kristen, who had been paralyzed in India from spinal tuberculosis and required major surgeries and blood transfusions, came in to hug Joe, and to offer: "Daddy gave me blood. I'm definitely related to my dad."

"Yep," Joe said, squeezing back. "We're blood relatives."

Joe does all the food shopping and Nancy all the cooking. "That engineering mind of his is fascinated by the challenge of coupons," Nancy told me. "'Buy One, Get One Free' really gets him going. Stores used to limit quantities per customer, so Joe would drive home, grab half a dozen kids, run back to the store, and line them up: they would each stand there, even the little-bitties, with a wad of coupons and, you know, a dollar seventy-eight tucked into their shorts, holding two cans of soup and two heads of lettuce."

"My record was the time I bought a hundred and fifty dollars' worth of groceries with forty-five coupons and a twenty-dollar bill," said Joe.

"Tell her I'm your Polish son," called Mark from the den.

"Mark is my Polish-Chinese son," Joe said. "He loves kielbasa and polkas. He and I say it's the result of 'airborne genes.'"

"It typically takes us a year to work in a new child, a year till he or she isn't 'new' anymore," Nancy said. "At first, when a new one arrives, all the other kids are really nice and helpful and supportive. Then, slowly, it dawns on them: 'Hey, this kid is kind of a pain.' It's an interesting dynamic, and it's always the same.

"I know everyone wonders why we want all these kids and all this responsibility. But I suspect that people who seek promotions at work that permit them to manage more people are not questioned in this way. Raising a family isn't so different."

Nancy and Joe Kayes were a happily married pair whose fantasies of old age included neither Florida condos, nor Arizona retirement communities, nor comfortable portfolios, but rather images of themselves still surrounded by lively young people. The Kayes would have nineteen children before they were through.

I learned that family systems therapists use the metaphor of a mobile to describe a family's delicate balance and how that balance is thrown into disequilibrium with the arrival of a new child. When the addition is an older child or a young teen, or maybe a three-kid sibling group or a child with cognitive or emotional challenges, the family mobile goes haywire—arms tilting precariously, threads tangling, and figurines colliding together like a wind chime crashing in the gales of a storm.

I also learned that not all mega-parents are as skilled as Nancy and Joe Kayes. Some seem to relish anarchy. I visited a house outside the Twin Cities where twenty-four children lived (eight by birth, the rest by adoption); kids screamed and tumbled about and rode in baby swings and hopped in baby bouncers. Two industrial-sized washing machines shook the laundry room. Broken toys littered the sunporch; diaper odor lurked in the air; the kitchen garbage can was overflowing; someone stomped up the stairs in fury; and there was not enough spare change for the ice-cream truck outside, leading to tears and tantrums. In the kitchen, the mom, whom I'll call Betsy, in a scrum of children, laughed brightly and humorously rolled her eyes, but I wasn't sure what was funny. After half an hour I felt eager to express (shout) my appreciation for the interview, zip my briefcase, and flee to my rental car, distributing coins for the ice-cream truck on my way out in order to tamp down some of the wailing.

In the name of saving the world's children one at a time, or perhaps dazzled by a vision of herself as the matriarch of a rowdy clan, Betsy had reeled in extras until the whole enterprise seemed about to collapse under its own weight. She saw sibling rivalry and fist fighting as the stuff of life, and her ability to rise above it, laughing it away, as the essence of fortitude. She was heroic, certainly—a bit heavy and perspiring, blotting her forehead with her sleeve, tucking several baby bottles into the pockets of her long sweater, squatting to open her arms to the nearest wailing youngster, making fun of herself—"*This* is what I do instead of jogging!" and "Can you believe I used to play *tennis*?" Her kitchen calendar was blocked out with visits to doctors and hospitals, to plastic surgeons and infectious disease specialists. Few people were lining up to adopt the world's neediest, loneliest, and sickest children. Betsy and her husband had saved these children's lives.

And yet I wondered, was this still a family, or had it become a group home? A few adoption agency directors, who had helped create the mega-families, had started to ask this question, too. Some looked back in dismay at what they had wrought, including within their own families. "The 1960s generation in the adoption world had the motto: We'll Just Put Up Another Bunk Bed—No Big Deal," said Barbara Holtan, former executive director of adoption for Tressler Lutheran Services. "People saw it as a way of changing the world. They got utterly caught up in the chase. 'If she's got eight, I'm going to adopt twelve!' Some became 'collectors': 'We've got one heart problem, one limb anomaly, two Down syndrome and two C.P.' Some became 'adoption addicts.' We were flying blind and didn't know what the endgame would look like.

"Over time we began to learn that it really *was* a big deal to add a child. The two-year-old with emotional problems grew into a seventeen-year-old with emotional problems. In the heyday of big families, if a couple came in and said, 'We'll take three kids, and it's okay if they have emotional problems,' we'd be falling over ourselves to make a placement. Not anymore. Now I'd say, 'Let's talk. What are your motivations? For whom are you doing this?'"

Dr. Barbara Tremitiere, the mother of fifteen children (twelve by adoption), also affiliated with Tressler, is the author of *The Large Adoptive Family: A Special Kind of Normal.* "During the 1960s, '70s, and '80s we celebrated new placements; we lived in the present," she said. "Now I wonder: Did *any* of us have realistic expectations about the future? The young handicapped children became older, heavier, and more difficult. Supportive friends became rarer as our children's 'harmless childish behavior' turned into 'teenage aggression' and 'sexual acting out.' The effects of lack of attachment, congenital issues, and problematic combinations of children caught up with us.

"And yet there are large families who do marvelously well! I'd be the last person in the world to give a maximum number. I worked with an absolutely glorious family who adopted and adopted, including many children with Down syndrome. When they got up to ten children, I thought, *I love this family, but how can I place any more children with them? They're on the verge of becoming a group home.* Then the mother came to me and said, 'Barbara, it's been great. We're finished.' They knew when to stop, without injuring what they had built."

To not know when to stop was to create a group home rather than a family. "Collectors" and "adoption addicts" pushed too far, losing sight of what was best for the children already in the family. Yet regarding the Minnesota mother of twenty-four, I wondered, *Well, so what if it's a group home? It's still better than the destitute orphanages the children left behind in Russia, Eastern Europe, and Haiti. Here they have food, medical care, and love. There are worse places to be than a cheerful and well-meaning group home.* I looked at Betsy with respect, although I didn't know whether her original eight biological children were part of the massive human construction project or estranged from it. And I knew it was not what I wanted.

17

Dogs We Have Loved

An animal lived in our house. Jesse was terrified of her. Franny was a rotund, freckled, well-meaning American rat terrier. She had short white fur, three large black spots, bulbous brown eyebrows, and a stub of a tail. In the park in Bulgaria, Jesse had wanted to embrace *kuches* and had been grabbed away from the feral mongrels by Petko. But this was different: this *kuche* was in the house, a bizarre situation that would have disturbed any thinking Bulgarian.

To save himself, Jesse pelted Franny with food whenever she approached, and he ran away screaming at the top of his voice. His anguished screams meant *Take this! It's all I have! Take this and don't kill me!*

Franny interpreted the hurled food and hoarse shrieks to mean *Every time you come near me, I will throw treats to you.*

Franny now dedicated her life to following Jesse from room to room as he fled in horror, bellowing and slinging hot dog slices over his back.

His screaming was driving me out of my mind.

"IN THE NAME OF HEAVEN, SHE'S NOT GOING TO HURT YOU!" I yelled.

He understood my words to mean *RUN FOR YOUR LIFE, THE WOLF IS GAINING ON YOU.*

But during the long school days, especially during my Gloomy Period, no one else in the house was so warmly curious about Jesse or so eager to spend time with him as Franny. The rapid wagging of her stubby tail no longer upset him. He began to talk to her and she listened with a cocked head and an intelligent look. One afternoon I watched them in the front yard kind of frolicking together, communicating. The child relayed: *We're friends now!* The dog relayed: *I was thinking it might be time for you to go inside and peel us a hot dog.*

I loved their budding friendship, as my deepest bond in childhood had been with a dog. He was a black-and-white blue-eyed Siberian husky with so dense a mane that it took the full length of my arms to embrace him. His pelt gleamed in all seasons, but when he tussled with my brother Garry and me in the snow, ice crystals dusted his black fur like diamonds. I was headed into the purgatory of middle school years and often slumped home after school with hurt feelings, but regal Chief leaped and barked in his outdoor pen in greeting. At school, I fumbled the social cues, but with him I was in the company of a world-class beauty. I took an apple, a candy bar, and some dog biscuits, and we loped off toward a pocket of woods. I sang "The Happy Wanderer" from music class, feeling, with Chief, that I was on the high road. He bounded, chested through the undergrowth, roved and returned, threw himself happily panting at my side. I gave him a biscuit from my pocket.

"You!" I said, holding his great head between my hands and looking into his pale, lively eyes; he gave a submissive lick.

Every night after dark, I let him out of his pen to wander. He sprinted away, panicked a flock of wild geese camping in a cornfield, and crashed through a stream. Before dawn he returned, made a racket with his tin water dish on the kitchen steps, and barked for food. Briars clumped the fur of his chest and legs; when I let him in, he smelled of earth and of the night air. His flanks were thin. He'd run for hours, for dreamless miles.

Later we'd hear reports that he'd chased a cat, knocked over some garbage cans, and scratched the paint off a garage door behind which a beagle in heat was cloistered, but he was a glorious dog.

Why this polar animal dwelled at 5569 Joyce Ann Drive, Dayton, Ohio, was a central mystery of my childhood. We drove to a breeder in Indiana one day to acquire the handsome pup. It was a happy day, a happy car trip. And it was a ridiculous mistake by my parents—I still think about it, their foolishness, my grief—to ask a sled dog capable of running seventy miles a day across frozen tundra to spend his life in a seven-by-seven-foot pen and shingled doghouse in a suburban backyard.

Neighbors complained about Chief's nocturnal mischief, so I was ordered by my father to lock him into his pen at night. He metamorphosed into the Houdini of backyard dogs. He dug out of his pen easily. He tunneled like a POW, wriggled free, and ran for joy under the stars. My father shoveled the dirt back into the escape holes, lined them with wood and then with bricks, but Chief still escaped. He could chew through most things and muscle aside the rest. Dog lovers in outlying townships waylaid him and called the phone number on the dog tag. "That's a beautiful dog you got there," they said, implying that the next person to find him might not call his owners.

My father always drove to retrieve him—once going as far north as the airport, ten miles away—and came home angry. Chief stood wagging his tail in the backseat, happy to see me through the car window, but I said, "Bad boy!" in an attempt to ingratiate myself with my father, and I dragged Chief by his collar to his fenced enclosure, dropping to hug him when we were alone.

My dad steered a wheelbarrow to Chief's pen and paved it over with cement. Now it was like a small parking lot or a treeless zoo exhibit. Chief could no longer tunnel out to freedom. Instead, the Siberian escape artist learned to climb, to jump. The leap over the chain-link fence in the moonlight must have been a thing of beauty. My father added inches to the fence, sweating and cursing while he twisted the wires into place, and he added a short length of chain to a steel post anchored in the cement, until finally it was done: Chief was our prisoner.

At 3:00 a.m., sleepless, homesick for the glaciers, Chief sat on his moonlit square of cement and howled. At 3:05 a.m. our next-door neighbor phoned to wake up my parents. "Shut the goddamn dog up!" roared my father from bed. "I've had it with that dog!"

My love of Chief turned into a forbidden love as Chief became an outlaw. Within a few years I would be the one restlessly pacing my square pink bedroom, longing for freedom. Secretly I cheered for Chief when he still managed to escape—the gate left open after a feeding, the chain unattached, or a last-minute bolt away from me when we returned from a walk. He came back, or was returned to us, wagging and unbowed. I cried into the great muff of his fur when he lay beside me in the shadow of his doghouse. I fondled his velvet ears.

One night Chief hurt his paw getting over the ever-higher fence. Was he heading for the North Pole, my blue-eyed wolf? Was he following the arc of the wild geese, the sparkle of the North Star? "I love you so much," I whispered, kissing the broad back of his head, brushing his thick tail. "Can't you stay?"

But it was in the nature of beautiful things in that period of my life to elude me. I lay curled on my side in bed, drawing my legs in close, feeling the coming blow. Chief escaped again one night, getting himself free of the chain, over the fence, and away. My parents told us that Chief reached a farm thirty miles out and that the very nice people there had called and offered to keep him. My parents told them yes. "Chief will be happier there," my father said.

I ran to my pink bedroom and slammed the door in time for the explosion of grief, a Big Bang of sorrow from which shards of melancholy blew across many years.

Chief was the dog companion of my childhood; Franny is the true friend of my middle age. She, in her own middle age, has become the kind of barrel-shaped, anomalous dog that appears in children's picture books and in *New Yorker* cartoons. Though lacking the royal bearing of a Siberian husky, Franny has a noble soul; there is kindness and intelligence in her soft brown eyes. Franny tries to spend every minute of her life with me. "Has any dog ever loved a person as much as Franny loves you?" my children ask. Sometimes they phrase it differently: "Has any living thing ever loved another living thing as much as Franny loves you?"

"We need a dog!" the kids complained. "Franny is only your dog! She only sits in your lap and she only sleeps with you!"

So we got a wirehaired miniature dachshund with a ferocious nature and a Napoleon complex. But Theo doesn't sleep with the children or follow them around, either. Theo is devoted to Franny. And Franny's with me.

When I push back from my desk to walk to the kitchen for a cup of coffee, Franny, on the nearby sofa, rouses herself from her midmorning nap. "Franny, really, no, I'll be right back," I say, wanting her to enjoy her rest.

No, I'm up already, she seems to say, hopping down with a small groan to waddle behind me down the hall. Theo trots behind Franny. The three of us pour a nice hot cup of coffee and return to my office together.

The kids started up again the other day: "*We* need a dog!" But I said: "Forget it."

Franny was born in a farmhouse outside Winder, Georgia, to owners who enjoyed squirrel hunting and, probably, squirrel stew. Pickup trucks with rifles sat in the gravel driveway; dogs on chains bayed in the side yard. Those people were wise to give away Franny because Franny respects squirrels—she loves to chase them, but would never kill one!—and because Franny HATES loud noises, like gunshots. When she was a puppy, a bursting balloon sent her careening, sliding, tripping down the front hall and up the stairs to the safety of my bedspread, under which she lay, trembling, for hours. Now, with age, she objects so violently to the very possibility of a balloon popping that we do not bring balloons into the house. We'll see her shaking, vibrating, unable to put one foot in front of the other to try to make her way to the staircase; only then do we notice that a visiting child has entered our house with a balloon and has started to blow it up. "NO! STOP!" we scream, tackling the innocent from all sides as if he were about to pull the pin on a grenade. Franny also hates guns, even though the only guns in this family are squirt guns and Nerf weapons. "Look at Franny!" someone will say, and she is having her own private earthquake under the coffee table. If someone has unthinkingly brought a squirt gun into the house, that child must run to throw it outside, then come back in to kneel and apologize to Franny.

Franny and I walk several miles together every day, rain or shine. Franny runs joyfully off her leash; in high grass, she pounces like a tiger. She chases squirrels up trees and then runs back to me, grinning, vibrating her stubby tail. I ruffle her old head. I bite into an apple. Franny may be slowing down a tiny bit; she may have gray in her anxious brown eyebrows, but to me, she is young. I don't lie about my own age; I only lie about Franny's. When anyone asks, I say, "Franny? Oh, she's two or three, I guess." But what's a dropped decade between best friends? Together, Franny and I are forever young, out on the open road.

18

The ABCs of Preliteracy

In the fall of 2000, Jesse started kindergarten: it was time to learn the ABCs. Having taught four children to read, I launched into the project confident in my ability. I spent a week on the letter *A* with Jesse. Then we spent another week on *A*. Three weeks into *A*, he still couldn't recognize it. Never before had the alphabet seemed so remote and inaccessible. It was as if Jesse and I stood in a dirt field in a rural county and I tried to direct his attention to a glittering city of splendidly shaped buildings on the far horizon. "Look! Can you see that? You'll love it there. Look at that one: that's *A*."

But he couldn't make it out, not the city, not the letter. It was like asking him to interpret a message made by yellow leaves on the driveway. "What's this letter?" I asked on his bed at night, showing him a letter we'd drilled all day.

He *so* wanted to get it right. "Don't tell me! Don't tell me!" he yelled. He leaned into me and whispered out of the side of his mouth, "What is it?"

"*D*," I whispered back.

"What?" he hissed.

"*D.*"

"Don't tell me, don't tell me!" he yelled again. And then, as if he had come up with the answer all by himself, he shouted: "*D!*" I hugged him and exclaimed, "You got it!" But he fell behind his classmates, some of whom had begun sounding their way into early readers.

When did my four older children learn the alphabet? We plucked letters here and there off stop signs and billboards, like picking mulberries. But I don't recall having to explain that the spidery lines scratched on the white spaces in picture books were called "words" or that the story was *there*, coiled within those letters.

Searching for ways to help Jesse, I discovered the field of "preliteracy." I pitched the story to a parenting magazine and began by interviewing Dr. Marilyn Jager Adams, a cognitive and developmental research psychologist at Harvard University and the author of *Beginning to Read: Thinking and Learning About Print*. I sketched Jesse's past for her: three years in an orphanage without books, posters, learning toys (or any toys), paper, or pencils. Jesse might not have seen a printed word until the car ride with us to Sofia, along roads that included street signs. No one had read to him until he arrived in our home at nearly five years of age.

"A line of print looks to Jesse like Arabic looks to most Americans," Dr. Adams told me. "Words look like elegant curlicues rather than a string of distinct items; and the ABC song sounds to him like it does to a younger child, like a stream of nonsense syllables, not a list of separate names."

A child's school success depends most of all on how much he or she learns about reading *before* getting there, she told me. Poor Jess was not poised for school success.

What *should* children learn before starting school?

Dr. Adams told me about the indispensable "prereading" stage enjoyed by young children who—unlike Jesse—have access to ABC puzzles, magnetic letters on the refrigerator, picture books, and *Sesame Street*, and who see their parents reading. (Flash cards for babies are unnecessary.) All these age-appropriate experiences shape important pathways in young brains.

A child whose parents read to him, beginning in infancy, for thirty to forty-five minutes each day will have enjoyed one thousand to seventeen thousand hours of storybook reading, "one-on-one, with his face in the books," before first grade, says Dr. Adams. A thousand hours watching *Sesame Street* and thousands of hours with puzzles and magnetic letters and writing and playing word games in the car and on the computer accumulate knowledge. A child gains the two vital prereading skills: (1) the ability to recognize the letters, and (2) the ability to hear and differentiate the phonemes—the specific sounds that go together to make a word. Those two skills take a child to the next level, the ability to grasp the "alphabetic principle": a story is made up of words, the words are composed of sounds, and the sounds are written by letters.

Although Jesse showed up, bravely and hopefully, on his first day of school, wearing a new backpack rattling with new pencils and crayons, he was, in hidden ways, unlike the other kids. Compared with his classmates, he'd grown up in a pre-Gutenberg era.

But Jesse loved picture books and loved having me read to him! He quickly learned to settle himself within the circle of my left arm at bedtime and study the smooth pages of *my* favorites: *Corduroy*; *The Runaway Bunny*; *Harry the Dirty Dog*; *The Story About Ping*; *Sylvester and the Magic Pebble*; *Pretzel*; *The Tub People*; and classic childhood tales. He grasped that there were small animals in distress! Frantically he formulated and pronounced new English sentences as best he could, trying to rescue them. When the Big Bad Wolf ate the first little pig, Jesse, panic-stricken, jerked the book out of my hands and flipped worriedly back through the pages. He found what he was looking for.

"What this name!?"

"Mama Pig."

"I need talk Mama Pig . . . Mama Pig!"

"Yes, Jesse?" I replied in a maternal porcine voice.

"No go! No pigs go! Bad wolf coming!" He sobbed.

"Oh! Thank you!" I snorted. "I'll tell the boys."

When we read through the story again, I altered the plot. Instead of "And he ate the first little pig up," I said, "And the little pig ran home very fast to his mama and he never saw the bad wolf again." Jesse went to sleep that night with the deeply satisfied feeling of having averted a tragedy.

Jack and the Beanstalk came as a huge revelation to him, headline news for weeks. Every night he tried to deter Jack from encountering the giant, while all I wanted was to finish the damn book and go back downstairs for the rest of my evening. He refused to let me push on with the story, refused to go to bed with issues of life and death unresolved, and refused to be read any book other than *Jack and the Beanstalk*. If I hid *Jack* in the hopes of introducing him to a work of more soporific literature, we lost more time because he ransacked his room looking for *Jack*. When I read it, he grabbed the book from my hand and spun back through the pages, wanting to try again to convince Jack *not* to climb the beanstalk. I wrangled the book back and turned the page, longing to finish. He snatched it back.

"I need talk Jack!" he yelled.

"Yes, Jesse?" sighed Jack in my voice.

"No go! Bad giant coming!"

"Nah, I'm going."

"No, Jack! No go! Giant coming!"

"I planted this darn beanstalk. I'm climbing it!"

"No, Jack, no!"

At this point Jesse and I were in a desperate tug-of-war over the book. He fought to save Jack's life, while I fought for a chance to see Donny and my other children again. I was bigger. I won. I pulled the book free, flipped forward half a dozen pages, and roared, *"FEE FI FO FUM!!"*

Jesse was all accusation now. He pointed his finger at Jack. "I told you, Jack! I told you!"

Night after night Jesse intervened on the side of the underdog. He delivered tongue-lashings to the persecutors of the Ugly Duckling, Peter Rabbit, and Pretzel. "Why you put Peter's daddy in pie?" he demanded of Mr. McGregor. "Why no love Pretzel?" he asked the pretty dachshund named Greta. Curious George was a hopeless case, refusing to listen to warnings from either the Man in the Yellow Hat or from Jesse Samuel.

In deep and important ways, the child understood literature. But letters evaded his grasp.

In the approach to literacy, letters must be memorized. But letters are hard to memorize! They look like one another, and it matters which way they face, and their names rhyme, and the lowercase letters don't always resemble their uppercase counterparts, but sometimes they do. "The alphabet was thousands of years in the making," said Dr. Adams. "It is just not designed for a crash course."

Showing Jesse the same letter day after day and drilling its name with him wasn't taking us very far. I next spoke to a developmental psychologist in Philadelphia, Dr. Barbara Z. Presseisen, who had retired from the educational research laboratory Research for Better Schools. She said, "Children acquire concepts through touch, movement, and sensation. Don't rely exclusively on visual teaching with Jesse. Learning letters is *motor* knowledge. A child must shape, write, feel the letters; use his body. Tell Jesse to lie down in the shape of a *C*, or to shape the *R* in the air with his finger. Use materials like clay, paint, and sand. He needs to talk, see, touch, and hear. Refer frequently to the letters: 'That's the color red, it starts with *R*, it says *rrrrr*.'"

So Donny and I did all these things. At bedtime Jesse and I read and laughed and yanked the book back and forth, but every few minutes I drew his attention down to the bottom, where the deepest riches lay embedded in the text. "Oh, look!" I said. "Here are the words, and they're built out of letters, and they're telling us the story." One night Donny and I helped Jesse shape the entire alphabet out of clay. On another night we asked him to make letters out of building blocks. We surrounded him with alphabet puzzles and alphabet place mats and alphabet pillowcases.

He began to see that letters weren't just silly look-alike squiggles, but referred to things outside themselves, even to people he loved. His special name for Lee was "Botco." (We'd thought it meant older brother in Bulgarian, but maybe not.) One day Jesse recognized the letter *L*.

"*L!*" he shouted. "*L* means Botco."

On another day he proudly pointed to a *W*. "Mommy's letter!" he yelled. "*W* for Mommy, *W* for Melissa."

I accepted these as real steps in the right direction.

And then one day, literally a red-letter day, Jesse wrote a word. He'd become a great fan of Disney/Pixar's *Toy Story*. The toy characters flaunt the fact that their owner, a little boy named Andy, has written his name on the bottom of their feet. It proves that he loves them.

Jesse had a *Toy Story* toy, a big, shiny, battery-operated white Buzz Lightyear. When Buzz said, "To Infinity, and Beyond!" Jesse echoed him while jumping off the back of the sofa, shouting, "To Fifteen, and Beyond!" Now he ran to show me that on the bottom of Buzz's shoe he had written "JᴲssƎ."

It was a breakthrough. And it was readable! From the incomprehensible curlicue river of decorative patterns and flourishes, the letters *J*, *E*, and *S* had made themselves known to him. These three, he now understood, could be pulled out of the stream and lined up in a certain meaningful way. That day, on the foot of his Buzz Lightyear toy, Jesse began to make his mark, to write his own name in the world.

19

A Continent of Orphans

One morning in 2001, I idled over the kitchen table with a tepid cup of coffee, delaying work, slowly turning the large pages of *The New York Times*, when I saw Africa referred to as "a continent of orphans." Africans were being felled disproportionately by the rolling destruction of the HIV/AIDS pandemic. In sub-Saharan Africa, twelve million children had lost their parents. In Ethiopia, eleven percent of the children were orphans.

I read the paper that morning, as always, as an interested and concerned world citizen. But I also happened to be a person aware that a perfectly good twin bed in the upstairs nursery was unoccupied. *Twelve million children without families?*

Is adoption a good response to a humanitarian crisis? It's not. Adopters cannot be among the first responders to hurricanes, tsunamis, earthquakes, wars, or pandemics, because children who appear to be orphaned might still have living relatives. Children should be sustained and protected as close to home as possible, giving their families a chance to locate them. Only after a country has had a chance to sort out which children are true orphans can adoptive parents be sought.

In any case, a little person is not a philanthropic project. Adults with the commendable urge to do good can join or support frontline lifesaving organizations. A humanitarian urge—when overlaid upon the life-time commitment of raising a child, especially a traumatized child—fades fast, often by the fifth tantrum.

Adoption is the appropriate response to only one situation: the need of a child for a new family, combined with a family's desire for a new child.

My interest in adopting again preceded the news that there were millions of African children in need; I was already interested, dabbling near the surface of the water. The news of the world's AIDS orphan crisis showed me where it might be possible to dive in.

But if we found another child to adopt, would I have the gift of making everyone feel loved and safe? Or was I on the verge of fomenting a mini-cyclone at home that would never die down or give anyone a moment's peace, like some of the mega-families I'd met? If we brought in another child, would we still be a family or would we be on our way to becoming a group home?

Cautious, but finally undeterred, I inched ahead.

Ethiopia was one of the only African countries with a formalized international adoption program, and Adoption Advocates International (AAI) in Washington state one of the only American agencies licensed to work there.

Before contacting AAI, we took time to consider the ramifications of adopting an African child. We asked friends and relatives of color. "Can we raise an African child? Is this the right thing to do for a child?"

"A child needs a family," everyone said. "If an African or African American family can't be found for the child, the child still needs a family."

"In *Atlanta*? Can you raise a black child in *Atlanta*?" asked our cousin Julian Haynes, a Morehouse College student. Atlanta was a historic African American city: an academic, business, civil rights, political, and music capital of black America; the birthplace and final resting-place of Dr. Martin Luther King, Jr.; and a cultural magnet for African immigrants, especially Nigerians, Ethiopians, Eritreans, and Somali. According to the 2000 Census, Atlanta had the third-largest African-born population in the United States, after Washington, D.C., and New York;

Atlanta was in the top tier of cities with significant Ethiopian-born populations. "Yeah," said our biracial cousin. "You can definitely raise an African child in Atlanta."

A shiny pixie of a girl with smiling eyes appeared in AAI's August 2001 newsletter. Her wide forehead gleamed in the sunshine. Her hair was drawn back into three sections. She had a wistful smile in which the tongue poked out shyly between the baby teeth. She stood in front of a cinder block wall, under a tree, wearing a long-sleeve white T-shirt under a blue-jean jumper. She was five years old, and her name was Helen.

Standing at the mailbox, I flipped through the newsletter and was struck by Helen's picture immediately, but it was nine-year-old Lily who claimed it. She came in after school, studied the pages of the newsletter at the kitchen table beside a bowl of Reese's Puffs, then looked up almost in awe and said, "I think I just found our new sister." She ran through the house to show Seth, Lee, and Jesse the cute face. Lily so wanted a little sister!

I requested a video from AAI, and a few nights later we watched it. We spotted Helen singing in a group of children and hopping in her excitement. After the song, she touched her front tooth with her index finger, a gesture of shyness.

Lily was beside herself with happiness. She drew Jesse out to the porch to speak to him privately; she wanted him to feel excited rather than threatened or jealous at the thought of another adoption. Jesse burst back into the house and raced to the kitchen to tell everyone the news.

"I going be *big brother*! I *bigger* him! I FASTER him!"

"Do the name *Ethiopia* ring a bell?" roared Donny, scooping Jesse up in his arms. "You NOT faster him. Him faster YOU."

We all laughed very hard the night we resolved to try to bring Helen into our family.

At bedtime Jesse promised, "I going be nice to him ONE HUN-DRED!"

We learned that Helen had lived in the orphanage for only a few months following the recent death of her mother. Her father, a soldier, had died when she was two. She was an only child. HIV/AIDS had robbed her of her family; she was HIV-negative, healthy.

I pitched a story to *The New York Times Magazine*, offering to fly to Ethiopia to report on the condition of some of the world's AIDS orphans while meeting one small girl in particular, and the story was commissioned.

Sitting at my computer, accepting the assignment and beginning to sort out my calendar and travel plans, I was seized by a panic so powerful it nailed me to my chair. My heart slowed to an audible bass thump. *I'm doing this to myself again?* An icy wave of the Post-Adoption Depression of 1999 doused my spirit. With shaking hands I searched through cyberspace for the only person who had done academic research into post-adoption depression syndrome, and I e-mailed her: "If you've had this once, you probably won't get it again, right? Isn't that true?"

She e-mailed back: "Not true. People sometimes experience it a second time."

I sat forward with my head in my hands. Adoption seems so theoretical, and fun, until you realize you will have to put one foot in front of the other in real time, through actual streets of a city with an impossibly exotic name, on a continent you've never been to, surrounded by people rapidly speaking in many languages of which you will understand not one word—all with the goal of bringing back a traumatized young human being from very far away to your everyday midtown American life. Unable to rise from my chair, I wrote a feeble e-mail to Nancy Kayes, mother of god-knows-how-many-now in Cincinnati.

"Nancy, I'm panicking!" I wrote. "We've just committed to a five-year-old girl in Ethiopia and I'm having second thoughts. I can't face post-adoption depression again!"

I hid out in the dank basement laundry room, witlessly sorting socks while hoping for an encouraging word from Nancy. *Maybe Nancy will adopt her!* I thought.

An hour later, Nancy e-mailed back: "Melissa, you will be fine. This little one has no one in the world. You are strong and capable and you have a wonderful family. You can handle this."

Her words calmed me instantly. I printed out the e-mail and put it in my back pocket. "This little one has no one in the world . . ."

20

First Trip to Ethiopia

November 2001

On my first morning in the mountaintop capital of Addis Ababa, the highest-altitude capital in Africa (and the third-highest capital in the world), I was awakened by the hollow-toned clop-clop of donkeys going downhill along paved streets, a sound like a cascade of wooden building blocks. A rooster erupted from beneath my second-floor window, and minor-key calls to prayer and early-morning chants drifted on the air from the Sunni mosques and the Ethiopian Orthodox churches. Though my perception the night before was of a dusty, chaotic city, now the early-morning sky blew overhead like freshly laundered sheets on a line, and the leaves of the eucalyptus trees flapped in the breezes as if they were applauding. I stood barefoot on the cement balcony, filled with a sense of well-being and adventure. A row of schoolchildren passed by in the lane below me; when I waved to them, they laughed and ran for their lives.

My driver and translator, a young man named Selamneh Techane, came for me. In the blue and white taxi we lurched through packed streets across hair-raising intersections lacking traffic lights and stop signs. The lawless speedways of cars, trucks, and buses were clogged by herds of goats and sheep followed by ragged boys flicking whips over the animals' heads to keep them trotting. Men ran by in flip-flops, with upside-down chickens in their fists. Women in heels and pantsuits, talking into cell phones, stood beside women in colorful peasant dress, sometimes with the faces of babies peeking out over their shoulders from within the knotted drapes of cloth; very few women wore burkas, though the population was roughly forty percent Muslim. We passed business towers and mud slums; there were luxury hotels with sheep nibbling on the flanks of their emerald-green lawns, and streets where sick and destitute beggars, from elderly people to toddlers, lived on the sidewalks. Falcons wheeled overhead, and vultures stood in the treetops, riding out the swaying of the branches patiently, as if with crossed arms, like businessmen calmly ascending the city by elevator. A million people were afoot.

Down a narrow, rocky lane we bounced, then parked outside the cement walls of Layla House, AAI's orphanage. Selamneh honked for admission. I was beside myself with excitement and a kind of stage fright. For the second time in my life I prepared to meet a child who was going to call me *Mama*.

There can be no other demarcation of time, no other "life-cycle event" as significant a crossing-over as this one. Marriage is momentous, but in most of the modern world, brides and grooms stand at the altar beside their beloved. Childbirth is a major event, but it, like marriage, follows a deep prior connection. Now the elderly guard pulled open the gates and I prepared to meet a person who would join, and change, my life permanently.

She was tiny! A scruffy, scared little girl who was now being half shoved, half dragged across the playground toward me by an exuberant crowd of children. She wore a baggy play outfit of turquoise elasticized shorts and a matching stiff cotton shirt, and her head shook with little beaded braids. I knelt down beside her as dozens of children surrounded us. The arrival of a new mother at an African orphanage is a very, very big deal.

But I was having a moment of misgiving—was this the bright, sparkly, intelligent-looking child of the photographs and video? I glanced up . . . was this actually the right . . . But then she touched her forefinger to her front tooth in shyness and I looked down into her big eyes. This was Helen.

I hugged her. She was shaking harder than I was. She had a round little tummy under her cotton shirt. She gave a small smile made of tears, happiness, shyness, and fright, but mostly she had a very worried look on her face. We were both squinting in the hot sunlight. I released her and stood up from my uncomfortable crouch. When I put my fingers to the dirt ground to steady myself, I felt my hand shaking. Helen skittered away across the playground and watched me cautiously from a distance.

I had brought toys for the orphanage in a canvas duffle bag. With a sense of unreality, almost of lunacy in the blinding sunlight, I began pulling things out. I shook out a colorful plastic mat for the game of Twister; I smoothed out the folds and stood back proudly as children came running to play. How to explain the rules to children who spoke Amharic, Oromo, Tigrinya, one of the Gurage (goo-rah-gay) languages, or one of the nation's eighty other Afro-Asiatic or Nilo-Saharan languages occurred to me as a problem for the first time. I jogged over to hand the spinner to Helen and gestured for her to come closer to the game. When I turned around, I beheld tumult on the mat. Eight or ten children had thrown themselves onto the play space and started wrestling. Helen gave the spinner a flick. "Left hand! Red!" I called idiotically to the non-English-speaking children thrashing one another for supremacy on the plastic. "Green! Right hand! Right foot, yellow!" A few disenchanted girls escaped from the wrangle and fled, while additional boys, spying a rumble, sprinted over and piled on. At the bottom, children were splayed and flattened like defeated wrestlers. Helen continued to flick the spinner happily. I looked around for adult help. Young Ethiopian women in aprons and headscarves were pinning up children's garments on the clotheslines, and others crossed the playground carrying trays of food for lunch; they nodded at me with kind smiles as they snappily passed by in their flip-flops. As far as they knew, this was how the game was played. "Blue! Yellow! Right foot!" Tough boys pounded one another. One child ran away wailing, with a hurt ear. A caregiver set aside her tray and knelt on the dirt to comfort him. She glanced up and across the playground at me with, I felt, concern. "Stop! That's not how you play!" I scolded. Some kids kicked and stomped; others howled. The goal was to own the mat. Finally it was over: a big boy with widely spaced front teeth and thick eyebrows repelled all comers and now stood spread-legged upon the plastic cloth. He reached his open hand to

Helen, expecting to be rewarded the spinner, and she gave it to him. Now he owned the mat *and* the spinner. He stood with a big, satisfied smile, exaggeratedly flicking the spinner. Game over. Twister: Lord of the Flies Edition.

I looked around again for guidance, but none was forthcoming; the teachers were on break; I must have arrived during recess. The children wondered what else I had in my duffle bag, but I believe their wonder included a touch of apprehension.

Well, I had brought whoopee cushions. I pulled out half a dozen of the red rubber platters, size large, and handed them out. When I described this scene in *There Is No Me Without You*, my book about Ethiopia's AIDS orphan crisis, I included the fact that people in the know had suggested I *not* bring whoopee cushions to Addis Ababa. "Ethiopians are very polite people," I was told. "They will *not* appreciate whoopee cushions."

I'd never met children that polite, I felt, so I packed them.

Now—pushing bravely on, as if my reputation hadn't been damaged by my having, upon arrival, invited children to pound one another for possession of a plastic ground cloth—I handed out my latest bit of fun. The children held the deflated whoopee cushions listlessly. Like uncooked pizza dough, the toys flopped over their hands. The children looked at me blankly. I realized that they had no idea what these things were, nor whether they were now supposed to fight one another for them.

There was a lone metal chair in the shade at the edge of the playground. I dragged it front and center amid the crowd of children, threw the whoopee cushion onto the seat, and sat down on it with resounding flatulence. The Bronx cheer blew from under my seat across the playground.

I looked up, chuckling to myself, and encountered a wall of stone-faced children.

Americans have to buy something to make that noise? some were thinking. And others had a look that expressed *But Helen's new mother... is insane.*

There was a long, universal moment of unhappiness. The children didn't like their gifts. They looked at me sadly. Behind me, Selamneh, the driver, made a move in my direction, then hesitated. He wanted to help but could not fathom my intention. *I'm going to be a failure in Ethiopia,*

I thought miserably. Most of all I hated to disappoint and embarrass Helen, who had been publicly linked to me.

There was no way to back out of this. Mortified, trapped, humiliated, I threw a second whoopee cushion onto the chair and sat on it. It made its big, prolonged, gurgling, blubbery snort. I jumped up as if startled, as if embarrassed, and—thank God—a boy burst out laughing. He caught himself and looked around in case it had been impolite to laugh, but I was already waving him over to try it for himself. I slapped the cushion back on the chair and stood aside. The boy seated himself gingerly on it. Nothing happened. I mimed the importance of sitting down *hard*, which was, in itself, a rather unfortunate sort of performance for me to offer at that moment in my international travels. He nodded, stood up, backed away, took a running start, twisted midair, and landed butt-first on the chair. He was rewarded with a fart noise at the volume of a backfiring bus. Now all the children burst out laughing! They got it! It was a joke! It was something ridiculous! Before they could begin punching each other to gain access to the chair, I pointed out that many of them were already holding whoopee cushions and that they could use the ground or the low cement wall. The children ran wildly all over the playground squashing their bottoms upon whoopee cushions with trumpeting results.

Now it was the caregivers' turn to look at me sadly.

From across the compound, shy Helen watched me, and—when our eyes met—she smiled behind her tooth and finger.

Before departing the compound, I was treated to a coffee ceremony, the first of many I would come to enjoy in this country, which is the birthplace of coffee and source of the richest and most stimulating brews on the planet. A young woman in a skirt and kerchief knelt in front of a coal-burning brazier on the floor, shaking a long-handled iron skillet in which fresh coffee beans were roasting. A stick of incense clouded the air. Long green grasses had been spread across the floor. When the beans were ready, the young woman circled the room with the smoking pan, and I followed the lead of the others in fanning the fragrant fresh coffee smoke toward my face with my fingers. The young woman returned to the floor to grind the beans with a wooden mortar and pestle; the coffee grounds were then added to water inside a spouted clay pot—a *jabena*—and boiled; and there was a series of elaborate pour-offs and filtering processes. Every step of this ancient coffee making and serving ritual was encrusted with tradition. A bowl of popcorn was passed around—part of the ceremony—and then a tray of fat, sweet hunks of bread. Each coffee serving, I would learn, had its own name. The first time fresh coffee was poured into tiny china cups waiting on a low four-legged tray was the Abol serving—I accepted my cup gratefully. The second round was the Huletegna serving, and if you lingered long enough, you might receive the Bereka serving; but it was time for me to retrieve Helen from the lunchroom and for us to depart.

The little girl came away with me in Selamneh's taxi, her eyes averted from mine, her bottom teeth gnawing at her top lip, yet seemingly not displeased. We would spend the next few nights together in the apartment owned by the adoption agency. I could not return to Atlanta with Helen on this trip, because our paperwork was not complete, but I was grateful for the chance to make this get-acquainted visit, as I had with Jesse in Bulgaria. It lessened a child's preadoption fright, as well as mine, to meet the new mother in advance of the adoption.

We drove to a pizza restaurant halfway up the Entoto Hills to the north. We were seated on a flowery patio overlooking the curve of the city against the mountains; at this distance, Addis Ababa seemed to lap up against the dry brown hillsides like a radiant lake.

Helen spotted a few discarded bottle caps in the dirt, and she ducked under the table to pry them out. Captivated by the archaeological glint of long-buried bottle caps, she surfaced for a moment only to seize a spoon from the table and then dove back to her work, declining the pizza when it arrived. In the coming weeks, in mud huts and tin hovels and circular straw-roofed houses called *tukuls*, I would grow acquainted with the toys foraged and jerry-rigged by the children of Ethiopia's poor. I could see that these bottle caps were a great find.

Affluent and middle-class Ethiopian families also lived in this city, and there were ambassadors and diplomats and UN officials and the Organization of African Unity (OAU) officials, for both of which Addis was the African seat. There were economists, urban planners, statisticians, public health officials, and development experts from every continent, who raised children in upscale homes with shady yards and television satellite dishes. But the numbers of private school children were dwarfed by the multimillions of poor children in the country. Bare-foot or in flip-flops, dressed in rags, too poor to go to school, at risk of being orphaned, they rummaged in garbage cans and dumps for the raw materials of toys; from throwaway cans, plastic bags, torn magazine pages, and bottle caps they fashioned playthings. Helen's little pockets bulged and clinked as we departed the restaurant. She wore the smug look of a squirrel who has set aside nuts aplenty for the coming winter.

Then we went shopping! Selamneh parked the taxi outside a narrow children's shop crammed amid a row of stores facing a busy street. The store was so small and packed with goods that many of the wares—toys and clothing and adult products, too—hung from hooks on the ceiling. Bicycles clogged the entrance. Diminutive Helen, in orphanage clothes and decrepit flip-flops, took possession of the shop rather quickly. She looked around, understood what was afoot, and began to make selections: she would like . . . hmmm . . . (finger touching tooth) . . . that blue adult bicycle! and she would like . . . yes, that shiny black electric guitar, and of course the sweetest little pair of red plastic sandals with buckles, and . . . a *gun*, a revolver in a glass-fronted display case . . . and a woman's bridal gown hanging from the ceiling like an angel. That's all! She was happy.

I said yes to the sandals, no to the rest, and yanked a dress off the overstuffed rack to show her. She turned her nose up at it just like Lily at home, who treated any item of clothing I removed from a shelf as poison. Just like Lily, Helen tossed her hair, ignored the dress I offered, browsed the racks, and settled on a dress more to her taste. It was a complicated winter jumper over a white cotton blouse with a lace collar. It came with a blue corduroy jacket with brass buttons. Yarn sheep stood out upon the wool plaid jumper. It seemed designed to be worn in Scotland. We also bought pink cotton pajamas, underwear, play clothes, and socks. While I paid the owner, Helen did some jumping. She opted to wear her new socks, with small pink ribbons on the cuffs, and her new sandals proudly out of the store. I would have liked to discard the flattened, filthy flip-flops, but Selamneh said they would be needed back at the orphanage.

Late that afternoon we returned to the apartment provided by the adoption agency; Selamneh wished us good night, and Helen and I began to set up homemaking together. I stood at a gas stove warming up the Ethiopian food that had been prepared for us by a housekeeper, while Helen busied herself in the bathroom, scrubbing her brand-new socks and her two dozen muddy bottle caps. Elbow-deep in suds, she barely paused when I looked in. Then she carefully carried her wet things out to the balcony to dry. Tenderly she draped each beribboned sock over the railing and hand-dried each bottle cap with a dishrag, polishing it until it shone.

She transferred the now-gleaming bottle caps to the lid of a shoe box and carried them to the floor of the living room. They jingled during the transport like bells. Suddenly she was scaling the wall, climbing up a bookshelf! I ran to intervene—she was trying to reach a decorative wooden candlestick on the highest shelf, so I handed it down to her. With a squeak of pleasure she ran to the kitchen with it. Strangely, she filled the candlestick with water and came back into the living room ever so carefully. Then, biting her top lip with her bottom teeth in shyness, looking down, she took me by the hand, led me to the living room, and gestured for me to be seated on the carpet.

With delicate and precise movements the little girl lifted the candlestick and poured its water into the many shining bottle caps arranged in two straight rows on the shoe-box lid. Then she lifted one bottle cap with two hands and presented it to me with a bow from the waist. I understood! She had prepared the traditional coffee ceremony! I bowed in thanks and used two hands to bring my bottle cap to my lips. Beyond the balcony, the long day turned to a smoldering dusk. Cattle lowed from their pens, and the car exhaust fumes were displaced by the woodsmoke from thousands of cook-fires. With many wordless sips and smiles of pleasure, my new daughter and I partook of the candle wax–flavored water brimming in the bottle caps. I never tasted anything sweeter.

At bedtime on our first night together, I sat on Helen's twin bed in the small room we shared—separated from the living room by a partition—trying to think what I could express without a common language. We both felt the uncomfortable newness of being together, but I was the adult. So with one finger I gently tried tickling her on the tummy through her blanket.

She churned and squealed with excitement and happiness. The glorious reaction was far more than a wiggling poke through a blanket should have generated. She kicked her feet up and down and wagged her head back and forth on the pillow. So I pulled down the blanket and pretended to ponder where to tickle next—shall I try here, under the neck, or perhaps here, under the armpit? I spoke aloud my dilemma: "Where shall I choose?" She wriggled in excited anticipation. I cried, "Armpit!" and lifted up her arm for a tickle.

The delirium! The joy! The hysteria! The happiness of a once-treasured child being offered a second chance, a new mother.

The following day, as Selamneh took us around the city, I had only to wiggle a finger at Helen to make her face light up with remembered laughter.

On our second night together Helen got into her pink pajamas, hopped into her twin bed, laid her arms on top of the covers, and waited expectantly. By that hour of my second full day on the Horn of Africa, I was hot and itchy, jet-lagged and eager for sleep. With big, round eyes the child watched me move around the room and grew worried that our bedtime fun was not to be repeated. Her little brow grew creased. She lifted both arms off the blanket an inch and spoke her very first and very high-pitched English word to me: "Armpit?" she asked.

I leaped to her bed, and the ticklefest began.

21

Old Friends

Selamneh wanted me to see more of the country, so he, Helen, and I set forth on a road trip southeast from the capital. We bounced downhill from the highland plateau onto the arid, rocky desert. The dry land was gathered, bunched up in the distance, like a khaki-colored blanket. Hidden in the folds of the barren hills, archaeologists had knelt and picked and swept away millennial dust with tiny paintbrushes, sweating and burning under the white-hot sun year after year for decades. Occasionally they uprooted a bleached fragment of bone that astonished the world and pushed back the time line of human evolution beyond reckoning. On this landscape, the skeletal remains of a 3.2-million-year-old hominid, hailed as humanity's oldest ancestor, was unearthed by Donald C. Johanson in 1974. He named her Lucy, but Ethiopians call her Dinkenesh, meaning "You are amazing."

By the time we rode across the sun-blasted land, a far older skeleton had been discovered (though it wouldn't be revealed to the world until 2009). Nicknamed Ardi, for *Ardipithecus ramidus*, the 4.4-million-year-old hominid was neither chimp nor human, but something in between.

We entered a dry, windy grassland. Camel riders suddenly appeared— men whose colorful woven headwraps circled their heads and lower faces. They were of the Afar people. They drew their animals up, slowing briefly when encountering the road, ignored us, then spurred the camels on and jiggled away. In round marshes, hippopotamuses marinated like watermelons floating in galvanized tubs of water.

This was the second time Helen had ever been in a car, and she grew carsick. Suddenly she was moaning, crying, and twisting in the backseat beside me. "She's sick!" I cried. Selamneh pulled over in time for us to burst from the car, and I stood beside Helen as she threw up repeatedly onto the shoulder of the road. Rural people glanced up and came running across the fields. The little girl gagged and coughed, and I felt helpless. As words were exchanged, I felt the locals were demanding: *What are you doing to this poor child? Where's her mother?*

And Selamneh must be saying, *That's her mother.*

And they, with Yiddish-like intonations, must be replying: *That's her MOTHER?*

We dabbed Helen's forehead, and gave her water, and thanked the concerned citizens, and drove on across grassland buzzing with insects. On the horizon, a lone walker, a woman in a long cotton dress, balanced a plastic jug of water on her head. Sometimes children appeared out of nowhere—black-skinned, barely clothed in ragged shreds of shorts and T-shirts, barefoot, and beaming with cuteness. They offered to sell small wooden things they had carved, or pieces of honeycomb, or a potato. I bought a couple of hand-carved wooden cars from one group, and they joyfully chased after our car, shrieking and waving goodbye. *What use is money to them out here?* I wondered.

Occasionally there was a dusty town with wooden storefronts and hand-painted signs. We pulled over and parked at a roadside café. We ordered three bottles of Coca-Cola—the distinctive name and logo recognizable in Amharic—and sat in front, at a small wooden table just a few feet from the road. Donkey carts raced down the main street, stirring up sand and dust; standing in the carts, yelling and shaking the reins, tossing their hair, were teenage boys. They were drag-racing, causing their families' produce to flop around in the back. They looked gloriously free and happy. Helen lowered her eyes in shyness and giggled. We walked behind the café and found ourselves on the rim of a volcanic lake: unmoving midnight waters of incalculable depth and age. The lake looked remote and forbidden, but there were great white pelicans here, colliding and splashing, and marabou storks, wild geese, and cormorants. Flamingos clattered overhead like long-legged pink-and-white clouds.

As we left the town and pushed on across more miles of blank sky and hot rock, Helen sprawled across the hot backseat, asleep. I struggled to stay conscious in the front, blinded by equatorial sunlight multiplied a million times by sand and dust and superheated air. *If only there were good schools, clean water, and health care for all,* I thought, *this country would offer one of the world's great childhoods.*

In Addis the next day, Helen and I visited an older couple who'd known her parents and her paternal grandparents. *Ato* (Mr.) Ayele Negussie and *Waizero* (Mrs.) Tsige Temesgen had taken Helen and her widowed mother, Bogalech, into their compound after Helen's father died. Bogalech, they told me, was fine-boned and beautiful; she did light housekeeping for them. Her husband had been in the army and must have returned from his years of service infected with HIV/AIDS. He died of the disease in 1998, at a time when antiretrovirals had begun to slow the mortality rate in the West, but not in Africa. The high prices demanded by the pharmaceutical companies ruled out Africa as a potential market. Western governments were mostly indifferent to the course of the disease across sub-Saharan Africa, and African governments were slow to react to the catastrophe. When Bogalech weakened, she had to know what awaited her—a certain death, unrelieved by medicine, and the full orphaning of her daughter.

The fine older couple—middle-class, residing in a handsome pink stucco house—welcomed me warmly. I didn't realize till much later that I was being interviewed. They had enrolled Helen, so to speak, in the American orphanage, on the lookout for better opportunities for her; and they felt entitled to veto any prospective parent unequal to the task of raising this exceptional child.

Ayele, who was dressed in khaki slacks and a plaid button-down short-sleeve shirt, had served in the Ethiopian air force for many years, followed by a long career with Ethiopian Airlines. He and his wife, who wore a white shawl, were well traveled. Two of their adult daughters lived in the United States. Ayele's English was excellent. We sat in their front room and a servant came in with a tray of coffee and slices of watermelon. "As Bogalech grew very sick," Ayele told me, "we heard her praying. She prayed for God to let her live long enough to raise Helen to the age of eleven. But she died when Helen was five."

Oh, but what a treasured child Helen had been, the older couple told me. A wanted and doted-upon baby, and such a beautiful and smart girl!

Then to business: "What are your plans for her?"

I encircled Helen in my arms. "We will love and raise her as our very own child," I said. "She will have five older brothers and sisters." Here I pulled out the small photo album I had created for Helen. "She will go to excellent schools. She will go to university."

When I glanced over at Tsige, I saw that she was crying.

Of course I didn't know that I was being screened, but I felt their approval. We exchanged phone numbers and addresses, promising to keep in touch (and we would). They covered Helen in hugs, tears, and kisses as we departed; and then they bestowed nearly the same quantity of these emotional gifts on me.

Though too shy to speak to me when we were alone together at the apartment, Helen was playful, watchful, and quick-witted. She instantly grasped the game of dominoes I'd brought her, and then beat me at it. Ditto the game of pick-up sticks. One afternoon, I opened a box of Sun-Maid raisins I'd brought from home and handed Helen a raisin. She accepted it appreciatively, examined it closely, sniffed it, and ate it, one tiny nibble at a time. I had one, too. Somehow that seemed like enough raisins for now, so I closed the little red box and gave it to Helen to keep. She slid it into the Dr. Seuss backpack I'd brought her.

Several nights later, she and I were the dinner guests at the home of a professional Ethiopian couple and their four teenagers. I'd interviewed the husband and wife for the *Times* article. Upon learning I had an Ethiopian child staying with me at my apartment, they insisted we come to their house for dinner. Helen wore her complicated Scottish winter holiday outfit, despite the heat of the evening. As we got seated in our hosts' living room, Helen opened her backpack and politely produced the box of dominoes I'd given her. She swiftly explained the game to the teenagers and then, just as swiftly, with several decisive clicks, defeated them. Then she taught and beat them at pick-up sticks. Then we were seated for dinner. As everyone finished and prepared to push back from the table, she asked in Amharic to be excused. She returned with her backpack, extracted the box of Sun-Maid raisins, carefully opened it, and with great seriousness and ceremony circled the table and handed each person in the family a single raisin. Then she closed up the box and put it away. That's how they do it in America, she figured.

Helen and I visited her previous orphanage, called ENAT, which housed HIV-positive orphans. Having lost her parents in the pandemic, Helen had been assigned to ENAT; when her blood test came back negative, she was transferred to an orphanage for healthy children and she became eligible for adoption. Most of the children here did not understand these distinctions, nor did they grasp that Helen could expect to live a long and healthy life, while her best friend here—a handsome little fellow named Eyob—had a life span measured in months.

The older ones among them—seniors eight or nine years of age—knew what lay ahead. Funerals here were as common as children's birthday parties in our world. The day before our visit, a special favorite, a seven-year-old boy— "another little prince of our country," the director had told me over the phone—had been buried.

The moment we entered the gates, Helen tore off in search of Eyob; they clasped hands and hopped up and down in joyful and laughing reunion. A girl approached and watched them. I tapped Helen on the shoulder, to direct her attention to this other friend wishing to be acknowledged. Helen glanced over, looked up at me, and rolled her eyes, clearly relaying something like *That girl is so annoying!*, and then returned to chase and giggle with Eyob.

The mood at ENAT was one of frolic and play, seemingly no different than at the orphanages for healthy kids. But on closer inspection, I saw that some of these children were beginning to unravel. When they stopped jumping rope or kicking a ball, I glimpsed bald spots, open sores, and the mushrooming warts of molluscum around their eyes and lips; I saw too-thin legs, and too-large heads on bony shoulders; and I noticed that there were no older children in these compounds at all. In the land of HIV-positive children, any boy or girl who achieves the age of eleven or twelve is an old-timer; to reach fourteen would require a miracle. There was also the chilling sense here of back rooms into which children disappeared, to and from which nurses came on shift, and from which cries were sometimes heard in the night.

I produced "rocket balloons" from my purse. These long, striped, curly balloons, when blown up and released, blubbered and rumbled and zoomed low overhead like dirigibles. Children healthy enough to run chased after the balloons ecstatically, and weakened children sitting on the playground's curbs laughed and clapped from their places. Children danced in mock terror when the balloons nose-dived and sputtered out around their ankles. Some children mastered blowing them up and letting them go; others not. Solomon was a particularly filthy, snot-encrusted, ragged, and cheery boy. When he came to me for help with his grimy, slobbery balloon, I gave it a dismayed look, covered as it was with heaven knows what fluids. I wiped it thoroughly on my shirt and secretly substituted a fresh balloon before blowing it up for him. When he returned to me a few minutes later with the snotty deflated thing, he looked at it rather sadly, then wiped it on his own filthy shirt for me before handing it over for a refill.

Helen and Eyob hugged each other long and hard when saying goodbye. She waved enthusiastically at him from the taxi's backseat as we backed out of the compound. I assumed they looked forward to their next playdate, but I doubted there would ever be another one.

Helen and I packed up our apartment; on a Tuesday morning, Selamneh came to get us for the last time. "Does Helen understand that in a few months she will come to America and be my daughter? That I'm not leaving her here forever?" I asked Selamneh.

"Yes, she understand," he said.

I walked with Helen to her orphanage dorm room. I hoped it didn't appear to the other girls that I was returning Helen, that I didn't want her. She'd picked out gifts for them: hair clips, woven bracelets, hard candies, and coin purses. I was teary, but Helen was very composed. I placed her photo album on her bed. On impulse, I unhooked a silver necklace from around my neck—it was a replica of an ancient coin from the Kingdom of Israel—and strung it around Helen's neck. "Keep it for me," I told her, and I glanced up to one of the older girls. "Tell her, Mekdes. Tell her to keep it for me; and, when we see each other again, she can give it back to me." I started to cry. Helen was looking down, stroking with delicate fingertips the edge of her picture album. I hugged her goodbye, turned away, and left.

22

Helen in America

On Valentine's Day 2002, nine-year-old Lily spotted Helen coming from the international gates to the main concourse at the Atlanta airport, accompanied by AAI director Merrily Ripley. "Oh my God, she's so cute," Lily breathed. When Helen spotted me in the distance, she gave a happy wave and then reached under her sweatshirt, pulled out my silver Israeli necklace, and jingled it at me—to show she hadn't lost it, to show she remembered. Then she ran down the corridor toward us.

I swooped her up and—having forgotten how petite she was—nearly flung her into the ceiling. Settling on my hip, she touched her front tooth with her index finger. As Donny, thrilled, leaned in to meet her, she pressed hard against that shy front tooth but emitted a small smile, too.

Molly was at Oberlin, but Seth, Lee, and Jesse were instantly charmed by the tiny pip-squeak with enormous eyes and a thousand-watt smile to whom Lily introduced them in the front yard. They led her down the driveway, lifted her onto the trampoline, bounced gently with her as she squealed, and then seated her in Seth's lap on the forty-foot-high rope swing and pushed off. She had a high-pitched giggle, a little "eh-HEH" with the "heh" ending in a squeak, almost like a gagging sound. The big kids mimicked the mouselike squeak, which made her squeak more. On the way into the house, six-year-old Jesse explained, "I Bulgarium. You Earth . . . you Earthy . . . you Earthyopium."

At the kitchen table for dinner, Helen began to speak, but only to Lily, and in Amharic. She scooted over and whispered directly into Lily's ear some long comments and important questions. Lily's face crumpled in empathy and love.

We tucked Helen into her bed in the nursery beside our bedroom, an airy yellow and white room with a steeply angled ceiling, casement windows, and a skylight. Having delivered a good-night kiss, Lily said, "I've got to make her something. I can't stand it. I have to make her a present."

"You have a kit for making hair clips," I said.

"That just doesn't hit the spot," the fourth-grader replied. She rooted around in her closet and produced a hinged shoe box and a bunch of Mardi Gras beads. She glued the beads in ornate patterns all over the box and wrote "Helen's Box" on it. She tiptoed into the nursery and left the box on the foot of Helen's bed before going to bed herself. As I headed downstairs, Lily called out to me, "She's so sweet and funny! I'm so happy!"

Lily stayed home from school the next day and the girls played together under the eaves in Helen's new bedroom. Lily hauled out all her Barbie dolls, two dozen Beanie Babies, and the new doll we'd bought for Helen: "Kyra," an African American toddler with brushable hair. While the Beanie Babies leaned in to watch from atop the bed and dresser, the most beautiful Barbie of all married the most handsome Ken in a ceremony that took up all the floor space and most of the day. I brought the girls lunch on a tray as the hour of the nuptials approached. The girls showed me that Bridal Barbie's friends were dressed in ball gowns and spiked heels, but Ken's best man, the only other male in attendance, wore, unfortunately, a tennis outfit and big white plastic sneakers. Probably the curvy Barbies with diamond earrings and well-toned calf muscles would choose not to date him.

After dinner that night, Lily dragged out the costume basket. She gave Jesse a silver astronaut space suit and robed herself like a princess of Persia. Helen selected a pink satin princess gown, granny glasses, a velvet jester's hat with bells, and a yarmulke that had fallen in there. Around her waist she buckled a belt that held an army-camouflage walkie-talkie. When she pushed its buttons, it made the sound of explosions. Lily put on music from *Grease* and the children danced to "You're the One That

I Want." While I took pictures, Donny said, "Let's send a photo to Ethiopia, saying, 'Here is Helen on her first day in the U.S. wearing traditional American attire.'"

At bedtime after her first big day in America, the granny-princess Jewish jester-sergeant insisted on going to sleep with her new Kyra doll, two Barbie bridesmaids, the shoe box Lily decorated for her, and the toy army walkie-talkie. At odd intervals in the night we heard the distant sound of explosions.

As Donny and I told Helen good night on her second night, she pantomimed her desire to show us something. We sat beside her on the bed as she opened the photo album I'd left with her of our house and family, a photo album she'd lived with for half a year in the orphanage and, evidently, memorized. Now she offered a game. She flipped the album open to an image of *this* room, where we sat, and she pointed to a green, jagged thing at the bottom edge of the photo. Then she looked at us with a big smile and an exaggerated shrug to ask *Where is it?*

We looked closer at the picture, glanced around the room, and shrugged back, not knowing what that shape was.

With a squeak of happiness she darted out of bed, ran to the far corner of the room, and showed us Jesse's Playmobil Pirate Island. The jagged green thing barely captured in the photograph was the tip of a plastic palm tree.

Ready to play again? she asked us with smiling eyes. She pointed to a slender spine of a picture book on a shelf—I recognized it as *PEOPLE* by Peter Spier.

"I've got this one!" I told Donny, and slid to the floor to scan the bookshelves. I couldn't find it. I turned back to Helen, shrugging in defeat.

With a giggle she got down on her tummy, squeezed halfway under the dresser, pulled out the dusty book. It must have fallen behind the dresser many months ago, after the photograph was taken.

I challenged her: I pointed out a framed print from *Winnie-the-Pooh*, a pastel image of Christopher Robin and Pooh heading hand in paw up the stairs. It was not on the wall where it appeared in the photo album. There was an empty nail there instead. Chortling, Helen lifted up a pile of picture books on the floor, exposing the *Winnie-the-Pooh* print on the bottom. She'd researched this question in advance in case it came up.

One night that first week, I asked seventeen-year-old Seth if he'd mind fetching a nectarine for me from the kitchen. He ambled downstairs—it was around eleven o'clock—and encountered Helen there. Suddenly he felt confused about which fruit was actually a nectarine. "Which one is a nectarine?" he asked the only person available. Helen led him to the fruit bowl on the kitchen table and pointed to one.

She, too, had a question. She took him by the hand, led him to the counter, stood on tiptoe, and pointed at the blender, then turned to him to express, through pantomime, *What is THAT thing?*

He replied in mime, as if the rule were No Speaking Allowed. He plucked a few grapes from the fruit bowl, showed her the grapes on his palm, dropped them into the blender, and pushed the button. At the start-up of the rummaging, grinding noise, she started to flee the room, but when he laughed, she spun on her heel and returned. He took off the lid and showed her the demolished grapes at the bottom of the glass pitcher. She nodded sagely. He held up the nectarine and smiled his thanks. Both thus enlightened, they continued on their separate ways.

The next afternoon, he lounged across the sofa reading a book. Helen crept up silently, snatched the sock off his left foot, and fled screaming through the house with it. He chased her up and down the stairs and around and around the dining-room table. She sprinted past me, her face flushed with happiness, threw me the sock to hide, and kept running. When he finally ambushed her upstairs and pried open her hands, she cackled with laughter as he discovered that the sock was long gone.

I'd hired a young Ethiopian woman, Hareg, to come several days a week to help with Helen's transition. Helen told Hareg in Amharic, "I forgot the name of the tall brother."

The babysitter also had a bit of trouble pronouncing it, as *th*'s don't occur in Amharic. She relayed it as well as she could.

That night Helen suddenly yelled "Tzetz!" at the dinner table, then dove out of sight with stage fright.

Here and there Helen dropped clues that she was more educated than we realized. Since Jesse had arrived from his Bulgarian orphanage almost without spoken language, we hadn't expected a lot more from a child coming from an orphanage in one of the world's poorest countries in the epoch of the HIV/AIDS pandemic. On Helen's third morning, Lily gave her a notebook and offered to write "Helen's book" on it. But Helen took the notebook and pen and wrote "Helen's book" by herself, in English, in cursive.

We all stopped what we were doing and looked at the notebook. It was the apostrophe *s*, I think, that surprised me the most. I looked at the two words through narrowed eyes, suspecting a trick. Before I could figure out how she and Lily had done it, Donny boomed, *"Does she know her numbers?"* because he is a proponent of speaking loudly to foreigners. Helen opened her notebook, picked up a pencil, and rapidly jotted the numbers from 1 to 100 in columns of 10. Now Donny squinted at the notebook, trying to detect the gimmick.

That night, Seth and Lee discovered Helen in bed studying my Amharic-English dictionary by lamplight. "Oh, right, like that's happening," the teenagers said to each other. Seth leaned over the book and saw that Helen was browsing in the *A*s, so he picked out a word . . . "accountant." "What does that mean?"

Helen read it silently in English, slid her finger across the page to look at it in Amharic, and then looked up into the air, considering how to act it out. She reached for a piece of paper and a pencil from her night table, jotted down some numbers, and added them up.

Seth and Lee looked at each other in confusion.

Seth leaned over to choose another word: "abundance." Again the small girl moved her finger across it in both languages. She laid down the book, then gestured grandly outward with her hands to display a great quantity.

"Oh, this is ridiculous. Give me the dictionary," said fourteen-year-old Lee, as if he would now put an end to this foolishness. "She obviously studied the *A*s already." He pointed to the word "onlooker."

She read the word in both languages, laid the book down, straightened her back, shielded her eyes from the sun, and looked back and forth like a person observing a tennis match.

"My turn," I said, having watched this demonstration from the doorway. I flipped to the word "intelligent," wanting to relay that this is what she was. She thought I, too, required a definition. She put one finger up beside her nose in a pose of serious thought, then yelled "Aha!" and held up her pointer finger like a person who has just had a brilliant thought.

During the day, she listened closely to everyone's conversations; at night, she pursued her research with the dictionary and me. One night she asked: "What this means: 'butt'?"

Then we had a standoff and it confirmed my worst fears: the fear that the child might be too traumatized to adjust to our family.

Helen was reluctant to go to bed; there was something she wanted in the kitchen. She sidled over to the broom closet where six-packs of Coca-Cola, for teenagers only, were stored, and she opened the cupboard door. I shook my head no. She edged closer. I said, "No, those are for the big kids." She reached out her fingers to tickle the rim of the can, watching me carefully.

"Helen, no," I said, which I knew she understood, but I added anyway, in Amharic, *"Aydelem."*

She encircled a Coke can with her fingers and extracted it. "No," I said, and began to approach her. "Don't do it, Helen. That's not for you."

She studied the lid, wondering how to open it, as I moved toward her, repeating, "No. I mean it."

She popped it open. "Do not drink that or you are in trouble," I said.

She put it to her lips and took a sip. "That's it!" I yelled. I lurched toward her, took the Coke from her hand, and slammed it down on the kitchen table, causing it to explode. She went berserk, screaming in fury. I picked her up and staggered across the house with a female tornado in my arms, crawled up the stairs, made it to her bedroom, sat down on the floor, and hung on for dear life. She was hysterical. I locked my hands around her back. She windmilled her arms and I dodged to protect my face from blows. I tried to recall the little I'd read about "holding therapy," a controversial attachment strategy in which an adoptive parent hugs a raging child until the child gives up and relaxes. Supposedly it relays to a child that the new parent will not give up. In theory, the child's surrender to the adult's authority leads to a peaceful plateau and a new emotional attunement between parent and child.

I was pretty sure Helen was far from surrendering. Her violent flailing and earsplitting shrieks escalated. Speaking as an Atlanta resident, I am not opposed to the occasional refreshing sip of Coca-Cola, but this was about disobedience and about whether there were any rules at all in this new American wonderland. There is adoption lore (I don't know if it's true or not) that a horse released into a new meadow will run and run to the point of exhaustion, until it discovers the fences, after which it will calm down and graze. It was necessary to show Helen the fences. Coke was for teenagers. When I said NO, I meant it.

She continued to holler as if beaten by tongs (a cliché I have never understood but have always liked). Everyone came running to see what the mean mother was doing to the sweet baby sister. "Leave us alone!" I cried. The children fled.

"What's going on?" yelled Donny.

"I have no idea!" I yelled back above the commotion.

Donny fled.

Then, as the girl in my arms continued to roil and screech, I was hit by a horrible revelation. I fell in an instant to rock-bottom despair. *Oh dear God, I've done it, I've done that bad thing. I've adopted a child with attachment disorder. The child is profoundly damaged. She'll never attach to us.*

The setting sun tossed mint-green circles of light through the leaves of the tulip poplar beside the dormer window. Helen and I sat on the floor, locked together by my straining arms, and howling like infants. I sobbed: *Life is ruined.* She bawled: *I really wanted that Coke.* As we neared the one-hour mark, I leaned my head back against her bed for a rest. Across the house, my loved ones prepared for bed, but I was trapped in this bedroom prison with a demon-child obsessed with carbonated beverages. But then the tumult in my arms began to die down. The kicking lost its homicidal clout. Helen rolled onto her side and fell asleep in my lap. I gazed down on her unhappily and tried to release my tense muscles without waking her. After her nap, she woke up, gave a little yawn like a kitten, discovered me looming above her, and smiled as if absolutely surprised and charmed to find me there. I kissed her wet face. "Ready for bed now?" I asked. She nodded. I helped her out of her Coke-and tear-spattered clothes and into a Barbie-themed nightgown with ruffles. In the bathroom I helped her wash her face and brush her teeth. She hopped all the way back to her bedroom. I tucked her in, smoothed back some flyaway strands of hair, and kissed her good night. Soon Helen and I were asleep in our beds, all thoughts of attachment disorder and of Coca-Cola forgotten.

That was the only tantrum we ever had out of Helen.

23

Questions of Heaven

Several times a week, Helen succumbed to waves of homesickness and sorrow. Donny and I could see it coming, as if from a distance. No amount of gentle teasing or playfulness could head it off once the storm clouds of grief assembled. We watched her resist, then surrender to rapid, shallow sobbing and intakes of breath.

"Is she hyperactivating?" asked Lily, heartbroken at the little sister's sadness.

"'Hyperventilating,'" I said. "But no, she's just crying."

Our friends the Sarvadys, across the street—with two girls the ages of Lily and Helen—invited our family to dinner, Helen's first social call. It began well, with the four girls playing with Barbie dolls on the sunporch and then sitting near one another at the dinner table to chomp into corn on the cob and hamburgers. But then Helen tugged on my hand and we went back to the sunporch, where she dissolved into sorrow, heaving with sobs. "Come back in!" my friend Andrea—Andy—called, so I carried Helen to my seat as she continued to weep, her huge round eyes drowning in tears. Melancholy flattened the smiles of the other girls. Our friends cleared the table and returned with brownies. I broke off a piece and offered Helen a taste. Without interest she opened her lips a tiny bit, then sat up, flabbergasted. The look on her face was *WHAT???? OH GOOD HEAVENS!! WHAT???* She recovered completely, returned to her seat near Lily, and selected three big, rich brownies from the dessert platter.

"Maybe she was crying because she was afraid we wouldn't get dessert," I offered.

"She's already Jewish," said Andy. "You know how our people love baked goods."

I reached out to nearby mothers with rising kindergartners and invited them over so Helen could start making some American friends. A nice little girl showed up at our front door. Helen took a long look at her, then ran to find Hareg in the kitchen to ask in Amharic, "Does she have a mother?"

"Yes, she has a mother," Hareg replied in Amharic.

"Is that her first mother?"

"Yes, that is her first mother."

Helen marveled at the child's good fortune. But it was true of the next child who visited, and the next, and of the children she met on the playground, and of her new classmates at school. Soon I was the one answering her: "Yes, he has a mother." "Yes, that is her first mother." Helen had a new mother now too, as she was eager to tell, but she didn't take it as a given about anyone.

Knowing how deeply Helen had been loved by her parents, I felt hurt on their behalf by the questions asked by strangers. "She's so cute," some people commented. "Why would her parents abandon her?"

"They didn't abandon her! Only sickness and death pulled them from her," I said.

One day, grieving, Helen spoke to me between sobs: "Why . . . did my mother . . . have to die?"

"I'm so sorry, sweetheart," I said, taking her into my arms.

"I know why . . . she died," she choked out. "Because . . . she was very sick. And we didn't have . . . the medicine."

"I wish I had known you then," I said, rocking her. "I wish I could have sent you the medicine."

"But we didn't have a phone," she wailed, "and I couldn't call you."

———

"What did your house look like that you shared with your first mother?"
I asked one night.

"Oh, okay!" she said eagerly. She emerged from her covers to sit
cross-legged and straight-backed to tell me the whole story. "Well, you
know your office bathroom, where there's the little outer room with a
sink before you get to the inner room that has the bathtub and toilet?"

"Yes . . . ?"

"Our house was the size of that!"

"Okay," I said, shocked.

"We had two things in our house. We had a shelf, and we had a baby
bed. The baby bed was too short for my mother so she had to sleep like
this"—and she showed me how her mother slept in the crib with her legs
drawn up tightly. "We slept in it together."

"When my mother got sick, she laid back like this and her voice was
very rough," Helen said, now demonstrating how her mother had weakened and deteriorated. Helen, at five, had been her mother's chief caregiver. This I knew already from Ayele and Tsige, in whose compound
Bogalech and Helen lived.

"How did you get food?" I asked.

"People brought food to us," she said. Perhaps it was Tsige, or Tsige's
servant; perhaps there were kind women in the neighborhood aware
that, in the little house, a very little girl lived alone with her terminally
ill mother.

Helen ran errands for her mother. "Sometimes my mother gave me a
coin and I ran to the shop to buy her a bottle of juice. But one time at the
shop I saw something so pretty! It was a pair of butterfly clips, for my
hair! I wanted them so much, but I bought the juice for my mother."

I knew by now how much Helen loved pretty things. She closely examined the headbands and hair ribbons in the drugstore's hair-product
aisle. She and Lily lay across Lily's bed, slowly turning the pages of teen
fashion magazines. They braided each other's hair and painted each other's
nails, and together they summoned the courage for me to take them to
the mall to get their ears pierced; they squeezed each other's hands while
it was done. One day, at the drugstore, Lily chose her first-ever deodorant, and Helen wanted one, too, so she could be like Lily. Helen opened

hers and used it on the way home. She sprang into the house, yelling at the top of her voice: "SOMEBODY SMELL MY ARMPITS!"

"Uh, no thanks," replied the resident teenage boys, but Jesse, the young gentleman, said: "I will." Helen raced to him and raised her arms as if she were being robbed at gunpoint. He sniffed politely here and there, and gallantly announced: "You smell like a *lady*."

So I could easily picture tiny Helen peering, on tiptoe, into the rack at the dusty kiosk down the lane and spying, for the first time ever, amid the sponges and detergent and cigarettes and plastic buckets, something *cute*! Something for her *hair*! She bought the juice, sprinted home, and asked her mother if she could have the butterfly clips. Bogalech said yes.

Surely Bogalech had no coins to spare for butterfly hair clips; but she also surely knew, as I did now, how much her daughter loved sparkly things. Racing back down the lane to buy them became Helen's last happy memory of her time with her mother, and the butterfly clips her most precious possessions, for Bogalech died not long after that day. "They put my mother in a taxi and she died," Helen said. "On the day my mother died, people came and took me away. I forgot to bring my clips. I tried to tell them to go back, but I never saw my house again."

Of course, when I saw a necklace with a butterfly pendant in a store one day, I bought it for Helen; and a long-sleeve T-shirt silk-screened with butterflies, and even some butterfly-shaped hair clips. There are things you can replace for your child and things you can't replace. I was a mother to this darling girl, but I was not her first mother; her new butterfly items could not compete with the beauty of those first clips that sparkled in the semi-gloom of a hut in which a gentle and devoted mother lay dying because she couldn't afford the medicine.

One day Helen told me, "You look like my first mother," and on another day she said: "I'm getting you and my first mother mixed up."

I'd asked Tsige and Ayele to try to find photographs of Helen's parents, and one day two five-by-seven-inch black-and-white portraits arrived in the mail. Helen's father had the high forehead and intelligent gaze she'd inherited, and her mother had the dark-skinned beauty and silky hair. I bought a hinged wooden triptych frame for their photos and slid the earliest picture we had of Helen in between them. Helen appre-

ciated the gift deeply and began carrying the wooden contraption everywhere, from night table to car, from kitchen to school. For a week I
watched her struggle with the folding frame. I wondered if this was
about more than the precious photographs; maybe the child was trying
to figure out if there was still a place in her life for her first parents. "Do
you want me to keep the pictures for you?" I gently asked one day, and
she, exhausted by the effort of caring for the framed set, nodded. I set up
the pictures on my dresser. I would be a caretaker of her memories, too,
this implied, and she accepted that. At the time of her conversion to
Judaism, we would give her the Hebrew name Bracha in memory of
Bogalech.

Jesse had loved converting to Judaism! Well, he hadn't loved the in-
hospital under-total-anesthesia circumcision, but he didn't really remember it. He *loved* going to the mikveh. To attain a state of ritual purity,
it is necessary to disrobe and immerse oneself in a cistern, a natural spring,
a flowing river, the ocean, or a very small indoor pool. Jesse fearlessly,
nakedly, cannonballed into the water of a tiled mikveh at a local synagogue under the gaze of an Orthodox rabbi; he immersed himself the
required three times and for good measure did a somersault, his little
white butt flashing briefly above the waterline.

Now, in the backseat of the car, he excitedly prepared Helen for her
visit to the mikveh. "The blue-green water will cover all your body and
make you Jewish!" he enthused.

"Really?"

"Yes! You take off all your clothes and you jump in!"

"Wait. You take off all your clothes?" she asked.

"Yes! And you jump in the blue-green water!"

"And the rabbi's there?"

"Yes."

"Then I'm not taking off my clothes."

"Yes, you have to," he insisted. "The blue-green water touches every
part of your body and makes you Jewish."

"I'll wear a swimsuit," she said.

"You can't! Right, Mommy? You have to be naked so the blue-green
water can touch every part of your body and make you Jewish!"

"I am not taking off my underpants."

"You have to!" he said again, alarmed by this unforeseen obstacle. (In fact, the ceremony would be conducted with modesty and privacy.) Jesse was nearly weeping now: "The blue-green water has to touch every part of your body to make you Jewish."

"Forget it," Helen pronounced, looking out the window to end the discussion. "I am wearing my underpants."

"FINE!" yelled Jesse. "Fine! But your BUTT is NOT going to be Jewish!"

Speaking of heaven, Helen worried terribly that I might be headed that way prematurely myself. I couldn't sneeze around Helen; I couldn't *cough*; God knows I couldn't get a headache, lest she race to my side with anxious watchfulness. She did not want to see me on a bike, or showing off on stilts with the kids in the driveway, or burning my finger on the teapot. Any stumble I took, any blow of the knee against an open drawer or stub of a toe, reduced her to tears. "Please, Mommy, no, you'll get hurt," she protested when I offered to accompany the kids on a bike ride through the neighborhood. One night, Donny and I took everyone to an ice-skating rink; harking back to my Ohio childhood and youth, I gleefully laced on a pair of ice skates; but suddenly Helen was beside me and then at my feet, trying to unlace the skates faster than I could tie them. I hugged her, and laughed, and laughed harder as she trailed me to the ice, begging me not to go. "Mommy, you'll get hurt, please don't go, Mommy, please." She was crying.

"I can *do* this!" I said, and took off, a bit wobbly but upright. I carefully circled the rink, placing my right foot to the left of my left in order to form the turns as I'd been taught long ago. As I steered around the last curve, I prepared to wave gleefully to Helen, and perhaps glide on one foot for a while, showing off for her. But then I saw her face. Woefully she clung to the wooden railing, watching me from the cement walkway with eyes bereft of hope. She wasn't even crying now, she was just dazed, and forlorn, and alone. I veered to her and stumbled onto the rubber mat, and onto a bench, and began unlacing my skates.

"Oh Mommy! Thank you, thank you!" she cried, covering my face with kisses. "Thank you so, so much, Mommy!"

Now that we had touched upon spiritual matters, Helen had a question. "Is there just one heaven?" she asked at bedtime. She tossed it out in a high voice, as if at random, as if it were just a religio-philosophical inquiry between intellectual equals.

"It's impossible to know," I said, "but yes, I'd assume there's just one heaven."

"I mean, is there like a heaven above America and a heaven above . . . um . . . Africa?"

Now I saw where we were headed. "Oh, I wouldn't think so. That seems overly specific for heaven."

"So you think the people in heaven from Africa live with the people in heaven from America?"

"I feel sure they do."

"But which continent is it over?"

"I would think maybe it just floats around," I replied desperately.

Finally she got to the point: "In heaven, will my first mother live with us?"

"Yes," I said. "Yes she will. We'll all be together. Now go to bed."

24

Why This Is Not a Cookbook

Helen hated my cooking. She could barely swallow the foods I offered, because they were so tasteless. She was like a person whose mouth and lips were numbed by a dentist. And she hated all dairy products. The smell of cheese in the air caused her to crumple up her little face and fan her forefinger back and forth in front of her nose as if scolding the very air. Her many little braids with plastic clips at their tips shook in protest. She suspected that I was using horrid ingredients like *butter* in my cooking. One dab of butter on a giant bowl of pasta could ruin her entire evening.

Unfortunately, I was accustomed to this degree of criticism. Hints that I might not be that great a cook had been tactlessly dropped by Donny and the children for many years. If, for example, the fire alarm suddenly blasted a warning, one of the children was bound to say, "Dinner's ready." Or sometimes, when I pulled a casserole from the oven and peeled back the aluminum foil, a teenage boy widened his eyes like a great idea just hit him. "I know!" he yelled out of the side of his mouth, his eyes fixed in horror on my casserole. "Let's order pizza!"

I wasn't sure when this happened, since many of these children, as babies, considered me a marvelous chef. Their glee, their splashing contentment at the appearance of my hand-stirred mashed banana-and-pear puree inspired me. Wrist-deep in warm homemade avocado pudding, I'd reach up and smooth back a stray hair with the back of my arm, feeling like a farm wife who glances out the window as if there were goats and pea plants out there. But that nice fruit compote–smeared baby— Lee, for example—grew into a twelve-year-old who prepared noodles with butter and cheese for himself every night of the year that I cooked, except on the nights that I served up noodles with butter and cheese, on which nights he would step outside to grill himself a hamburger. He did this cheerfully, uncomplainingly, but I got the message.

I gained emotional sustenance over the years by my children's friends. *They* liked my cooking. *They* sometimes appeared uninvited at dinnertime with expectant looks on their faces and happily fetched an extra plate when invited to join us. I despaired of seeing those same eager and optimistic looks on my own children's faces. Once, Molly, at fourteen, peeked into the oven to see what was for dinner, then disappeared. I found her sitting alone at the dining-room table, fighting back tears.

Naturally, I grew demoralized, and defensive. Anyone would. To the question "What's for dinner?" I now snapped, "Who wants to know?" Their other frequent question, "What is that *smell*?" I refused to dignify with an answer.

There are inevitable mishaps in any kitchen, aren't there? I pulled a crisp, bubbling lasagna from the oven one night, felt the dish burning my fingers through the old oven mitts, yelled, "Ouch!" and tossed the lasagna high into the air off my fingertips like a volleyball. It landed top down on the floor, and the glass dish cracked. From the stricken, almost tear-filled faces around the dinner table, I knew I had their sympathy. But when—refusing to admit defeat (refusing to face the fact that I would have to cook something else)—I scraped and coddled the sprawling lasagna back into the dish and made a move to place it on the table, the children ran screaming from the kitchen.

Do you know that eggs in a pot from which all the water has evaporated will explode?

I am a restless cook. Standing at the stove makes me feel trapped. With a whisk in my hand and a white sauce on the burner in front of me, I feel I can take a moment to run to the basement laundry room and move the wet clothes to the dryer. Alarmed by dire warnings on a box of pasta, "DO NOT OVERCOOK," I obediently set the timer for eleven minutes, but then—with the feeling that someone else is handling it (the timer)—I step outside for the mail. If kids are playing catch in the front yard, I pause to throw a few high pops or grounders to them. If only the kitchen timer would turn off the water and drain the pasta while I'm outside, everyone would be happier!

Hoping to find something Helen wanted to eat, I took her to the grocery.

From her backward perch in the child's seat in the grocery cart she commandeered the expedition, pointing at the items she required *immediately*. I compliantly steered as the cart filled up with oddments: a container of Nestlé Quik Strawberry mix, a Barbie notebook, a bottle of Original Mr. Bubble, a bottle of Pepto-Bismol, and a box of Dreft laundry detergent. When she waved wildly and enthusiastically toward a greeting card that said "Happy Birthday, Grandma!" I suddenly grasped that she was picking out things that were *pink*.

I put everything back on the shelves other than the Barbie notebook and the bubble bath and steered into Produce.

There she recognized an actual food: a hot red chili pepper. "Whoa!" I cried, stopping her from chomping into it at that moment. "Wait, just wait." She held it happily on her ride through the store, the way most children that age hold animal crackers. At checkout, I searched for an Ethiopian cashier. No problem: all the cashiers were Ethiopian. "Excuse me," I said to a small, middle-aged woman. "Umm, this is my daughter. Can she eat that?"

The cashier took us both in for a long moment, then said, "Yes, she can eat."

I borrowed the hot pepper from Helen, paid for it, wiped it off, handed it back, and she crunchily devoured it.

By the next afternoon she was hungry again, and glum. My friend Sue Fox and I buckled Helen into the backseat of my car one night and drove in search of an Ethiopian restaurant. There are perhaps fifty thousand Ethiopians and Eritreans in Atlanta. Ethiopian churches, restaurants, markets, and businesses are everywhere. We chose a restaurant and entered shyly, unacquainted with the local immigrant community, but the hostess and waitstaff sprang into action with what seemed to be a long-planned reception specifically for Helen. They recognized her instantly as a little girl far from her home. They spoke with her in Amharic, complimented her, and fussed over her. Once she was seated, the hostess knelt beside Helen to gently ask her to name her favorite foods, and in a tiny, whispery voice, she did.

Before this night I'd known nothing of the link between an Ethiopian's vitality and joy in life and his or her ease of access to *injera*—the flabby, cool, sour, thick, spongy brown pancake that is a staple food of Ethiopia, made from the grain *teff*—and to *wat*, the spicy Ethiopian stews made from beef, chicken, lentils, potatoes, vegetables, or other ingredients. Sue and I sat back and watched as the small girl tucked into the baskets and platters that were brought to her, putting away more food than anyone would have thought possible. All week I'd been thinking, *There is no more dainty and feminine creature on earth than a little Ethiopian girl.* But she ate like a sumo wrestler. She gulped down everything in sight—scooping up the stews with torn scraps of *injera*—and then she sagged back in her seat like a bag of cement. The staff kissed us goodbye on both cheeks and pressed take-home containers into our hands. I guided the five-year-old—almost too sated to put one foot in front of the other, woozy with excellent nutrition—across the dark parking lot.

In the backseat on the way home, Helen began to laugh hysterically. She cackled like a madwoman. Sue and I began laughing uncontrollably in the front seat in response. How ridiculous and wonderful was life when there was a tummy full of *injera* in the car.

The next day, at an Ethiopian grocery, I bought the spice mix called *berbere* (burr-burr-ee), which is ground cayenne pepper, red chili pepper or red pepper flakes, and fenugreek, often with paprika and with or without allspice, cardamom, cinnamon, ground cloves, coriander, cumin, nutmeg, or black pepper. Sometimes it is mixed with oil and sold as a paste rather than as a dry spice.

I poured the dry *berbere* into a sugar bowl on the kitchen table, and Helen sprinkled it on every food. I carried a baggie of it in my purse in case we were away from home at mealtime. The Ethiopian babysitter concocted spicy Ethiopian stews for Helen.

Hector Perdomo, a carpenter from Honduras, was renovating our basement. He sat down beside Helen at lunch one day and she offered him a bite of *doro wat* (chicken stew), wrapped in *injera*, from her fingers. He happily accepted a taste, then looked up with bug-eyed, puffed-cheek astonishment. A strong man with a liking for spicy food, he took one swallow of little Helen's lunch, then ran to the sink for water, cursing in Spanish.

25

Married to the Defense

The mother of one of Jesse's school friends phoned me. She wanted me to know that Jesse was walking around with a cigarette lighter in his jacket pocket and was showing it to kids. "Oh, no!" I cried. "We'll deal with it right away! Thank you for telling me!" I ran upstairs, looked through Jesse's jacket pockets, and there it was: a bright green Bic Classic Disposable Lighter.

But that night after dinner, when Donny and I sat down to discuss the matter with Jesse in the front room, he declared himself innocent! He didn't know what we were talking about! No, he said when I produced the lighter, he'd never seen it before. He couldn't believe it came out of his jacket pocket. What would have been a minor case and teachable moment—Fire Is Dangerous; You Are Not Allowed to Play with Fire—was enlarged by the lying and denial.

"It's not mine, I SWEAR," Jesse said in the classic words of children in trouble all over the world.

It was often hard to get a rise out of Donny. A man obliged to spend his daylight hours in windowless high-security prisons visiting accused drug dealers and sex offenders did not panic in the face of an N for deportment on a young boy's report card.

"You're failing ART?" asked an older brother in predatory delight, leaning in from the doorway as I waved the report card at Donny.

"What's an N?" asked Donny.

"What's deportment?" asked the older brother.

"It means he doesn't know how to behave!" Donny happily roared. "Maybe he'll get that award at graduation we've always wanted: Most Improved in Social Skills!"

I signed the younger child's report card and sent him on his way.

It was hard to provoke Donny, but not impossible. He knew better than most parents that terrible things can happen when kids violate rules and teenagers break the law. On the big topics, he was tough: No hitting, no stealing, no lying. Be polite. Study hard, work hard, pull more than your own weight. Don't be mean to other kids. Invite the social outsider to the party. No drinking, no drugs, no guns. No carelessness with fire. No driving under the influence. No swearing. (Wait, I'm kidding about "No Swearing." He's a criminal defense attorney, not a friggin' saint.)

The kids knew that if one of their transgressions merited *Dad's* attention, it was serious.

Despite spending thirty years working on behalf of accused criminals— or maybe as a result of it—Donny's moral compass is bright and sure. He trusts in the wisdom of the Founding Fathers and the U.S. Constitution. The right of American citizens to be considered innocent until proven guilty is the bedrock of our freedom, he will tell you. Unlike millions of people around the globe, we are safe in our homes; we will not be seized by unwarranted government agents, we will not disappear into hidden prisons, we will not confess under torture. Every one of us is entitled—if accused—to have our day in court.

Yet everyone reproaches him: "How can you defend those people?!" Donny tolerates the abuse good-naturedly. He knows that the next middle-of-the-night phone call—"I may be subpoenaed at work tomorrow." "Our college son was arrested for selling drugs." "Federal agents just came into my house and seized my computer!" "My husband drove drunk again!"—might well come from a former critic. Besides, his job is not always about turning the dial from *guilty* to *innocent*; it's about help-ing a defendant present a coherent defense, and about seeking a verdict tempered with compassion: not *murder*, but *manslaughter*; not *death*, but *life without parole*.

Donny defended sociopaths. He defended men accused of gang rape, of murder, of drug and arms trafficking, of child molestation, and of ter-rorism. Sometimes he came home from prison visiting hours depressed and nauseated. He shielded his computer screen with his hand, not want-ing the children or me to see what he had to see, or to know about what he had to know about. But he believed in the workings of a criminal trial and in the just decisions often rendered by judges and juries.

Donny's line of work impressed our children. One day when Molly was little, she and her friend pretended to be lawyers. They set up an office with stationery, staplers, rulers, rubber bands, Elmer's glue, and a sign that said THE LAWYEr IS IN. But the other little girl snared the role of attorney, with Molly as her secretary! When I put Molly to bed that night, she wailed, "I didn't *want* to be the secretary!"

"I know!" I cried in instant feminist solidarity and then asked smugly, "What did *you* want to be?"

"*I* wanted to be the defendant," she said.

As they grew older, the children loved their father's stories.

Defending a marijuana dealer that morning (he told the kids one night), he was sitting beside his client at the defense table while the pros-ecutor interviewed the potential jurors. "Now, does anyone here believe marijuana ought to be legalized?" the prosecutor asked the citizens who had been summoned to jury duty. The prosecutor would dismiss anyone who voted yes, because he did not want a sympathetic jury. One or two local citizens began hesitantly to raise their hands, but then the entire panel burst out laughing.

Donny didn't have to look far to find something funny: his client, the man accused of drug dealing, had raised his hand.

"Did I tell you about the time—" he'd start. "Ten weeks into a lengthy drug trial in Tampa, Florida, an angry phone call came into the judge's office. It was a juror's husband, calling to complain: 'I haven't seen my wife for *months*! I'm sick of her being sequestered! Can't she at least have weekends off?'

"That was news to Ed," said Donny of his law partner, Edward T.M. Garland, "and it was news to the judge. The jury was *not* sequestered; they were *not* required to stay at night in a hotel. The missing wife had evidently started an affair with a male juror on their first day in court. They each told their spouses they were sequestered, and *they* spent every night at a hotel. The case ended in a mistrial."

Nothing was more exciting to the firm of Garland, Samuel and Loeb than to be hired by the most powerful and highly paid NFL defensive player of all time, the Baltimore Ravens middle linebacker Ray Lewis.

On January 30, 2000, Super Bowl XXXIV was held in Atlanta: the St. Louis Rams versus the Tennessee Titans. After a postgame party, Ray Lewis and two friends sat in a limousine outside a nightclub when a group of assailants reached the car, continuing an earlier dispute. Lewis's friends blew out of the car and into a melee of fists and knives, at the end of which two of the assailants lay dead of stab wounds. The two men, plus Lewis, were arrested and indicted for murder and aggravated assault.

"Dad, you've got to let me skip school and come to the trial. Please, Dad, please!" begged twelve-year-old sports fan Lee. Donny said no. But he agreed to deliver notes to Lewis from Lee, along the lines of "Dear Ray Lewis. You're my favorite player. From Lee."

One night I found Lee on the floor of my office amid a quilt of paper scraps and cutout *Sports Illustrated* pictures. "Your social studies project? You started it early?" I asked in surprise.

"No! Look!" said Lee. He was creating a huge, colorful poster of football scenes, upon which he glued printouts of the words "Not Guilty" in many languages. *Non coupable! Nicht schuldig! Non colpevole! Ikke skyldig! Não é culpado!* Donny dragged the poster to court the next morning and later reported that the NFL Defensive Player of the Year was very touched.

Donny enjoyed his time with Ray Lewis, too. Lewis hated having the eye of the television camera on him all day in court, feeding the proceedings live to CNN, ESPN, and other networks. Lewis positioned himself so that Donny blocked the camera's line of sight. But every time Donny moved in his chair, the camera zoomed in on Lewis again. In order to stay hidden, Ray Lewis began bracing himself against the moments that Don moved.

"I hear you're pretty fast," Don whispered to him during one of the interminable days in the courtroom.

"Yeah, I'm fast," said Lewis.

"Sometime in the next ten seconds I'm going to move. Let's see if you're fast enough to stay out of the camera."

They both tensed, ready to leap, while pretending to listen to the interminable courtroom proceedings. Then Donny *shoved* himself backward in his chair and Ray *shot* backward next to him, and the commotion drew everyone's attention to the fact that the bearded middle-aged Jewish lawyer and the six-foot-one African American superathlete had the giggles.

Lee longed to invite Ray Lewis to his bar mitzvah in February 2001. Having had all homicide charges dismissed, the superstar might have considered it. But now I was the one saying no, feeling unable to grasp the relationship between the Baltimore Ravens and Judaism. Lee was crestfallen, fearing his only chance to meet Lewis slipping away. Then the Ravens owner, Art Modell, on behalf of an appreciative organization, gave Donny and Ed Garland two tickets each to Super Bowl XXXV in Tampa in January 2001, where the Baltimore Ravens would meet the New York Giants. The possession of these tickets shot Donny and Lee into a stratosphere of joy I'd never even heard of before. I was pleased for them, but uninterested in the tickets until Lee made the mistake of bragging, "Fifty-yard-line Super Bowl tickets are going on eBay for ten thousand dollars apiece."

"What? Ten thousand dollars?" I asked.

"Apiece!"

"Are those the kind of tickets *you* have?"

"The fifty-yard-line runs *between* our seats!" bragged Donny.

"May I see those tickets?" I asked slyly.

"WHY?" they cried, suddenly alarmed, looking at each other.

"Twenty thousand dollars? TWENTY THOUSAND DOLLARS!! We could pay for the bar mitzvah! We could pay for Lee's freshman semester of college! Give them to me! Where are they? Are they in Dad's sock drawer?"

Donny, Lee, and I raced for the stairs. "No, that's not where they are!" roared Donny, obviously lying, from a few steps behind me on the stairs. Lee, being a twelve-year-old athlete, got to our bedroom first, darted in, grabbed an envelope, and sprinted down the hall to his bedroom, slamming and locking his door.

"Twenty thousand dollars," I whined.

A local TV news reporter covered the story of Garland and Samuel going to the Super Bowl, compliments of the Baltimore Ravens. He asked the law partners to meet him in front of their office building with the tickets, so he could film them. Don showed up without his tickets. "I can't get my tickets out of hiding," he told the TV reporter. "If my wife sees the Super Bowl tickets, she's going to sell them on eBay to pay for our son's bar mitzvah." The story aired with the two lawyers holding up just two Super Bowl tickets instead of four.

I didn't get a look at *our* family's two Super Bowl tickets until Donny and Lee ran across the front yard to the taxi that would whisk them to the airport. "Love you, Mom!" yelled Lee, waving goodbye with the tickets.

A few hours later Donny called from his cell phone. "This is the most beautiful place I've ever seen," he said. "The sky is so blue, the grass is so green, there are birds overhead . . ."

"Where are you, the Everglades?" I cried.

Lee took the phone.

"Mom! We're sitting *right behind* Chris Berman!"

"Great! Who's that?"

"And Art Modell is in the box right behind *us*!"

"Great! Who's that?"

The Baltimore Ravens won Super Bowl XXXV, and Ray Lewis was named MVP.

Two weeks later Lee stood in a suit and tie and prayer shawl and yarmulke in front of the congregation to deliver his bar mitzvah speech. As he reached the traditional "thank you" section, he began, "Ray Lewis, thank you SO much for our Super Bowl tickets. I had a really amazing time . . . oh . . ." He pretended to be startled and confused. He looked up, looked down, shuffled the papers, and said, "Whoops! Wrong speech!" He crumpled that page, threw it over his shoulder, took a deep breath, and began anew: "Rabbi, thank you SO much . . ."

One of the major lessons Donny tried to relay to the children was the importance of being honest and of facing the consequences if they'd done a wrong thing; or, as it used to be said back in the day, *Don't do the crime if you can't do the time*. Trying to escape justice through lying and cover-ups was a bad strategy and invariably led to worse problems.

Now Jesse was anxiously explaining away, wishing away, the green Bic lighter that lay on the coffee table between us. "I think someone put it in my pocket to get me in trouble!" he said.

"We just want you to tell us the truth," I said. "You're not in terrible trouble. We want to explain to you about fire."

"It's not mine! I never saw it before!" he insisted.

"I hear you, brother!" said Donny, taking over. "So you think you were framed? Someone did this to get you in trouble?"

"Yes, because I know I didn't put it in my pocket. I never saw it before."

"So you've mentioned," Donny said. "I've got an idea." He left the room for a moment and returned with tissues and a baggie. He delicately lifted the Bic lighter with a Kleenex, elaborately inserted it into the baggie, and sealed it. "I'm going to the FBI office tomorrow for a case—you know what that is? The Federal Bureau of Investigation. Those are the secret agents. I'm going to ask them to take fingerprints from this lighter and we will find out who is framing you! Good idea?"

Jesse nodded miserably, went upstairs to bed, came back downstairs in his pajamas, stood at Donny's side, and burst into tears of confession. "I found it on the sidewalk!" he wailed. "I'm sorry!" Sobbing, he asked, "Am I just like your clients now?"

"No, Jess!" said Donny gently. "Here's the great thing: you just told me the *truth*. Now we can deal with it and move on. My clients do bad stuff and they lie about it and they *keep* lying about it; they wake up every day and their crimes are still there, following them. They don't tell the truth, so they can never make it straight. But *you*: you're going to wake up tomorrow with a clean slate. You get to start all over and be good. And not play with fire."

Grateful, Jesse fell on him with hugs and tears. "I'm never going to lie again," he promised (classic words, children in trouble, worldwide).

"Don't worry about never," said Donny. "Never is too big to promise. Just don't lie the *next* time."

26

A Boy Moves Out, a New Boy Heads Our Way

In the fall of 2003 Seth left home for the Oberlin Conservatory of Music, to study composition, trombone, and piano. He was six feet tall and as skinny as a pencil, a natural comedian with eyeglasses and hair in tight curls. Molly had returned from fall break her freshman year and asked Seth, "What if you could go to a college where you did nothing but music all day?" But Donny and I, fellow alumni from the Oberlin College class of 1975, were ahead of her; we'd been hoping for many years to see him accepted by the world-class conservatory affiliated with the college.

As a one-year-old singing at the top of his voice from a high chair on the back porch, Seth had attracted the attention of a neighbor from two doors away: she, a performer on the viola da gamba (a Renaissance stringed instrument), had cut through the backyards and startled me by popping up outside the screen to say, "Excuse me, but I believe your baby has perfect pitch."

When he was in fourth grade, Seth came to visit me in my bedroom on the Sunday night before the Monday morning that the children would choose their instruments for the school orchestra. "Am I going to play upright bass?" he asked, his voice in its highest and politest register, not wanting to be difficult. "Because Molly does?"

"No, sweetie," I said. "You pick whichever instrument you want to play."

"Can I pick *trombone*??"

"Of course."

He tore out of the room in excitement.

The following afternoon he stood in the front yard, cheap rental trombone in hand for the first time, and blasted brass notes of joy at the heavens. Our across-the-street neighbor phoned to say he had woken up her baby and could he please move whatever he was doing to the *back*-yard. That night, Seth marched through the house playing "Seventy-Six Trombones" recognizably, though he'd never held a horn before that day. Molly, Lee, and Lily marched behind him, aware that something exciting was being revealed, even if they didn't know what.

Seth grew troubled that part of the trombone's range eluded him because his arms were too short to extend the slide to its greatest length. He couldn't reach a B natural. To achieve it, he propped his slide on the foot of our bed, secured it with a pillow, and slowly backed up with the rest of the instrument. Seth told his teacher about his technique. "Interesting," said the young man, trying to address Seth as a fellow musician. "Um . . . no one is really doing *that*." Then there was the night that Seth raced into our bedroom and announced, "Listen!" Standing in the middle of the room, he played a B natural. His arms had grown.

He began composing and arranging music in middle school, using composition software like FruityLoops. He'd invite me into his bedroom for a concert; I'd lie back on his pillows and close my eyes while he angled either the loudspeakers or the trombone, or both, at me, and I'd sail away on his often funny and sometimes moving music. One time, as the final notes died down, housebuilders in the distance dropped a load of wood planks onto a driveway. Seth looked up and said, "Hey!—that's in the same key."

Now Seth was at Oberlin, too, overlapping with Molly during her senior year. On Sunday nights they cooked dinner together at Molly's house. Conservatory students had no required classes at the college, but Seth did have one: Molly oversaw his enrollment in Professor Van Nortwick's class on the Homeric epics.

That fall we received a report card in the mail from AAI's orphanage school in Addis Ababa about a nine-year-old boy named Fisseha (FISS-uh-huh).

The addition of Helen to the family had been so joyful that it was easy to consider adopting again through the same program in Ethiopia. I knew that school-age boys waited the longest for new families, as most adoptive parents requested infant girls. I told AAI's director that we were open to a boy age ten or under. She was thrilled and recommended Fisseha Mengistu. His parents were deceased and his grandmother, too poor to raise him, had turned to the authorities eight months earlier begging for a place to be found for him in an orphanage. She could not even feed him, the grandmother had said. It seemed that Fisseha, like Helen, had once known the love of a family. We said yes.

Upon receiving news of another adoption, most friends and relatives replied, "So what took you so long?" while our children, especially the older ones, laughed in tones of incredulity and mild alarm.

Fisseha's report card arrived in the mail from a young teacher trying his best to relay nice impressions in English:

DID THE CHILD GO TO SCHOOL BEFORE COMING TO THE
    ORPHANAGE?
Yes he have, grade one.
CHILD'S ABILITY TO GET ALONG WITH OTHERS?
he is well done and he has good activity in class
and better between others
Fisseha is very decent boy.
HOW IS THE CHILD'S ENGLISH WORK?
He got good rank in exams. He identify English letters.
HOW IS THE CHILD'S SCIENCE WORK?
He is faster to understand new concepts.
HOW IS THE CHILD'S WORK IN AMHARIC AND CRAFTS?
He is happy in the class and well done in both Subjects.
WHAT DOES THE CHILD LIKE TO DO?
cleaning, *futball*, English
WHAT DOES HE DO WELL? WHAT DOES HE DO POORLY?
cooker, loundery

DOES HE HAVE ANY SPECIAL FRIENDS? WHO?

Yes, he have. his name is Mitiku.

DOES HE PAY ATTENTION IN CLASS?

Yes, he has a good attention in class. He is good and strong boy. He do
   what I give to him.

WOULD YOU DESCRIBE HIM AS A FOLLOWER OR LEADER?

No, he has not.

HOW IS HIS BEHAVIOR WITH OTHER CHILDREN?

He has good behavior,

and cool.

DOES HE FIGHT A LOT, CRY, ETC.?

Not alot, but sometime he fight.

and he is not cry.

WHEN HE IS IN A CONFLICT SITUATION, HOW DOES HE
   RESOLVE IT?

He is resolve by asking apologize

& with big hug.

WHAT IS YOUR IMPRESSION OF THE CHILD?

He is lovely boy

and he has smiley face.

I have alot of love to him.

We all loved this report card very much. The older kids loved "He
has good behavior, and cool" and pretended to believe that the teacher
meant he was a cool dude. (Now that we know Fisseha, we surmise
that is *exactly* what the teacher meant; perhaps only President Obama
himself is more "chill" than Fisseha.) While "He is well done . . . and better between others" was a little hard to interpret, I was thrilled to hear
that "cleaning" was higher on the boy's list of favorite activities than
soccer (this turned out to be bait-and-switch advertising) and that
he did well at "cooker." Best of all—really leaping off the page—were
the words "He is lovely boy and he has smiley face. I have alot of love
to him."

We couldn't ask for anything more.

We got more anyway. An adoptive dad, visiting AAI's orphanage
from Florida to pick up his new baby, e-mailed that he had met Fisseha:
"We started kicking a soccer ball to each other on the playground and
smaller children watched us. I was okay with just volleying with Fisseha,

but he made a point of gently kicking the ball to the other kids, to include them."

He has a good heart, I felt. *Anything else we can handle.*

Fisseha, second from left, holding letters from his new family in Atlanta

I arranged with *Good Housekeeping* to report a story from Ethiopia about a foster mother raising scores of children in a hillside house. Mrs. Haregewoin Teferra was among a new generation of unofficial, unsubsidized foster mothers coping with numberless bereft children in the era of HIV/AIDS. Fisseha could stay with me for the week, then—like Jesse and Helen had done—return to the orphanage to await the legalization of the adoption by the national courts and the American embassy.

On a hot, dry afternoon in November 2003, I sat again in the passenger seat of Selamneh Techane's taxi outside the orphanage gate and experienced my typical adoption feeling of mind-voiding terror.

The elderly guard yanked open the rusty gate, dragged it inward, and waved us onto the playground.

Children ran screaming in all directions, calling, "S'ha! S'ha!" Suddenly I remembered that we didn't have enough bedrooms at home to add another child! I was suddenly awash in confusion, longing for home. I got a grip by reminding myself that the boy must also be in a state of shock, about to be handed over to an insanely grinning strange American woman laden with camera equipment. The kids found Fisseha pressed against the far wall of the school building, out of sight, afraid to present himself. Senseless with a kind of out-of-body hysteria, I sped up and frantically traversed the blazing-hot playground.

27

Meeting Fisseha

He was a handsome little boy—much smaller than I'd expected—with feathery eyebrows in a tall, rectangular forehead, soft tufts of hair, and an infected eye. He seemed about the size of a six- or seven-year-old. I encircled him with my arms, kissed the top of his warm head, then knelt and put the flat of my hand against his chest, all while murmuring motherly nothings. "It's okay, it's okay," I found myself cooing, exactly as I had cooed to each of my crying babies moments after giving birth. "Don't be scared. It's okay." He hunched his shoulders in a kind of prolonged shrug while I fluttered about him. He looked away from me, both the good eye and the red eye squinting into the distance, the eyebrows drawn in and tense, but then he relaxed the stern look into a smile.

Over the next few days I learned to watch when he turned away from me and squinted into the far distance, knowing he was about to release a dazzling smile. He was shy.

Dozens of children mobbed us, eager to greet me. Those who had been matched for adoption yelled out the names of their future homes in their sweet accents: "I New York!" "I Denver!" "Alaska me!" "Family me!" Thumbtacks marked their future cities on a U.S. map in the schoolroom. I'd carried manila envelopes for a few of them from their waiting families in America, and these kids became, for the moment, the Homecoming Kings and Queens, the chosen ones. Each "matched child"—surrounded by a circle of curious and wistful friends—opened his or her packet of letters, photographs, and small gifts. Some urgently introduced me to their friends who still needed families. Two young teenage girls presented many children to me, saying "No family she" or "No family he" while gesturing toward my camera. I took pictures of everybody: some clowned with their friends, some gave huge smiles to greet their waiting families, but others—the not yet chosen—offered the most tremulous and poignant smiles of audition.

Selamneh called Fisseha and me to the taxi and drove us into the smoky, tumultuous city. The boy felt too abashed even to wave goodbye to his friends through the window. We bumped through streets streaming with humanity and livestock, the air dusty and colorful.

At the gates of the Ghion Hotel, uniformed guards admitted us into a green oasis. The Ghion was a glass-and-stucco rectangle on the site of an old palace. We drove up the curving blacktopped driveway through famously lavish flower gardens twittering with exotic birdlife. The giant stalks and fronds looked prehistoric. In a wood-paneled lobby I was given a brass key on a string for a third-floor room.

We said goodbye to Selamneh for the night, and I rolled my suitcase, with Fisseha following, to the elevator. I pushed the button and a steel door opened in the wall, a magic trick as neat as any my young friend had ever seen. Fisseha followed me into the metal room, and when the doors closed and the elevator lurched into ascent, his knees buckled. I said nothing. We stood side by side vibrating, and then the doors opened upon . . . a completely new scene! We'd risen through the center of the building! Fisseha glanced sideways at me with, I thought, admiration.

Two single beds awaited us; I showed him that one was mine, one was his, and I removed from my suitcase a stack of clothes I'd brought him. He donned the Atlanta Hawks headband immediately and eagerly slipped out of the dusty communal orphanage clothing to try on new things: khaki pants, a belt, and a blue Tennessee Titans football jersey. When we left the room in search of the hotel restaurant, I headed for the stairs, but he ran and waited outside the metal box, eager to exercise the Miracle of the Elevator in reverse. This time he braced his muscles and didn't flinch.

In his new clothes and my sunglasses, he looked like an American kid on vacation. He didn't remove the sweatband or sunglasses when we were seated in the dining room for dinner. When the waitress tried to take his order in Amharic, he didn't respond. I was surprised at the rudeness emanating coldly from behind the sunglasses until I realized that he was pretending not to understand Amharic. He was pretending to be an American, my American son. She didn't buy it. She leaned close to his face to demand, *"Amaregna t'nageraleh? Ethiopia weenesh?"* (Do you speak Amharic? Are you Ethiopian?)

The sunglasses slid down his nose as he dropped his head and softly confessed, *"Ow."* (Yes.)

Back in our hotel room, I showed him that most of my suitcase was taken up by a single thing: a boxed LEGO castle set. He couldn't begin to fathom that it was for him, or that it was a toy. Together we carried it out to the small cement balcony; we sat cross-legged and opened it. Dusk tamped down the yellow-gray smog beyond the tall hotel gardens; birds made a squawking racket in the bougainvilleas. I turned to page one of the directions and showed Fisseha how to look for the prescribed pieces and click them together in the assigned way. He got to work, and I moved to the deck chair and opened my book, Ryszard Kapuściński's brilliant *The Shadow of the Sun*, about the Polish journalist's four decades of reporting from Africa. After a few pages I glanced down at the start of a brown plastic castle. It seemed to me that Fisseha had misplaced some foundation stones and that a wall veered off at an odd angle. I leaned over to point out his mistake. He leaned in closer to study the blocks, then wordlessly held up page four of the twenty-page direction booklet, showing me that on the contrary, it was I who was mistaken. After that, I read my book and let him build in peace.

The next morning, I awoke in the sweet mountain air and the tea-colored sunlight strained by the palm trees in the garden. Fisseha was already awake. He'd crisply made his bed and was sitting on it, dressed in his American clothes, his Atlanta Hawks headband, and my sunglasses; he sat politely waiting for me to wake up. "Well, good morning!" I said, and he softly repeated, "Good morning." I went to the bathroom to dress; by the time I returned, he had made my bed perfectly, too, and was again sitting on his own. As we left the room, he insisted on carrying everything—the brass key, my purse, the camera bag—so that I should not exert myself. He ran ahead to the elevator and pushed the Down button. He ran ahead again to the hotel restaurant and found a table for us; he pulled out a chair and patted a seat to show me it was for me. With all his might, he was relaying his intent to be a good son.

As we left the breakfast buffet, I began walking faster and faster, with a conspiratorial smile at the boy, and I beat him out the front door and into the colorful garden that was buzzing with bug life. After that, we racewalked every time we entered the hotel lobby from any direction. He'd glance at me for permission, for the nod that meant *Go!* and off we'd pedal, walking furiously, pumping with our elbows and then sprinting the last few steps to be the first to touch the finish line—the elevator, or the banister, or the doorframe of the restaurant. I sensed his eagerness to have a go at the new world into which I was bringing him and his willingness to interact with me, a mother, his second mother.

Each of these unfortunate children—alone in the world through no fault of his or her own—must accept whatever new mother is sent by the gods of the orphans, or by the directors of the adoption agencies. Will the new mother be nice or stern? Humorless or playful? Will she employ corporal punishment—perhaps breaking limbs off a tree to use as a whip—which is widespread in the discipline of children in Ethiopia? Will the child have fun in his new life, or will it be mostly hard work, long hours, and boredom? Will the expectations be too high for him to meet, with the chance that he will disappoint or fail entirely? Will leaving the orphanage be a step *up* in terms of companionship and good times, or a step *down*, away from friends, into a non-Ethiopian hollow world of foreignness and loneliness?

Despite my increasingly frequent trips to Ethiopia, I could speak only a few words of Amharic, and he had even fewer in English. There was no chance for us to engage in verbal banter or joking. I could scrunch my fingers through his soft hair and he could swing my backpack onto his own shoulders; I could offer him a bite of fried fish from the breakfast buffet and he could whip out the room key from his pocket as we returned to the hotel in the evening, but . . . then what? These nonverbal conversations lasted mere seconds. And he was shy. I didn't want to impose myself on him; we weren't about to spend long minutes gazing into each other's brown eyes. Our camaraderie had to be constructed in the physical realm, and yet I couldn't hold hands with him as we walked or bring him onto my lap—he wasn't a four-year-old like Jesse or a tiny, squeaky five-year-old like Helen; he was a nine-year-old boy with great self-possession.

My racing him became our nonverbal repartee, our times of comedy and absurdity. The joke took off instantly and never lost its humor for either of us: that I, a middle-aged North American white woman, would pretend to think I could be faster than a young East African runner. The first of the dominant world-class Ethiopian runners was the marathoner Abebe Bikila, the first black African ever to win an Olympic gold medal. In the 1960 Summer Olympics in Rome, he ran his race barefoot, becoming a hero of legendary stature. In the 1964 Tokyo Summer Olympics, Abebe won the marathon again and became the first athlete to win gold in two Olympic marathons. In 10,000-meter races, Ethiopian men and women have won nine Olympic gold medals since 1980. A king's ransom of golds, silvers, and bronzes has been amassed in other distances, and modern heroes have arisen, such as Haile Gebrselassie, who won Olympic gold in the 10,000 meters in 1996 and 2000. Once, as we traversed Addis, Fisseha spotted the great runner coming out of a hotel. He stopped in his tracks and breathed one word: "Haile."

Now let's count the Olympic medals and marathons won by fifty-year-old Jewish women from any country . . . oh, right: zero.

So foot racing was a broad joke we could both enjoy. During one race I suddenly stopped, looked at Fisseha sternly, shook my finger, and said, "No running indoors. Not good." He halted, chastened. Then I race-walked away and just beat him to the elevator as we both slammed into it, laughing.

The dash to the elevator, after I cheated, was the last race I would ever win against Fisseha on land.

But I found another venue for our competition, and that was the hotel pool when I correctly guessed that Fisseha didn't know how to swim. He wore ballooning new swim trunks I'd brought him and had the goggles on upside down, and he seemed amazed to find himself waist-deep in turquoise water. Before I taught him the basics of flotation, I challenged him to a race across the shallow end. He ran through the water waving his arms while I swam.

I beat him easily! Then I taught him how to swim. Now I would never win another race against Fisseha on land or sea.

28

Searching for Grandmother

In the backseat of Selamneh's taxi, Fisseha and I rattled across the hot, noisy city, up to the Entoto Hills for a hike. We steamed along in bumper-to-bumper traffic on a barren strip of industrial highway that ran alongside piles of gravel, vacant lots, and haphazard markets where people seated on blankets offered a few onions for sale, or ears of corn or bars of soap. Fisseha suddenly sat up very straight, grasping his door handle; he seemed hypervigilant. As we edged past the roadside merchants, he pressed his face to the window. More than once he seemed to be eyeing someone, and then he swiveled to watch the person disappear from sight through the rear window. Was there something he wanted to buy? I patted his shoulder, preparing to pantomime the question, *Do you want to buy something?* but he jumped, startled, when I touched him. He shook his head. Sometimes roadside merchants offered cheap plastic soccer balls, so I began watching closely, too, in case we saw a bunch of them captured in rope netting like a bouquet of helium balloons; I'd be happy to buy him a soccer ball! He remained glued to the smudged window as the raggedy, haphazard panorama unrolled alongside the car.

Suddenly he tightened, looked harder, gripped the door with both hands, and *shouted*! He'd found something, the thing, whatever it was he wanted! *"Ahyatey kazee now yemi-t-no-row!"* he yelled to Selamneh once, twice; he pointed out the window. I'd never seen him this animated. He whirled in the seat and got up onto his knees to look out the back window.

"What's going on? What's happening?" I cried.

"He say that, um, there is street of his grandmother. He live here with grandmother."

The unnamed, unpaved road that excited the boy looked exactly like a thousand other anonymous dirt roads tangling through the city. "How can he recognize it?" I asked. In a capital of more than three million people, with numberless districts, upscale neighborhoods, slums, and shantytowns, with roads ranging from manicured boulevards to mud sloughs running with sewage, what were the odds that we'd driven by the precise unmarked dirt lane of his memories?

Selamneh didn't know.

"Should we go?" I asked.

"That is you," he said.

"He wants to go," I said, looking at the wide-open face of the eager child bouncing beside me like a puppy. "Let's try."

"Maybe we will take her a gift?" Selamneh asked.

"Like what?"

"Maybe some foods from a bakery?"

"You know," I said, "let's call the orphanage and make sure we have permission to do this."

Selamneh wheeled onto a gravel lot, phoned AAI, and handed me his cell phone. "Fisseha thinks he sees his grandmother's street," I told the orphanage director, a Canadian woman. "May we stop by to visit her?" The answer was yes. Selamneh made a U-turn and took us back into the traffic and the yellow haze of unfiltered car exhaust. Fisseha was wide-eyed with excitement, looking in every direction now, then keenly focusing on the skinny dirt lane as we passed it again on our left. Soon we encountered one of the randomly situated shopping strips, built of glittery sandstone, that arose suddenly out of the dust—some émigré's hopeful idea for development—and there was a bakery within tall glass windows. *What is the appropriate pastry for this occasion?* I wondered. I deferred to Selamneh, who deferred to Fisseha. I waited in the taxi, face-down on the ripped backseat to avoid luring desperately poor people with the flutter of my white face within the taxi's dark interior. After ten minutes my two males emerged from the bakery with a sheet cake in a white box so big it took both of them to tenderly carry it down the steps. I sat up and scooted over to make room. It was ornately decorated with white icing aflutter with pink and yellow flowers; it belonged at a wedding reception.

The literary phrase "the objective correlative of an emotion" crossed my mind.

The three of us, with cake, drove back to the nameless dirt road. Fisseha, now in the front seat, craned his head in all directions to catch every detail. We drove a long way downhill under scrawny pine trees that threw intermittent shade like handfuls of pins onto the deep dust. On either side of the lane stood tall, rusty corrugated metal barriers; they concealed modest dwellings of cinder block or stucco, perhaps of scrap wood and plastic tarps.

Suddenly, at a corrugated metal fence that looked like every other banged-together scrap-metal yard enclosure in East Africa, Fisseha yelled, *"Ah-koo'm! Yih bet-now!"* (Stop! This is the house!) This seemed as unlikely to me as the premise that this was the right street, and of course street numbers, like street names, are unheard of, but I was touched again by his enthusiasm. Selamneh pulled over and parked, then turned around in the front seat to ask, *"Ayahte-h se 'mwa mano?"* (What is your grandmother's name?)

"Tsehai," said Fisseha.

The two of them got out, stepped across the dirt lane, and banged at the enclosure's metal door while I tried to calm down by admiring the delicate flowers and curlicues visible through the plastic window on top of the cake box.

After a few moments a young woman squeaked the door open a crack and spoke with Selamneh. *"Tsehai zee-now-y'mit't norrow?"* he asked. (Does Tsehai live here?)

No, she said, shaking her head, sorry; she bowed politely, withdrew, and closed the door.

The boy turned around with a face stunned into blankness. He squinted as if sand were blowing into his eyes.

I thought, *Oh God. This is the archetypal child's nightmare. His family took him to an orphanage and then moved away.*

"Maybe it's the wrong house?" I asked Selamneh when they returned to the car. "Because really, look at this city, and he's only nine. How would he know his way? How can he be sure this is the right yard or the right street or even the right part of the city?"

"Maybe," he acknowledged.

Fisseha let himself into the backseat and sat up close to the door, silently staring through the window. I was aghast at what had just happened to him. I cast about in my mind for some precedent, for some note of reassurance, but I couldn't come up with one . . . *I'm sure your family still loves you? Let's go buy you a soccer ball?*

A door in the compound across the road opened and people stuck their heads into the lane to look at us. Taxis bearing white women didn't often park here. There was a quiet hubbub of misgiving and discussion among the people, and then they all poured into the road and hurried toward us with their arms outstretched. *Now what?* I began to think, until I realized they were calling Fisseha's name. They knew him! They were his former neighbors! He'd been absolutely correct about this dirt road and this unmarked tin compound. This was my first indicator of Fisseha's preternatural navigational skills.

He slipped out of the car and sheepishly accepted their warm handshakes and kisses on the cheek. But they said it was true: Tsehai had moved away and they didn't know where. Fisseha let himself back into the taxi and gently closed the door. Desperate to stem the grief of the child I'd met the previous day, I whipped out paper and pen. "Let's leave a letter here for his grandmother," I cried to anybody who could understand me, "in case she comes back for a visit!" I wrote out in English block print—and then Selamneh translated it into Amharic—the news that my husband and I were in the process of adopting Fisseha, that we lived in Atlanta, Georgia, U.S.A., and here was our street address and our phone numbers, fax numbers, and e-mail addresses. (I might as well have written, "Second star to the right and straight on till morning.") We added Selamneh's mobile number on the bottom of the paper, and then I folded up a photograph of Fisseha inside it. "Please," we said to the neighbors, "if you ever see her again, give her this letter. We want her to know what has become of her grandson." We shook hands all around, and they bid us farewell, promising to take good care of the letter.

Sometime between six months from now and never is when we'll hear from this woman, I thought. We dropped off the wedding cake at the orphanage.

The next day, Selamneh and Fisseha led me into the bewildering, fluttering, cacophonous aisles of the Mercato, one of the largest open-air markets in the world. Lift off the roof for an aerial view of Macy's at Herald Square to get a hint of the colors, textures, scents, and allure of a thousand consumer items and the rustling migrations of shoppers through and around the displays. In single file, along well-treaded dirt paths, we shuffled up and down narrow rows between mountains of shoes, hillsides of T-shirts, stacks of cheap TVs and plastic radios, tethered goats, jars of honey, pyramids of thread and yarn, towers of handwoven baskets, fresh piles of coffee beans, hand-carved wooden mancala boards with hand-carved wooden marbles, a sheep, a row of prickly pineapples balanced on a card table, bins of gold-threaded umbrellas for religious ceremonies, and vertical Peg-Board displays of wallets, jackknives, plastic kitchen utensils, socks, brassieres, wristwatches, nail clippers. Every day was market day here; the exhibits smelled and bleated like a county fair. Selamneh held my wallet and money, as I was a natural target for pickpockets. "Allo? Allo?" I heard him yelling into his mobile phone and pressing his hand against his free ear to try to hear. He turned around with a sweating, beaming face and bid us turn around and wind our way slowly back to the market's outer boundary, beyond which the taxi was parked.

"What's going on?" I yelled, but he gestured that we should keep walking, and quickly. When we found his taxi, he said, "They found her! She wait us there."

Fisseha's former neighbors had fanned out across the city in search of Tsehai. They had found her and brought her to their house for a reunion with her grandson.

"Cake?" I asked, but Selamneh snorted.

29

Tsehai

We rattled down the narrow dirt lane again and parked; the moment we opened the car, a tiny, wrinkly, beige-colored woman wearing a traditional white dress and shawl shot out of the compound door, screeching and laughing and holding several fingers to testify to God about miracles, and I thought she tripped over her hem and fell, until she began cradling my sandaled feet in her hands and kissing them and I realized she had prostrated herself on the ground before me. "Oh please, no, no, please," I said, helping her up; she kissed my hands fervently, fervently, looked up to God again, hollered something in joy, rained blessings on me from heaven with both hands, kissed each of my cheeks, and then descended on the boy like a hawk seizing a rabbit in its claws. She kissed, hugged, cried, and nuzzled. She drew back in order to examine his infected eye—it was better now, I'd been putting drops in it—but it worried her greatly, and she stroked him all over his face and hair and shoulders. Under this onslaught, he smiled a childlike smile. When she grabbed him close again, he rested his head on her shoulder.

Our hosts warmly invited us into a weedy compound. Their redbrick house had a cement porch and cement floors. In the main room, there was a cocktail bar of polished laminate, with bottles lined up on mirrored shelves behind it. Their income, I gathered, came from serving wine and beer. Tsehai, Fisseha, and I were invited to sink together into a low-bottomed sofa, and the family pulled up barstools and kitchen chairs into a haphazard circle facing us. Tsehai was hoarsely talking, raucously laughing, and praising God nonstop. Our hostess brought us cups of coffee and a bowl of grapes on a brass tray. I pulled out my notebook, eager to gather as much information as possible about Fisseha's life and family. I waited for Selamneh to begin translating the nonstop gravelly onrush of syllables coming out of the exuberant little lady with the wrinkly, beaming face. But he wore a look of dazed delight and would not translate. "What?" I gestured to him, and he laughed and whispered, "I can barely understand her! I understand almost nothing!"

I heard a chuckle from the doorway and looked up to see the owners' son, a good-looking young man in jeans, T-shirt, and sneakers; he and Selamneh exchanged words behind the backs of the others. "He can't understand her, either," whispered Selamneh to me.

Tsehai came from the countryside, from a village near Jimma in southwest Ethiopia. A navy blue tattoo encircled her chin from ear to ear, like an old-fashioned seafarer's style of beard, and a tattooed Orthodox cross decorated her forehead. As she sat and held forth—declaiming, cackling, swaying back and forth in prayer—she amused the whole room; she was for them like a visitor from the Old Country, from their grandparents' era. It was her rural accent that made her Amharic hard to understand. As word spread down the road about these unexpected guests, neighbors and friends of the homeowners stepped into the room, bowed in silent greeting to Tsehai, Selamneh, and me, or breached the circle of chairs to shake our hands. The host stood behind the bar drawing glasses of beer, happy to host the reunion. I didn't know who was the greater draw—the diminutive, bossy peasant woman, the bashful, polite American woman, or the handsome Ethiopian boy on his way to becoming American; or maybe it was the fact that we were somehow all related that made us an attraction not to be missed.

Tsehai, shouting to one and all and to God, seemed to believe that I could understand her. Increasingly she faced me during the delivery of her hoarse and detailed soliloquy. I nodded with the gravest empathy. Later our hosts would say, in mistaken admiration, "You're the only one who understood her!"

Then she was ready to hear all about Fisseha. Were they good to him at the orphanage? she wanted to know. Selamneh, rapidly mastering her dialect, translated. Did they mistreat him? Did they feed him enough? Did he go to school? Had he learned to read? "Speak English!" she yelled at him in Amharic. "You are American now! Speak English! Don't be too shy or sad! Dress properly! Why aren't you talking? How will you support me if you don't get an education?"

Under the barrage of questions and orders, Fisseha sank down on the sofa a little deeper, with a rueful smile.

"He can write his name in English," I offered, and Selamneh translated. For an illiterate peasant woman, this was headline news. She stopped breathing as I gave Fisseha my notebook and he painstakingly inscribed his name.

"This is his NAME????!!!!" Tsehai screamed. "In ENGLISH?????"

Yes.

She RIPPED the page out of my notebook, stood up, folded the page into smaller smaller smaller sections until it was a fat little packet, and then she stuck it deep into her bosom.

"What is she saying?" I asked Selamneh.

"I think she say: 'My eyes do not even know how to look at this!' " he said.

I was still caught on the words, translated by Selamneh, "If you don't get an education, how will you support me?" Did Tsehai understand that she had transferred custody of Fisseha to the Ethiopian government, which had sought an adoptive family for him? Perhaps she saw the orphanage as more of a boarding school, believing that he would graduate from it with an education and come home to support her. "Does she understand that he will come with me to America and be my son?" I asked Selamneh. "He will take my husband's name; he will be Fisseha Samuel rather than Fisseha Mengistu."

She grew very, very still. She listened silently as this was translated, betraying no emotion. If her eyes had not known how to perceive English letters, her ears did not know how to take in this information. Or perhaps she had understood all these things—after all, she had finagled a place in an American orphanage for her grandson; he wasn't in an overcrowded government compound—maybe she was trying to comprehend where *she* fit into this picture.

"I want her to always be part of his life. A boy needs his grandmother," I said.

She had lowered her head to take in the news; when this was translated, she lifted her face to us, her eyes bright with tears. She raised one hand, as if testifying, and solemnly pronounced in Amharic, "God is good to me! Look what God has given to me before I die!"

"Oh, Selamneh! The photo album!" I said, wishing I could share with her the family photo album I'd brought for Fisseha. "But I've got my camera! There are digital images on the memory card." I pulled out my Sony DSLR, flipped it over, and clicked to activate the LCD screen. I pulled up a photograph of our house in springtime, in pink-dappled light as sunshine fell across the branches of the flowering Japanese cherry tree in the front yard. Selamneh translated for Tsehai: "This is the house in America where Fisseha will live with Melissa's family." Tsehai took the camera out of my hands, studied it at arm's length, and then mashed the screen right up to her eye. She gripped the camera so tightly and began yelling so loudly in excitement that I had no chance to correct the situation: she seemed to believe she was seeing *through* the LCD screen or the viewfinder all the way to our front yard in America. She aimed the camera up, down, left, right, squinting for a better view, as if through binoculars. She returned the camera with a bow of her head. Its screen was now thickly blurred. I wiped it off and clicked to bring up an image of Fisseha's future brothers and sisters, but Tsehai declined to try to see it. She sighed, hand over heart, to express that her heart was full, she had seen enough.

Now she took my hands, turned to face me, and addressed me directly. "Selamneh, help," I muttered out of the side of my mouth, and he pulled his chair in closer.

"She say . . . she want you to understand . . . that she did not abandon the boy but . . . she had not enough food to feed him. His father has died when Fisseha is very small boy and his mother has died one year ago.

"She say . . . 'It is right for the child to live off the adult, but it is not right for the adult to live off the child.' "

"She say . . . 'We had nothing. We were very, very poor. We slept on the ground and had nothing.' " She looked around anxiously, pleading for forgiveness, feeling guilty for having taken the boy to an orphanage. Although he called her Grandmother and she referred to herself as his grandmother, she was not literally his grandmother, though there was a close family connection. "I am the matriarch," she said, tapping her chest. She had kept him as long as she could. She loved him. She bowed her head when she finished speaking, waiting for divine or local punishment.

I squeezed her hand. "I understand. Let us help you."

"We'll help her," I told everyone, especially Selamneh. "How can my family help her to support herself?"

Everyone, while regarding Tsehai fondly, appeared stumped by this question. How could an older, illiterate, tattooed countrywoman earn a living in the capital, where tens of thousands of people just like her were destitute and homeless?

My late friend, Marjorie Shostak, was the author of a classic work of anthropology, *Nisa: The Life and Words of a !Kung Woman*. To thank the woman she called Nisa for becoming her guide to and informant in a !Kung-San community in the Kalahari Desert in southwest Africa, Marjorie had given her a few cows. The cows made Nisa a wealthy woman among her people, bestowing much higher status than was to be gained by being the subject of a highly regarded work of nonfiction. Inspired by Marjorie and Nisa, I asked, "Should I buy Tsehai a cow?"

Translated, this produced hearty laughter and the shaking of heads throughout the room. "A cow?! No, a cow is too big for her."

Everyone lapsed back into bewilderment.

I broke the silence again. "What about a goat?"

"What would she do with a goat?" people asked, some in English, some in Amharic, and all chuckling.

"Well . . . she could sell its milk, or use the milk to make cheese," I said.

This produced an outburst of laughter.

"Goat's milk cheese is a delicacy in America," I retorted, but they scoffed, finding this unbelievable.

Again we engaged in group meditation.

"Chickens?" I offered.

"Chickens!!!" everyone cried in agreement. "Chickens! Yes, yes, of course, of course, chickens!! She will raise chickens!! Chickens are the right thing!!"

"Does she know how to raise chickens?" I asked, and this was translated and bandied about the room with great hilarity.

The unanimous answer flowed back from the crowd: "She's from Jimma. Of course she knows how to raise chickens!!" To my Georgia ears it sounded like, "She's from Moultrie!" or "She's from Gainesville!" (Gainesville, the Chicken Capital of the World, is the home of the Georgia Poultry Park, in the middle of which stands the Chicken Monument, a twenty-five-foot-tall marble obelisk topped by a bronze rooster.)

"Chickens are complicated," I said. "Chickens get diseases."

"She's from Jimma!!" everyone yelled in reply. *She's from Moultrie!*

"Okay, well, how much money will she need to start a small chicken business?" I asked.

Selamneh translated the question, and everyone looked respectfully at the citizen from the East African Chicken Capital of Jimma.

Tsehai thought hard for a moment, squeezing her eyes shut, and then shouted, "A thousand birr!"

Later I would learn that she had pulled this number out of her butt, as my children say. She'd never seen this much money and had no idea what such riches could purchase. She was basically shouting *A million dollars!!*

A thousand birr came to a little over a hundred dollars.

I had that much in my purse. But I didn't want to insult everyone in the room by simply handing over a roll of money.

Through Selamneh, I told Tsehai that I would try to reach my husband in America tonight by phone and we would discuss her business venture together. If he agreed that we should invest in it, he could wire the money from America and I would go to a bank tomorrow morning and withdraw the funds. With our hosts' permission, we agreed to meet back at this house in twenty-four hours.

On our taxi ride back to the hotel, Fisseha napped against my shoulder, exhausted by happiness.

The next day, the chicken summit meeting took place. Many of the previous day's guests returned. Tsehai was in a sober and businesswoman frame of mind. She greeted me with a kiss on each cheek, and then again on each cheek, before we were all seated. She knew a man to ask about building a pen, she said; and she knew of an apartment block where she could sell fresh eggs.

"You're sure you know how to do this?" I asked, with Selamneh translating. "You don't need advice?"

She looked around at her supporters, who used the cue to remind me: "She's from Jimma!!!" *She's from Gainesville!*

With formality, I pulled out a business envelope stuffed with birr; she accepted it in the traditional way, using both hands, bowing as her hands received it.

"Please tell her she will always be part of Fisseha's life," I told Selamneh as we finished our coffee and prepared to depart. "She is his grandmother." I promised that Fisseha and I would visit her again in a few months, when I returned to bring him to America.

"Then you will have to fly by airplane to America to visit us," I told her. After Selamneh translated, Tsehai held her hands up to her cheeks and looked around the room, then covered her eyes with her hands and bent forward, shaking with laughter. From within her bent-over posture, she called out something. Selamneh translated: "She say, 'If you take Fisseha to America, my heart will fly there behind him.'"

I flew home the next day, promising to return in a couple of months.

"Tsehai has bought her chickens," Selamneh told me by phone one day, and we chuckled with satisfaction.

But several weeks later Selamneh called again, with news: "Um . . . the chickens of Tsehai are dead."

"All of them?" I cried.

"Yes, all."

"But, but . . . she's from *Jimma*!"

I wired another hundred dollars to Selamneh, which he converted to birr and drove out to give to Tsehai, and again he was able to report, "She has bought chickens."

The following month, another phone call: "The chickens are dead."

"I'm not that impressed with Jimma," I replied. Donny and I decided that after the adoption was finalized, Fisseha could send occasional contributions to his grandmother. We could all spare a few hens their premature deaths.

On my next visit to Ethiopia, twenty-three-year-old Molly came along. We visited Tsehai in a new mud house. As we sat upon a mud bench covered with newspaper and she caught us up on the gossip, a chicken actually wandered into her dirt yard and peeked into the house. "Uh-oh! Look!" whispered Molly, who knew the saga of Tsehai and the chickens. "Shoo! Shoo!" she whispered to the bird, fanning it. "Run! Run for your life! This is no place for a chicken!"

30

The Labyrinth of Nightmare

Jesse hit a rough patch in fourth grade. Impulsiveness overwhelmed judgment, and he often found himself in trouble, grounded for an hour here or an afternoon there. The day he attempted to explode a beach ball in the backyard by pouring bicycle oil into it and then lighting it (because boys on the school playground had told him how to make a bomb) resulted in his being grounded for weeks. "Can I ever let you leave your *room* again?" I cried in despair. "I can't even trust you in the *backyard*!" He was sorry. He was always truly sorry, but the regret came too late.

He passed the long, grounded hours on the lower bunk bed in his room arranging his dozens of decks of Yu-Gi-Oh! cards. He had hundreds of these brightly colored Japanese manga dueling cards—some "rare," some "super rare," some "rare ultimate with foil"—and all with marvelously strange names: Blue Eyes White Dragon, Crossroads of Chaos, Left Leg of the Forbidden One, Chainsaw Insect, the Deity of Poisonous Snakes, Obelisk the Tormentor, and (my favorite) the Four-Starred Ladybug of Doom.

Yu-Gi-Oh! cards were the obsession of many boys that year; Jesse's teacher finally imposed a moratorium: no Yu-Gi-Oh! cards during the school day or they would be confiscated. Jesse struggled to pay attention in this class; it was an elderly teacher's last year before retirement and she was easily rattled. Jesse, a fabulous mimic, portrayed for us at the dinner table her stream-of-consciousness teaching style. In a high nasal quavering voice he said, " 'The Pilgrims settled Plymouth Colony in Massachusetts in . . . RANDALL!!! RANDALL WHAT ARE YOU DO-ING??? STOP THAT RIGHT NOW! RANDALL!!! and then Thomas Jefferson did the Louisiana Purchase . . .' And I'm like, *Wait, weren't we talking about the Pilgrims?*"

The day after Mrs. Smith's moratorium on Yu-Gi-Oh! cards, Jesse ran home wailing, "Mrs. Smith took my deck!" We'd seen that one coming; Donny and I stood back to let natural consequences set in. Jesse went to bed that night feeling bereft, and maybe vulnerable, too, as he loved the magical significance of the cards, their arcane curses and unfathomable spells able to summon dark and mythical powers to his side.

The next day after school was worse. Jesse trudged down the side-walk from school so slowly, his head so low on his chest, that I thought someone had hurt him. I ran to meet him in the driveway and knelt down. "What happened?"

"I'm going to be grounded forever," he said in a voice so low I could barely hear him. "I'm never leaving my room again."

I guessed instantly: "You took your cards out of Mrs. Smith's desk." He tilted his hand to show me the deck.

"GET IN THE CAR!" I roared, shaking with disbelief and fury that he'd screwed up again so soon.

"I'm sorry," he said with a quavering voice.

"I DON'T WANT TO HEAR IT. GET IN THE CAR."

"Where are we going?" he asked, buckling himself into the backseat.

"BACK TO SCHOOL."

"Why?"

"*I DON'T KNOW!*"

I pulled up in front of the school, jerked to a halt, and noticed that children were still pouring out of the building. Technically, the day wasn't quite over. "Jess!" I said, turning around. "Do you think you can get back into the classroom and put the cards back on your teacher's desk?"

"Really?" he gasped.

"Try to do it," I said. "If Mrs. Smith is there, tell her the truth: that you took your deck and you realized that was wrong and you brought it back. If she's not there, just put it back."

In a flash, he was out of the car. He looked both ways; exited the car, staying low; darted through crowds of kids; pressed himself up against the brick wall; sidled along behind the bushes; and then vanished into the building, a ten-year-old James Bond. Five minutes later I spotted him through the rearview mirror coming from the opposite direction, out the school's side door, running hard and low. He flung open the back door and dove to the floor, hissing, "Drive!"

"Did you do it??"

He had. He'd undone his crime. He was exultant. At the stop sign he slid up into the backseat and got buckled. "Mom, you can't believe, all the way home after school my heart was pounding so hard and I was saying, 'Please God, please God, please God, somebody help me.' And you helped me!"

"You knew you did the wrong thing, and that's really important," I said, starting to feel exultant, too. "It's best if you can stop yourself from doing a bad thing. But the fact that you realize it afterward is really great, and it means that sometimes, you can fix it."

He stuck to my side all afternoon, flying high with happiness. He insisted on running errands with me. In the grocery store aisle he reached over to hold my hand as he had done as a very small boy. "You can always come to me when you're in trouble," I reminded him. It would become my most important message to this impulsive child: no matter what happens, come to me, tell me the truth, and we'll move forward together. "Daddy and I love you and we're on your side."

"I know," he said. "I love you, too." Together we had defeated the Dark Crisis; the Winged Dragon, Guardian of the Fortress; and perhaps even the Ancient Prophecy.

That night Jesse came into my bedroom for a last kiss good night and to give me a present: the Ladybug of Doom was mine.

31

The Professor Gives Birth

One of my kindest and prettiest friends, an attorney, was hard-hit by the dour (and false) predictions of the 1980s that a college-educated woman over thirty was more likely to be crushed by a meteor or killed by a terrorist than to find a husband. She scarcely knew whether to scan the rotundas of the county courthouses for a good man or to keep an eye on the sky, prepared to duck. Thus it promised to be an April evening full of flowers, piano arpeggios, small nieces in tulle, and every kind of loveliness and happiness when, at forty-six, my friend prepared to wed the handsome, gray-templed attorney and sailboat owner in a Victorian house in Atlanta. Old friends flew in from around the country and some stayed with us. With an hour to go before the seven o'clock wedding, my friend Andi Casher from Philadelphia and I tore back and forth along the upstairs hallway looking for missing earrings and for hose without holes.

At 6:35 p.m. on that warm evening in 1995, Donny stood in the driveway twirling the car keys while friends began to climb into the car. From the front door, I called up the stairs to thirteen-year-old Molly to remind her to start a Disney video for Lily and to fix hot dogs for the boys. At that exact moment, in a sawdust-lined glass tank on Molly's dresser, a black gerbil named Professor Otto von *Schnitzelpusskrankengescheitmeyer* went into labor (we hadn't known she was pregnant), emitted ten trans-lucently pink babies, and died.

Wails arose from Molly's bedroom. Lee was crying especially jag-gedly. Dressed in a taupe linen suit and pearls, I ran back up the stairs while in the driveway Donny tooted the car horn as a friendly reminder that we had a wedding to go to.

The Professor—"Otto" for short (her name came from the animated TV series *Animaniacs*)—was a doted-upon gerbil triplet, one of three beady-eyed recipients of tasty treats and interesting hairstyles. The chil-dren had erected a cardboard wall in the tank when the animals reached sexual maturity, which had happened ten minutes after we brought them home. The divider was intended to keep Otto safe from the incestuous predations of her brothers, Goniff and Knuckles. But the boys resolved not to be defeated by the cardboard barrier. Inspired, perhaps, by Presi-dent Reagan's clarion call eight years earlier—"Mr. Gorbachev, tear down this wall!"—the males clawed, gnawed, shoveled, dug tunnels, avoided the searchlights, dodged bullets, leafleted, demonstrated, petitioned, held candlelight prayer vigils, appealed to the Western democracies, and threw their furry shoulders against the wall until, on a fateful night twenty-four days earlier (if I may count backward based on the gesta-tional period of the gerbil), they tore it down. The rest is history.

Now it was 6:40 p.m. At the top of the stairs Andi took my upper arm, looked me sternly in the eye in the way that only someone who has known you since childhood can look at you, and warned, "We are NOT going to be late to this wedding." Yelps of grief were coming from Molly's bedroom. "Mousie dead!" two-year-old Lily shouted. "Worms here!"

I peered in close, hoping that the Mother Professor was just resting, but she was an island of stiffness in the midst of a seething pink sea. Lily was right: the squirming babies looked like shiny pink worms with ap-pendages. They waved their tiny fists and opened their tiny mouths. In the driveway, Donny honked the horn a good long honk.

From head-down on Molly's dresser next to the gerbil habitat, seven-year-old Lee raised a stricken, tear-streaked face to me. Skinny, curly-topped Seth, age ten, was doing a joyful dance of vicarious fatherhood on Molly's bed. The actual fathers, Goniff and Knuckles, dozed belly-up in their half of the tank, the plump face of each seeming to sneer *Look, man, I got nuttin' to do with this. Sleep with my sister? What do you think I am, some kind of pervert? It musta been that guy.*

"We have to feed the babies," said Molly. "They have to nurse or they'll die."

"Why are you looking at *me*?" I cried in alarm. "It's been a year since *I* breast-fed anybody!"

"Watch *Aladdin* now?" asked Lily anxiously. In the driveway, with everyone else in the car, Donny was simply *leaning* on the car horn. With, I'm pretty sure, his *face*. As I dashed out of the room and back down the stairs, the four children sent up a clamor of grief.

"Go! Go on! Go without me!" I called from the front door, waving them away.

Donny said, *"What??"* at the same instant that Andi said, *"DRIVE!"*

"The babies will die if we don't feed them!" I called.

"What babies?" asked Donny.

"I'll fill you in. GO!" yelled Andi. It was 6:55 when my husband and friends zoomed off to my dear friend's wedding. Though unhappy, I really had no choice. I didn't see it like this: *Friend v. Rodents,* but more like this: *Well-attended Ceremony v. the Moral Imperative to Preserve Life.* Yes, they were minuscule gerbils, the color and size of pencil-tipped erasers, but with that spark of life in them, wasn't each unique and irreplaceable? Brilliant scientists dabble in the stuff of life, manipulating genes, molecules, atoms, but no one has yet stumbled upon the formula from Genesis, the initiating thunderbolt, the creation of a living thing ex nihilo. Between suffering and a social event, one must hasten to relieve suffering.

Back upstairs, the neonates, in a pulsing mass, were trying to suck on each other but couldn't get purchase on those sleek heads. I ran to phone the veterinarian's office—it was closed on Sunday evenings, but the recording listed an emergency number. I reached an animal urgent care hospital as it was closing. The receptionist offered to hang a can of baby rodent formula on the back door. At 7:18, I squealed the tires backing out of the driveway. I found the animal ER, ripped the bag from the door, and sped home. "Here! Run! RUN!" I yelled as I blew through the front door. In the upstairs bathroom, Molly, Seth, Lee, and I read the instructions, mixed the formula into a cup of warm water, fished out a couple of gerbils from the tank, leaned them back on our palms, filled up eyedroppers with formula, and hosed the babies. They came to life with a start. It was like adding water to those little sponge capsules they hand out at birthday parties; when the capsule melts away, little pink dinosaurs and green rhinos spring out. The gerbil infants squirmed, coughed, gagged, and finally began licking and swallowing. "All right, are we good? Can you do this? Can you do this?" I asked. Molly said they could.

I flew down the stairs and out of the house and drove to my friend's wedding. I let myself in the back door and squeezed into a tightly packed, sweating mob of wedding guests in the standing-room-only kitchen, where, if you stood on tiptoe and were very, very quiet, you could hear the last soft "I do" from the living room in the distance.

The children and I kept nine of the ten babies alive, feeding them every four hours for a month. They looked a bit sketchy, as if they grew up on the wrong side of the tracks or had been outside in high wind. They looked like the three tough-guy Munchkins of the Lollipop Guild in *The Wizard of Oz*. They needed to be groomed, by tongue, but even *I* have limits. Molly remembers: "The survivors were scrawny, ungroomed, and covered in minuscule cowlicks. When we brought them to that crazy pet store with the insane Eastern European owner, the guy who lived with goats, some other customers announced that ours were the cutest gerbils there."

Friend wed, lives saved.

The whole episode took a lot out of me, though. Weddings are so stressful!

32

The Young Hunter-Gatherer

On his second night in America, in May 2007, Fisseha followed the noise of shouts and cheering into the basement rec room, where sixteen-year-old Lee and friends were watching the NBA Western Conference semifinal game between the L.A. Lakers and the San Antonio Spurs. PlayStation controls lay around on the tiled floor, radiating a magnetic appeal to a ten-year-old boy. Fisseha picked up a control, eager to play, and looked hopefully to Lee for instruction, but the older boys didn't want to miss the play-off game, so they pantomimed to Fisseha that he controlled the televised game, specifically that he controlled Shaquille O'Neal. Every time Shaq made a basket, the high school boys pounded Fisseha and yelled their approval, so he wildly pushed the buttons and jerked the levers with a huge smile on his face as the Lakers pulled ahead. *What realistic graphics!* he must have thought. After the game, when Shaq hugged his coach, twelve-year-old Lily said, "Fisseha thinks he just pushed the PlayStation button for 'hug.'"

He fell for it, but soon revealed that he, too, had a few tricks up his sleeve. "Mom!" yelled Lee from the driveway the next afternoon. "Come out here! You've got to see this!" Fisseha had found a skinny white metal flagpole in the bike shed; its neon-orange banner allowed bikers to be seen in traffic, if bikers would ever let the flagpole remain attached to their bikes, which mine did not. "Watch!" called Lee as I looked down from the porch. With a nod to Fisseha, Lee threw a Frisbee into the air—a heavy-duty regulation Frisbee—and Fisseha raised the bike flag-pole like a spear, hurled it, and pierced the Frisbee midair.

"Do you know the *strength* that takes?" said Lee. "I can't penetrate the Frisbee if I've got it in one hand and the bike pole in the other. And watch *this*!" Now Lee sent the holey Frisbee skimming across the back-yard. Fisseha hoisted the bike flag–spear again, tracked the Frisbee, launched the pole, and lanced the Frisbee to a tree.

That night at dinner, when Fisseha politely declined a nice helping of cheese lasagna, Seth, nineteen, said, "Hmmm, no. I *definitely* have the impression that he prefers to spear live game."

After dinner I hauled out the reliable old *Macmillan Illustrated Animal Encyclopedia.* When Molly was young, she and I had loved turning the glossy pages to scrutinize the many jeweled species of humming-birds, the fiercely snouted variety of bats, the hunched and whiskered rodents. Now, sitting with Fisseha in the den after dinner, I turned the pages with him along the research theme of "Mammals I Have Killed and Eaten."

Penguins, no . . . Porcupines, no . . . Toucans, no . . . Old World Monkeys, *now* we were getting somewhere! He turned the wide pages care-fully, peered in closer, then tapped triumphantly upon an image. The gelada baboon. "That one?"

Yes.

"You hunted that one?"

Yes.

Name: gelada, *Theropithecus gelada.*

Range: Africa: Ethiopia.

Habitat: mountains: rocky ravines, alpine meadows.

Well, he seemed to be accurate. "You *ate* this?" I asked.

He laughed, shook his head no, built an English sentence to explain: "Monkey . . . eat . . . farmer . . . corn."

The next day, our Ethiopian babysitter, a middle-aged woman named Azeb Arega, spoke with him and elaborated: Fisseha had stood on a rickety wooden structure above a farmer's crops, on the watch for in-vaders. When he spotted monkeys or baboons or antelope coming to eat the crops, he scared them off. When in charge of goats, he could defend himself and the herd against hyenas, jackals, wolves, cheetahs, foxes, or wild dogs.

One summer afternoon Fisseha came into the kitchen, took a huge carving knife from a drawer, and hiked into the woods with nine-year-old Jesse. I barely had time to think *Uh-oh!* or *Initiation ceremony?* when the boys emerged from the trees with two slim fresh fishing poles over their shoulders. "String, Mom?" barked Fisseha in his loud voice. I opened my sewing box and he selected a spool of thread and two straight pins. He bent the pins into hooks and tied them to the poles. Then he led Jesse across the street and up the steep sidewalk in search of a good stream. The boys leaned their fishing poles over their shoulders. From the kitchen window I watched them hike away, thinking, *We've adopted Huckleberry Finn.*

We visited the coast of Maine that summer. Beside a whitecapped inlet, the kids picked up smooth stones and began skipping them. Seth's and Lee's stones went bippity-blip. Lily's went kerplunk. Fisseha's stones created tidal waves, whizzing and dipping across the lake like flying saucers, somehow speeding up rather than slowing down as they spun toward the horizon. A wild duck paddled out from the reeds just as Fisseha let fly a stone. The stone skipped once and hit the duck in the head, and the duck rolled over, died, and sank. The kids screamed in horror. *"Sorry!"* said Fisseha in his low voice, with real regret.

On another day Fisseha pulled stringy strips of bark from the trees, brought it to the back steps, and twisted it into twine. From this shaggy rope he braided a thick, hairy bullwhip. With my kitchen knife he carved and smoothed a wooden handle and attached it to the whip. The first *thwack* of the bullwhip ripped open the sultry summer air like a firecracker. *Thwack!* The curl of cracking rope drew smoke from the driveway cement. *Thwack!* The bang had a metallic edge to it—it was actually a sonic boom, I looked it up. Boys of all ages came running. Lee's friends in particular—high school varsity baseball and football players mostly—lined up to try. Their attempts made the rope lazily twirl like a drowsy snake. They were like old cowpokes circling a lasso at their feet. Patrick King got some speed and power going, and the rope licked around and slashed him on his neck, drawing blood. *"Ouch!"* he yelled, dropping the whip and fleeing back up the driveway.

Through it all, Fisseha stood by with a mildly perplexed half smile. Every rural Ethiopian boy had this skill. It was as basic as building a shelter, starting a fire, foraging, and catching and grilling a fish for dinner. What *did* American boys spend their time doing?

In August, Fisseha started fourth grade at Fernbank Elementary School. Soon we had mobs of fourth-grade boys visiting the house. In their eyes, in their cute, sweaty, freckle-faced towheaded friendliness, "Fisseha" became "Sol," from his middle name of Solomon. These boys, who would become his great friends, loved the slingshots, the bullwhips, and the spears. But their favorite game was How Many of Us Will It Take to Pin Sol? The average, as he threw and bucked them off left and right on the sofas and floors of the basement rec room, was nine.

Fisseha also wove slings, like biblical slings, like the weapon with which David slew Goliath. On his wooden platform above his employer's fields, he had stored rocks and pelted the invading monkeys and baboons. "Mom, see!" he barked at me one day in his hoarse, boyish voice. He stood on the driveway and I watched from the screened porch above him. He held up the sling he'd just finished braiding or knotting, and I went out to examine it. The sling was a more complicated weapon than I'd gleaned from the Book of Samuel. There was a kind of rope trigger to be pulled, releasing the stone. Fisseha looked around, picked up a rock, inserted it, and swung the rope around and around over his head with a fantastic whistling wind, an ancient sound of speed before there were things like engines in the world. I backed away. Suddenly he released the rock and it flew—*BANG!*—like a bullet, straight through the Plexiglas basketball backboard. The two of us looked in amazement at the clear, round hole; then the whole backboard slowly, sadly crinkled, folded inward, and rained in pieces onto the driveway.

"Mom! Sorry!" barked Fisseha.

"Can you be *careful?*!!" I cried. "You could *kill* somebody with that thing!"

Now we had boys of all ages lined up on the driveway taking lessons. Fisseha demonstrated by pointing to a sapling deep in the backyard, whirling a pebble overhead, and hitting the tree dead center with the rock. He then directed all those in line, other than the first man up, to hunch down behind posts and trees and the AC unit, to keep themselves out of the line of fire of rocks slung by the uninitiated. As with the bullwhip, no one else mastered the high-velocity precision art of the sling-shot, though all had a great time squatting and screaming as badly launched stones boomeranged at them from all directions.

One afternoon Lee and Lily climbed the rope ladder to the tree house deep in the neighborhood woods. Lee reported: "We found seven carved and sharpened spears, three bullwhips, two slingshots, a pile of stones, and six wooden daggers, all carefully arranged like in a military bar-racks. It looked like Fisseha was planning a coup."

This rugged boy, this one-man Outward Bound expedition, explored the streams and woods of our midtown Atlanta neighborhood. He found wilderness wherever he looked, the way other people have a knack for spotting parking places. But at night he came in search of me, hoping I would read him a book. "Story, Mom? Mom, story?" he barked, holding up one of his favorites, *The Berenstain Bears*. I wondered if the middle-class bear family's well-appointed tree house struck him as an architec-tural halfway point between the mud-and-straw hovel of his recent past and his current suburban address. I wondered if he thought, *They're bears. And yet they have electricity, indoor plumbing, telephones, and cars.* After a day spent fishing and foraging, slinging and whipping, he liked to lean against me and hear more about them. His favorite was *The Ber-enstain Bears Get Stage Fright.*

Sol trotted downstairs one morning that fall wearing a bright green T-shirt. "Wow! You look really handsome in that color!" I said. "That is really your color, kid. Green is great on you!" I ruffled his hair. He knit his brows as if angry, looked away, and smiled.

The next morning he came downstairs in a green shirt belonging to Jesse.

"There's that green again!" I exclaimed. "You look so handsome!" I gave him a sideways hug.

The third morning, here was another green shirt, a polo he'd taken from Seth's room.

On the fourth morning, another.

On the fifth morning he started over with green shirt number one.

I took this in appreciatively. It seemed to me that Fisseha was shyly trying to tell me something like *Thanks for all this. I have a lot of love to you.*

33

Identity

In 1999 we had adopted, without a thought about race, a brown-skinned boy. Jesse was a handsome four-year-old with laughing black eyes and a flop of shiny black hair. We thought, *Dark eyes, dark hair, he looks just like us.*

He came home from his first day in kindergarten and announced, "There are two boys named Alex and they're both brown like me!"

I doubted it. I'd escorted him to class and had seen black boys and white boys, but no brown boys. I knew that the first Alex's parents were white. But I later learned that he had been adopted from Texas, the child of a Hispanic mother; and then I learned that the second Alex's father was from Mexico. Jesse was already, unconsciously, far more sensitive to color than I was.

He liked to hear about his adoption, about how we needed another little boy in our family. "But did you need a little *brown* boy?" he always checked.

"Yes!" I'd say. "We really needed a little brown boy!"

He asked me this every few weeks for a year, until we made the decision to adopt Helen from Ethiopia. He was shocked when shown her photograph. "She's brown. Like me!" he gasped.

Months later, when we brought Helen home from the airport, Jesse took one look and then dashed happily to my side to report, "Mommy, she is *really* brown!"

He never asked again: "But did you need a little *brown* boy?" I think he felt, *They might have made this mistake once, but I don't think they would make the same mistake twice. They must be doing this on purpose.*

When in the presence of people of color, white people tend to approach the conversational topic of skin tone gingerly or defensively, or avoid it entirely. Helen and Jesse talked about it easily. One night I found them side by side at the bathroom sink, studying their reflections in the mirror. "You look like Pocahontas," Jesse said admiringly.

"I do," agreed Helen, tossing her long hair, "but I'm not really her color. You're more her color."

And Jesse agreed.

This was nothing, less than nothing, yet I would remember this conversation for years, suggesting it was something new for me then, heralding a new frankness of tone.

Helen was a classic Ethiopian beauty. Westerners were drawn to her loveliness but didn't know what she was. White people often asked if she came from India. Ethiopians recognized her instantly. Even in her sweatpants that said SOCCER across the butt, and her hoodie, and her flip-flops, laughing with Lily at the checkout counter of Publix as they bought ice cream and hair products, she was recognized by the Ethiopian cashiers. They asked her, *"Amarigna menager techiyalesh?"* (Do you speak Amharic?) She laughingly replied, *"Amarigna alinagerem!"* (I don't speak Amharic.) They were sorry to hear it, but they liked her very much anyway and gazed after her wistfully as she danced away. Later they must have wondered, *If that child doesn't speak Amharic, how in the world did she answer that question?*

For Helen's and then Sol's first year in America, I forced them to speak Amharic to the scores of Ethiopians we constantly ran into in town. "Look, Ethiopians!" I enthused, spotting entire families browsing the racks at Burlington Coat Factory. "Let's go talk to them."

None of my children are keen on public humiliation. "No, Mom," Sol said. He had seen Ethiopians before. Where Sol grew up, there were

Ethiopians as far as the eye could see. The novelty for Sol was not making chitchat with Ethiopians, but shopping at Burlington Coat Factory.

I was trying to follow the guidelines I'd gleaned from the experience of international adoptees my own age. The South Korean adoptees of the 1950s, '60s, and '70s were the first generation of internationally and transracially adopted children in America; as adults they are shaping adoption policy and guiding the national conversation about transracial adoption based on their pioneering experiences. From their work I've gained many insights. For example: a child would prefer *not* to be the only person of color in a family or in a classroom or in a school system. It's *not* true that young children don't notice race; and if a child is slow to notice that he or she doesn't resemble Mommy, his or her classmates will be eager to enlighten. It's *not* true that children who have been adopted transracially are best raised by white parents claiming to be "color-blind." And adoptees should not have to wait until the age of eighteen or twenty-one to be offered a chance to reconnect with their countries of origin and their biological families.

I want to know about my first parents, an adopted person will think at some point, possibly at many points, in life—perhaps as a four-year-old a little shaky at bedtime, afraid her first mother can't find her; or as a thirteen-year-old, wondering if he's going to grow tall enough for the NBA; or as a thirty-year-old, thinking, *I'm about to become a parent. Yet I've never even seen pictures of the people who gave birth to me.* An adopted child who never brings up these issues may truly not be interested; *or* the child may remain silent to spare the feelings of his or her adoptive parents.

It seems that growing up in a loving family is enough to help a child thrive in almost every way but this: the natural need to feel part of a deeply rooted people; the desire—when gazing upon a world map—to be able to say, "My ancestors came from *there.*"

We graft our adopted children's names and school photos onto the family tree posters when those pesky family tree assignments are handed out in grade school. On the posters created by adoptive families, the trunks of the British, Italian, Russian, or Scandinavian founders rise into branches flowering with Chinese and Guatemalan and African American great-great-great-grandchildren; the Lithuanian-Jewish immigrants'

American descendants were born on the rocky hills of Ethiopia. These family trees stand in the forest of the heart.

But: our children have other trees, the ones whose little twigs have fallen far afield. Those trees stand in the forest of kinship.

A person's sense of self rises out of a simmering stew of traits, talents, events, sensations, looks, chance, discoveries, books, relationships, beliefs, and memories, from nature and from nurture. A person's racial, ethnic, and/or national identity is one ingredient. It's not necessarily the most important element in structuring one's character, but neither is it irrelevant, dispensable. How can a child arrive at a deep sense of self when his or her family history and ancestry are unknown? How does one construct an identity upon a formless past?

We start by telling a child that, like everyone else on earth, you had, or have, a living biological mother and father. You grew inside your mother; you were fathered by your father; you were born. These may seem like staggeringly obvious truths, too basic to be told, but we have the testimony of adult adoptees that it was confusing, in their childhoods, when those details were skimmed over. It was unsettling to grow up with baby scrapbooks that began with "The Day We Met You." Some children surmised that all babies started life on airplanes. Some believed that all Koreans were adopted, especially if the only Koreans they ever saw were other adopted children with white parents at adoptive family picnics.

So we tell our internationally adopted children: You came from this place on the globe. This is your birth country, filled with people who look like you. Do you remember living there? Maybe you were too little to remember. Let's look at pictures of your country, and at YouTube videos. Let's wave your country's flag during the Summer Olympics. Why don't you make a poster about your country for the social studies fair? We'll visit your country in the future, hopefully many times. And there are thousands of people from your country living in America; they emigrated here, too, just like you.

Sometimes adoptive parents can get even closer, as in the zoom function on Google Maps. Sometimes it's possible to know a child's regional, ethnic, tribal, language, or religious affiliation. Here the thread of a child's ancestry begins to thicken, to gain texture and color. Knowing that Jesse came from the Romani people, Helen from the Amhara, and Sol from Amhara and Oromo gave us a lot to work with: landscape, history, language, cuisine, religions, art, and literature. Still, it's material we work with from afar, as outsiders. We gaze at photos of people in traditional costumes performing folk dances; we cook up traditional recipes; and we fill our homes with traditional works of art or literature from our children's countries. But we may have little useful knowledge about how twenty-first-century citizens live in that country or how they live as immigrants in America.

Can love make up for the complicated web of connections lost to the child through international adoption? If it cannot, or not completely, what should we do for the children we're removing from the lands of their birth?

As I rode in the taxi with Selamneh to meet five-year-old Helen for the first time, I wondered how I would make it up to her for removing her from this populous vivid landscape, from her ancient country, of which she was indelibly a part. I imagined an overturned world . . . What if it were not Helen, but Lily who had been orphaned and left all alone at five? What if new parents couldn't be found for her in Atlanta, or even in America? What if a nice couple from rural Nigeria were the only new parents stepping up? What if there were few Americans, Jews, or whites in their village, but they were kind people who said that color and nationality didn't matter to them?

What would I want for my daughter?

I'd want her to be adopted by this family rather than grow up in an institution. But I'd be grateful if her new parents would seek out Americans in the vicinity, maybe hire an American babysitter to speak to her in her native English, and prepare Pop-Tarts and macaroni and cheese, and bring over Disney videos. It would be nice if she could go to school with a few kids who looked something like her, even if they came from Greece or Scotland. If there were a Jewish community in the village willing to include my daughter in holiday observances, it would be a fine thing.

I'd hope that these new parents would live in a diverse community, so that Lily wouldn't stick out as an exotic transplant on every walk to the market or the playground and she wouldn't hear her parents congratulated everywhere on the grand thing they'd done by bringing in the poor little orphaned American girl. I wouldn't want my daughter to be an ambassador of color at every gathering, to be the one child whose skin color made her preschool or Brownie Scout troop "diverse." I would want her to be welcomed and treasured, symbolic of nothing.

I thought about this while preparing to meet Helen. She had been wanted and cherished by her first parents; we wanted and would cherish her, too, for herself. We hoped to raise Jesse, Helen, and now Sol to be and to become richly and complicatedly and uniquely themselves, with the widest possible range of American elements at their disposal and—however conceivable with white parents in America—Bulgarian and Ethiopian ingredients.

We also wanted to teach them that their truest selves were deeply their own, independent of all borders.

Meanwhile, the kids explored their identities in unique ways.

"Our family is weird," Lily said one night in the kitchen as I brought serving bowls to the table.

"Oh, sweetie, really? Is that how it's feeling to you?"

"Yes."

"Is 'weird' really the word?"

"What would you call it?"

"I don't know . . . 'different'? . . . 'special'? . . . 'unique'? Are you having a hard time with this? Do you want to talk about what feels weird?"

"*Look* at them." She waved one hand toward the window seat. Three identical Zorros sat on the bench: Helen, Jesse, and Sol were dressed all in black, with black capes, broad-brimmed black hats, and black eye masks. They'd checked their swords at the door. I'd somehow missed their arrival.

Jesse was engraving a *Z* in his mashed potatoes with a spoon.

"Oh, okay," I said. "That is weird."

34

Sandlot Ball

During the summer of 2004 in Atlanta, instead of seeking a conventional summer job, Lee created a neighborhood baseball clinic for kids from about seven to thirteen. The news was spread by a single flyer tacked up at a neighborhood pool and by word of mouth. I was unsure such a last-minute ad hoc approach would work; I figured that most neighborhood children had been booked into their summer camps and enrichment programs six months earlier. I also knew that an entire generation of children was being raised to expect their sports training to resemble that of professionals, unfolding on well-maintained fields under the direction of paid coaches.

But in the steamy, buggy late-afternoon heat of the Fernbank School playground, Lee, Andre Mastrogiocomo, and twins Palmer and Matt Hudson showed up and waited. And starting just before 5:00 p.m. on the first day, a swarm of children appeared, on foot or on bike, at the top of the grassy hill leading to the playground. They swept over and down the hill, fanning out into the field. From that day on, their numbers increased daily. I sat in a beach chair at the far edge of the playground in a singing haze of mosquitoes. I kept the books. Or rather, the shoe box. Also, I kept the box of Band-Aids. The charge was five dollars per kid per day. Each child, running or biking past, pulled a balled-up five-dollar bill out of a pocket or backpack and tossed it to me. I turned and waved at parents peeking over the crest of the hill; mostly I waved them away. Starting on day two, I shook the box of Band-Aids at them to show I was on top of the first-aid situation. Many parents were still in work clothes; they signaled their gratitude and drove away.

A few of the obviously sporty boys drew back, balked, even shed some anxious tears on the first day. "He's never played baseball before," a mom would explain apologetically. Or just one word sufficed: "Soccer." I understood. The outdoor lives of modern children had fallen under adult dictatorship. Early and intense specialization was part of the package. Twice- or thrice-a-week practices plus two games a weekend sent young players barreling across green fields, fit and competent. But parents sometimes forgot to pencil in the days on which the child was allowed to dabble in hopscotch, roller-skating, jump rope, jacks, fort building, hide-and-seek, or a pickup game in a sport other than the one of primary focus.

Here's what the young coaches didn't require of their players: previous experience, advance registration, tryouts, birth certificates, assignment to teams by age, gender, and skill level, snack schedules, parental phone trees, commuting to fields in distant counties in search of the appropriate level of competition, picture day, and any commitment beyond taking it one day at a time.

Here's what the players didn't miss: any of the above.

The high school guys hoped to relay the pure fun of throwing and catching a ball, of swinging the bat, of loping across the green, steamy field yelling "Mine mine mine!" There was a quarter-generational transfer not only of baseball skills but of a few hallowed childhood truths. What doesn't matter: that all your teammates should match you in gender, age, and talent. What does matter: that you should yell your head off if one of them gets a hit.

Lee divided the players into two opposing teams like this: he told them to stand in a line and count off by twos. *Hey, I remember that technique!* I thought. *I haven't seen it for forty years, but I remember it.* The batting order was youngest-to-oldest or oldest-to-youngest. The high schoolers pitched.

Here's what the kids *did* care about: not striking out. But no one ever struck out. The rule here was: Swing until you hit something. The young coaches didn't care if a kid racked up ten strikes before getting a hit, or flying out, or getting tagged out. There was no humiliation in flying out or getting tagged out. At the end of one game I heard a boy yelling all the way up the hill as he ran to meet his dad, "I hit a home run!"

Had he? It didn't ring a bell. Then I realized: he had. He'd swung at so many pitches I personally had lost interest and was reading the newspaper, but he had finally connected with the ball. I watched him join his dad at the top of the hill and head for the car, walking with just a trace of a swagger.

The baseball coaches taught drills with great seriousness: how to crouch, how to stop a grounder, how to call for and catch a fly, how to run the bases. From their high school varsity coach they borrowed a tarp with the drawing of a batter on it, with which to teach pitching. Every day they played Pickle, a base-running game in which the herd of kids sprinted back and forth between home plate and first, as two basemen attempted to tag them out. Seth helped out, taking aside any child who lacked catching and throwing skills completely for one-on-one tutoring.

At night Lee, Andre, Matt, and Palmer sat around like big-league managers to discuss what each player needed to work on. They didn't have films to review, but their approach was the same. They loved the two smallest kids, Walker and Jacob, ages six and seven. "They have no skills, but they are totally into it." The coaches chuckled with pride. Walker tended to run in the wrong direction from home plate after a hit, but he was learning. A few kids stymied them: the kid who pouted when he wasn't on his best friend's team for the scrimmage; the kid who yelled "loser!" at his teammates; and the permanently unhappy kid who said it was too hot, baseball was stupid, and he'd rather be home playing Play-Station 2. The coaches matter-of-factly collected these issues under the category of "attitude."

I loved the way the high school players talked to the little kids. "Nice swing, man," Lee would say. Or, "Good stop, man." "Good speed, Walker, but could you go *that* way?" The children thrilled to this semblance of equality with bona fide young men who owned baseball cleats and who shaved. For some, their first sports-hero crushes began.

By midweek I was dressed in long pants and thick socks and a long-sleeve shirt and doused with mosquito repellent, and if I'd owned a mosquito net, I'd have worn it. From a distance I marveled at the *Bad News Bears* quality of the games. You had your twins; you had your mix of white kids, black kids, and brown kids; and you had your tiny, shy, feminine eight-year-old Ethiopian girl named Helen, who turned out to have a phenomenal throwing arm. You had your nine-year-old boy with "issues"; you had a few out-of-shape players; you had an eleven-year-old boy from Kazakhstan and the usual bunch of athletic fourth- and fifth-grade boys.

I wondered why the motley quality of the teams wasn't more familiar to me—why they reminded me of *The Bad News Bears* and *The Sandlot* and *The Big Green* and *The Mighty Ducks* and other misfit-to-champion-team movies for children. Then I remembered: children's teams don't look like this anymore. Adults, who organize the tryouts and draw up the rosters, don't allow for such teams. I had seen them only in the movies.

A nonathletic older girl timidly poked the bat across the plate when it was her turn, and the ball touched the bat (nice aim by the pitcher) and bobbled a few inches. Her teammates screamed themselves hoarse urging her to first base. She didn't make it, but she got many pats on the back and offers of "nice hit" and "good try" from her teammates.

A big boy with developmental issues was at bat one afternoon. The first pitch sailed right by him. But as Lee wound up for the next pitch, the boy suddenly put down the bat, reached into his pocket, and produced a twenty-dollar bill. "I have twenty dollars," he yelled to Lee.

"Great, man, that's cool. Pick up your bat, okay?"

"Look! Twenty dollars!"

"Great, man. You're up."

"Do you want it?"

"Not right now, thanks. Can you put it back in your pocket?" The game came to a complete halt as the boy carefully folded his money and neatly squeezed it into his hip pocket. Lee threw a slow underhand pitch, and the batter slowly swung the bat, and there was a lovely pocking sound, and the ball majestically arched into the air. This kid was strong! This kid had a future as a power hitter. The outfielders started running in circles, and the batter's teammates began cheering. But the big boy didn't run. He carefully put the bat on the ground again, reached back into his pocket, and turned around to show the catcher: "I have twenty dollars."

One day there was a meltdown at third base. The chronically angry nine-year-old boy—I'll call him Chris—who was playing third base lost his temper with the base runner. He didn't like the way his opponent was standing on the bag, or something. Chris threw down his glove, threw down his cap, and began stomping and shrieking. Then he gave the base runner a hard shove. Coach Andre, a tall, solid fellow headed for Georgia Southern University in the fall, left the pitcher's mound and lumbered over to third base. He didn't have a clue what to do with Chris. He wasn't a professional coach or a special ed teacher; he was eighteen. He studied the tantrum for a moment, then picked up the raging baseman, threw him over his shoulder, strode across the field with him thrashing and screaming, set him down gently in the woods beyond the baseline, and returned to the pitcher's mound. Chris stormed off into the woods. Andre told another kid to go cover third base. The game continued. We could hear Chris bellowing and storming about deep in the woods. After about ten minutes I noticed that a calmer Chris had emerged from the woods and was watching the game. His side was now at bat. "Hey, man, you're on deck!" Lee called from the pitcher's mound, and Chris ran to get ready. When he got his hit, his teammates cheered for him.

Chris's parents said to make sure to let them know if there was going to be a clinic next summer. The child with developmental issues evidently made more progress with eye-hand coordination in those two weeks of baseball than he had in eight years of one-on-one with an occupational therapist. A handful of boys told Lee they would go out for baseball next spring instead of soccer. Helen asked for a baseball glove for her next birthday. The heavyset girl whose bat once touched the ball no longer feared PE at school. And in school hallways the former teammates said hi to each other; regardless of age, race, gender, grade, or sports ability, they once played on the same side.

While I sat at the edge of the sweltering, itchy playground on the last day, parents descended the hill again and again to thank me, to thank Lee for this chance not only for their children to learn baseball but for their children to play baseball in a sandlot pickup walking-distance neighborhood game at least once in their lives.

35

Squirrels We Have Known, Also Insects

Over the years, we've had turtles, tropical fish, mice, an ant farm, and a free-flying parakeet. As a teenager, Molly had a guinea pig named Mug-wump who sported a natural Mohawk and shrieked in time with the punk music blasting from the stereo. In Seth and Lee's room lived two green anoles. The elegant lizards moved in nanosecond jerks, as if we were glimpsing them through a strobe light. We bought live crickets at the pet store for Pip and Squeak, and brought them home in a crisply rolled paper sack that looked like somebody's lunch. It was somebody's lunch. The feed crickets made scribble-scrabble sounds against the walls of the bag, like a moviegoer's fingers rummaging for popcorn. When we poured a few into the tank, the green anoles froze into hypervigilance. Their scales silently angled toward the unsuspecting insects like rows of solar panels subtly tilting toward the sun. Only a retinal speck of light narrowed in the silent tableau. Then, in a flash, the pair of them leaped, faster than we could see but evidently openmouthed, because, when they stopped moving, Pip and Squeak were on the floor of the tank, each gulping and choking a whole live cricket down his throat. Each had a somewhat sheepish look on his face, like a Thanksgiving guest caught in the act of trying to swallow the entire turkey when left alone for a moment in the dining room.

Molly came home with a duck. Attending a wilderness summer camp in rural Pennsylvania, she'd hiked through an open-air market in Amish country and spotted a booth with a hand-lettered sign: "Ducks. $1." And she had a dollar. The duckling instantly bit her, so, in honor of the hit movie *Reality Bites*, she named him Reality. A dollar a duck was one thing, but getting a live duck home from Amish country to Atlanta was another. Delta Airlines required a duck carrier, which, strange to say, we didn't own. It cost fifty dollars. Then we had to purchase baggage space for the duck carrier. That was another fifty dollars. Molly flew home with her one-hundred-and-one-dollar duck and a new sort of life began for us. First, there was the way Reality looked at you. Inconvenienced, being poultry, by one eye on either side of his head, he couldn't look you straight in the eye like a stand-up guy. Instead, when you came into the room, he immediately turned his head away, as if flirtatiously. In fact, he was paying strict attention out of the side of his head. Then there was feeding him. I was referred from pet shop to pet shop until I reached a rural grain-and-feed store in Pike County. They told me what I needed was a water-soluble powder called "duck starter." What a great product! Why hadn't we ever started a duck before?

I liked having the chance to experience the habits and opinions of so different a species, the *Anas platyrhynchos domesticus*, or domesticated duck. I liked how earnestly he adapted to our world; small-brained he might have been, but having been plopped down in this cavernous house peopled by giants, he carved out a busy small life for himself about five and a half feet below eye level. When everyone gathered in the kitchen for dinner, Reality showed up, too, though I don't think he knew what the hubbub was about. Maybe he thought we were sitting down to nice bowls of cement-colored human starter. And Reality was good company. He quacked constantly, but it wasn't loud and obnoxious like the barking of dogs; it was like muttering under his breath. Imagine a waiter in a nice restaurant who has an impossible customer who has just complained for the tenth time about the food and service: "The tart is bland and the berries are not fresh." Smiling broadly, the waiter returns to the kitchen with the rejected dessert, repeating mockingly to himself under his breath, *"The tart is bland and the berries are not fresh."* That's what Reality's quacking sounded like. Reality lived with us until he was fully fledged, at which time he relocated to a nice family's backyard pond.

A nest of baby squirrels blew onto our front yard in a storm, killing the mother. Lily, Jesse, Helen, and I caught the startled-looking babies and reinstalled them on the back porch in a borrowed parrot cage. Given my extensive gerbil- and duck-starting experience, I started the squirrels with a tiny bottle-feeding kit. Theo, hyperactive with happiness that we'd brought *squirrels* into the *house* for *him*, got on his hind legs, nipped a couple through the bars of the parrot cage, and ate them. Only one agitated little fellow remained. Jesse and I bottle-fed and guarded him; he scampered up and down our arms and perched on our heads while Theo, now leashed to the coffee table, barked wildly in high alarm, trying desperately to tell us *That is a squirrel!* and *That is a squirrel on your head!* Finally released to the front yard, Theo ran in circles, shouting, *There is a fucking squirrel in our house and it's sitting on these people's heads!* Fearing for the squirrel's life, Jesse, Helen, and I drove the baby squirrel to the home of a squirrel rehabilitator. How, before the Internet, would we ever have known of the existence of such a person? Who knew that was a career option? Her entire house was devoted to—and smelled of—squirrels. Tunnels, like dryer vents, ran from her windows into the backyard so squirrels could come and go between her bedroom and the tree canopy, depending on their stage of transition back to the wild.

In full disclosure: I didn't totally think she was insane.

One of our favorite thing about flying off for vacation together is the *SkyMall* catalog. From our seats up and down the rows, we pass copies of it overhand and across the aisle, pages folded down to such wonders as the $49.99 Inflatable Pet Spa or the $39.99 DayClock with a single hand pointing to the day of the week (*"Do you have little trouble keeping track of the hour and the date, but the day of the week eludes you?"*) and the Solar Powered Bible for $119.95 (*"The Greatest Gift . . . fits in the palm of your hand and speaks all the books of the Old and New Testament, in a real human voice."*)

Despite these fabulous offerings, the only item I ever ordered from *SkyMall* was, several years ago, the Bark Free. For $29.99 it promised to extinguish outdoor barking, which happens to be the sole occupation of Franny and Theo, aside from napping. Dozing under the kitchen table, they react to every distant outdoor sound of pedestrian, dog, squirrel, UPS truck, chipmunk, bird, and autumn leaf. The dogs' feet begin to scramble before they even wake up completely; they yelp and carom and skid across the slippery kitchen floor, blow through the flapping dog door—*pow! pow!*—and race howling down the kitchen steps and around to the front yard. They've engraved deep trails in the yard through years of loudly chasing innocent passersby along the length of the wooden fence. They're the most obnoxious dogs in the neighborhood. "Oh," people will say primly after I've given directions to our house. "The yard with the *dogs*?"

I eagerly unwrapped my Bark Free and set it among the flowers in the front garden. Equipped with a wide funnel, it looked like the 1921 Victrola, represented in the company's logo by the image of a Jack Russell terrier peering into the funnel, hearing his master's voice. The funnel of the Bark Free was designed to emit unpleasant supersonic discouraging beeps in response to barking. I set it up and went back into the house.

Suddenly here came a stormy-tempered neighborhood senior citizen! Our dogs go insane when they see this lady, as if she were a bipedal squirrel with a hairdo. They yap frantically and snarl at her through the slats of the fence as she marches past in sensible shoes. My screaming at the dogs through the kitchen window—"Franny!! Theo!! Stop it, stop it, goddamn it!"—has not burnished our family's image in her eyes.

The dogs heard her coming and exploded out the dog door while I hunched down by the kitchen window to watch. I waited for them to freeze in their tracks, cover their ears with their front paws, smile feebly, and then offer to carry the woman's groceries. I couldn't wait to see them halted and transformed by the Bark Free!

Instead they bayed like hounds after a fox. *Go on! Get out of here! Go on with you, you stupid squirrel-woman!* they barked. Grim-faced, she endured the verbal assault until she was out of sight beyond the mailbox.

Concerned, I hastened out to check my Bark Free. Its green light was on. I aimed it at the dogs and pushed the button. Nothing. I aimed the Bark Free at my own face and pushed the button. Nothing. But then it wasn't supposed to stop *me* from barking at the lady. I didn't care whether she walked past our yard or not. Over the next few days I saw the dogs hop back and forth over the Bark Free in pursuit of innocent pedestrians; I saw them stand right next to the Bark Free, barking; and I saw Franny peer into the Bark Free funnel—just like the Victrola ad!—and bark right into it. I think it acted as a megaphone, broadcasting her woofs across the neighborhood.

Seth and Lee felt I'd misunderstood the *SkyMall* ad, that "Bark Free" meant *"Bark for Free!"* or *"Free up those Barks!"*

Naturally one is intrigued, on family trips, by offerings like "Remotely Control Your Existing Umbrella!" for a mere $109.99. *"You don't need to brave the elements to collapse your table umbrella on windy or rainy days. Open or close it remotely from 40 feet away, even through walls and doors."* But after five years of no discernible impact from Bark Free, I'm never going to order another thing from *SkyMall*.

I enjoy pointing out the wonders of the outdoor world to my reluctant children. I welcome any feathered, tufted, furry, plated, exoskeletal, bipedal, and/or quadrupedal animal that comes our way. When a child (Lily) screams that there is a bug under the bed, I rush in with a magnifying glass and a field guide for identification. Bird identification books are piled up around the kitchen, more numerous than cookbooks. (Too bad for the family!)

Late last summer, on a hot, dry day, I heard a remarkable sound coming from the flower garden in the front yard: the rusty hinge–like seesawing croak of the seventeen-year cicada!

How I knew it was the seventeen-year cicada—of the species in which all the adults emerge at the same time after seventeen years underground—rather than a member of a regular old annual cicada species that comes out anytime, I can only marvel.

I couldn't find the animal, but I showed the children photos of a humpbacked creature with spherical red eyes and orange-veined wings, so we could all look for it together. Was it standing upside down under a prickly leaf of the rosebush? *Rrraaawk! Rrraawk! Rrraaawk!* it blurted, contracting and expanding the creaky abdomen of its exoskeleton. Soon the bushes and trees would be full of them, I told the children. It would sound like a thousand tiny musicians shaking maracas. It was one of the great sounds of summer, I told them. The writer James Agee compared the powerful song of cicadas to the music of the sea. But the kids, finished with that enlightening lesson, had already buckled themselves into the car and were waiting for me to drive them to Target for some miniature electronics they urgently needed.

When we pulled back into the driveway, my little insect friend was still there, grating away in hoarse splendor. "Wait, are there two of them now?" I paused at the gate. The kids were fleeing toward the front door with their purchases. "Come on!" I pleaded. "Let's find it! A seventeen-year cicada! You don't meet one of *these* every day of the week! Yosef, come on! You'll be . . . thirty the next time one of these comes out. Helen, you'll be thirty-one! Lily, that's thirty-five for you! Come on, guys! This is special!"

They stopped at the front door and very, very slowly turned around, weighed down by their profound lack of interest. Lily sweetly tried to work up some enthusiasm. They fanned out across the yard and flower garden, following the sound while I hunched low, looking for the creature along individual blades of grass. *Rrraaawk! Rrraaawk! Rrraaawk!* it razzed.

Of all the gardens in all the towns in all the world, I was thinking, *the seventeen-year cicada walks into mine.*

"Oh, Mo-om!" called Lily in a singsong voice. "I think we found your bu-ug." I bounded over like a puppy.

Lily untangled something from the leaves and then held it up. Its green light was dimmer now, blinking through a few years of encrusted dirt, and its ultrasonic beep had been altered and lowered to a mechanical, rusty yawp within the range of human hearing. *Rrraaawk! Rrraawk! Rrraaawk!* it said. It was the Bark Free.

36

A Wonderful Number of Children

The family was complete. The houseboat was full; I cast off the ropes. Oddly, it was *now* that my friends said—thinking they'd gotten the hang of our family—"You're not finished."

"Yes, we are," I'd say.

"No, you're not."

"Yes. Really. We are."

Big smiles. "No, you're not."

We'd become a neighborhood reality show. But we *were* finished. Seven was a wonderful number of children to have.

In the fall of 2005, Lee, a high school senior, was the oldest of the five children at home. At seventeen he had reached his adult height of just under six feet, with a head of black curls, a jaunty air, and the sunniest of laughs. He played varsity baseball, ran cross-country, and was co-editor in chief of the school newspaper. He had retained his childhood knack of savoring happy moments. When his dad, his friends, and his siblings lounged on sofas near him and there was a Braves game on TV and a plate of nachos on the coffee table, Lee sighed, leaned back, laced his hands behind his head, and looked around with supreme satisfaction. He loved to ride along to meet Seth's friends for Ultimate Frisbee, from which the two of them would return bare-backed, with sunburned cheeks and shoulders. He called Lily "Pad" or "Padarooni" from her younger days as Lily-pad. He called Helen "Missus." "The tiniest Missus!" he exclaimed when she entered the room; either he or Seth would pick her up, twirl her around like a baton, and toss her, screaming with delight, onto the sofa cushions.

But then Lee grew restless. He'd spent the spring semester of eleventh grade at a high school in Israel, studying and hiking. The desert air, the Mediterranean sun, the antiquities, and the friends from many countries intoxicated him. He was hungry to see more of the world. He counted up his courses and discovered he had sufficient credits to graduate from high school after first semester. "You want to come with me to Ethiopia in a few weeks?" I asked.

"What would I do there?"

"You want to volunteer in a couple of the orphanages I'm writing about and stay behind when I come home?"

"*Could* I?"

Dr. Jane Aronson, the New York City international adoption doctor whom I'd profiled in *The New Yorker* and the founding director of Worldwide Orphans Foundation (WWO), had become a friend; she interviewed Lee by phone and in person. All of WWO's volunteers were then medical students and health-care professionals, but Dr. Jane accepted Lee as her youngest-ever "Orphan Ranger," as an experiment in putting a sporty young man into the field with grieving and sick children. She could provide a room, a food subsidy, and a shared driver in exchange for Lee's working at three orphanages. His assignment: "*Play.* Go play with the children!"

Thinking he would set up a program like his neighborhood baseball clinic, he packed a duffle bag with plastic bats, small gloves, and Wiffle balls.

"I don't know if they play baseball in Ethiopia," I cautioned.

"All kids love baseball!" he said. "I'll teach them!" On February 10, 2006, Lee's eighteenth birthday, we flew to Ethiopia. He leaned back in his seat, picturing the future first-ever Ethiopian Little League team.

I thought I'd be his guide to Addis Ababa, but I was hit by a bad cold and low-grade fever that worsened across the two days of travel: Atlanta to New York, New York to Frankfurt, Frankfurt to Addis Ababa.

Neighborhood roosters woke us at sunrise in our room in the small modern Yilma Hotel. Cool mountain air fell from the heights like a waterfall. My sore throat and head cold persisted. I told Lee he had to go without me. Even if I'd had the strength to drag myself out, I couldn't visit the HIV-positive children while sick. Immunocompromised children are at far greater risk *from* healthy people than we are from them. In front of the little hotel, the WWO driver, nicknamed Baby, waited in a scraped-up blue van. Lee, in jeans, T-shirt, and sneakers, offered some kind words of concern, turned off the overhead light, and headed out. I went back to bed.

A few hours later he gently woke me; he had brought me a bottle of cold lemonade. He was flushed with excitement and awe from his first bright, dusty intersection with Africa, and he had a cell phone.

"A phone?? Where'd you get a phone?" I asked, propping myself up in bed.

"I asked Baby to help me find a cheap used phone, and we got one on the street near the airport. It was like thirty dollars."

I was so impressed! On all my trips to Ethiopia I'd been hampered by the lack of a phone, yet it had never occurred to me to buy one. Lee was going to have an ease on the streets I would never know. He already had a funny story. He'd been wearing a white T-shirt that displayed a big color photograph of the rapper Jay-Z. An Ethiopian in his thirties had approached Lee on the sidewalk, stopped, and pointed at the shirt. In English he said, "This man, I know he."

"Oh yeah?" asked Lee.

"This man, he name: Niggah."

Lee burst out laughing. Pleased, the stranger shook Lee's hand and then walked on.

Later that week, I took Lee to meet *Waizero* (Mrs.) Haregewoin Teferra.

She was a short, round, and opinionated woman with an upright hedge of graying hair. She had first opened her door to AIDS orphans in the early years of the pandemic, when there were few safe havens for them. Haregewoin had lost her oldest daughter, Atetegeb, a young wife and mother, to AIDS; in the deepest part of her grief, she listlessly opened her door to a few teenagers and children orphaned by the disease. With nowhere else to turn, hundreds of needy, bereft children followed. Haregewoin felt joy in the children's company; she, a grief-stricken mother, felt her heart stirring to life again.

Now she had moved from a muddy hillside compound to a middle-class residence in which four simple brick houses faced a clean cement courtyard. She named her program Atetegeb. Later, she opened a second compound for HIV-positive children; she called it Little Atetegeb, and the first house became Big Atetegeb.

Haregewoin's children at Little Atetegeb, like the children at Helen's former orphanage, ENAT (now called AHOPE), were terminally ill. In rich countries, HIV-infected children were now sustained by brilliant new drug combinations, but those medicines were expensive. Their sky-high cost represented the difference between life and death for African adults and for African children. When, in 2006, Dr. Aronson's organization, Worldwide Orphans, opened a free pediatric AIDS clinic in Addis Ababa, it was one of the first on the continent. Under the medical oversight of WWO, the Little Atetegeb and the AHOPE orphans were among the first infected children in Africa to be offered the lifesaving "triple cocktails."

For a couple of the AHOPE and Little Atetegeb children, the medicine arrived too late. They died, and the grief of their caregivers was mixed with dark suspicions of the new drugs, as if the pills were just the latest murderous conspiracy from the West. Grieving the death of a baby girl, Haregewoin opted *not* to give any more medicine to her sick children. No, she didn't believe in it, she announced with crossed arms, and she barred her door to anyone coming from the WWO clinic. She would nurse the children back to health herself, with love. The doctors and nurses begged her and I begged her to give the medicine a chance to work with the other children, children less fragile than the baby who had died.

No, she didn't trust it. She sealed her lips, bolted her door; her decision was final.

But at AHOPE, which was not Haregewoin's orphanage, the medicine began to work its miraculous transformations, restoring dying children to health. A skeletal child gained a pound in a week. A dull and listless child recaptured a gleam of light in her eyes. A long-bedridden child sat up in bed; and the next day he sat up and put his feet on the floor; and on the third day he put his feet on the floor and crept slowly to a chair in the lunchroom; and the following Monday he showed up at the door of the classroom, ready to learn a lesson.

In the face of this evidence, Haregewoin reluctantly allowed the WWO doctors and nurses to come back into Little Atetegeb with their kits and their pills. She wasn't happy about their presence, especially when they scolded her about issues of cleanliness and nutrition, and when they reprimanded her for carelessness in administering the complicated regimens of pills. She didn't like being told what to do by outsiders. She kept close oversight over the visiting medical caregivers, generating a mood of mutual suspicion; a frown pulled down all the features of her face. But no more children died. Instead, the children lived.

All of this was unfolding as I took Lee for the first time to meet Mrs. Haregewoin. It was an open question whether she would welcome him as my son or keep him at arm's length as another WWO staffer intent upon berating her and issuing orders. I hadn't mentioned this uncertainty to Lee.

As always, when I stepped through Haregewoin's gates after an absence of many months, I was mobbed by the children. They screamed my name—"May-LEESE-ah!" Some sprinted toward me, some ran in the opposite direction; the ones who ran away were fetching something—a half glass of grainy water, a kitchen chair, a short length from a peeled banana—so that they could draw close to me and win a smile or a word of praise or thanks in my language. The ones who ran toward me began formally with handshakes, then moved forward for kisses; the kisses—one on each cheek, then repeat, in Ethiopian style—were fervently given and gratefully received. Children pressed in close to me, lingered, inhaled. It wasn't so much about *me*—though in part it was—as about the fact that I was a woman, a mother. They knew I wasn't *their* mother, but in embracing me, or in relieving me of the weight of my purse, my backpack, my camera bag, or the paper sack of fresh oranges or bakery rolls I had brought them, a child could pretend for a moment that he or she was the light of my life. The winners of my purse, camera bag, and backpack would wear them all day, if permitted. *Look how I help May-leese-ah,* each one hoped to imply to the others. *Look how I help you,* each showed me, turning so that I could capture a glimpse of my backpack still safely being carried. Some hurried to bring their school notebooks to display their good work; they presented graded papers from four months earlier. "I'm so proud of you!" I said with a hug. "Look how smart you are!" Even though the children didn't understand all my words, they shivered with pleasure, then ran to ransack their rooms for something else that might impress me and win a moment of my undivided attention.

On her front porch at Big Atetegeb, Haregewoin greeted Lee with her warmest crinkle-eyed smile and invited him to take coffee with us in her sitting room/bedroom. He seated himself happily, looking at everything with admiration. She sensed that he was an innocent, a guileless and playful boy. Among all her children, she loved best the scamps. She loved, for example, Tsegay, a small boy who could have been Pigpen in the *Peanuts* cartoon strip. Dirt sought out Tsegay and accrued to him; and he always did the wrong thing, like accidentally farting during evening prayers. Beneath the multiple layers of dust and morsels from his last meal, he had the endearing smile of an imp. Haregewoin could not look at Tsegay without her chest going up and down in suppressed laughter. Though Lee was clean-shaven and wearing a fresh T-shirt and blue jeans, Haregewoin detected a rapscallion within. "He is *all boy,*" she told me, and I agreed, and that was it: she accepted him.

Lee stepped outside to stretch his legs and have a look around. The sunbaked cement courtyard was clean and empty. An enlarged photograph of Atetegeb hung as a framed poster, under glass, above the porch of the boys' dormitory. Some forty children lived here, but it was boring. There was little to do here after school, on weekends, and through the long summer months. A few kids, having just come in after school, leaned dully against the wrought-iron banister in front of the boys' dorm; others were napping on thin mattresses in hot rooms. Girls took down and rebraided one another's thick hair. Toys *had* been donated to this foster home many times over the years—*I* had brought them!—but Haregewoin displayed rather than distributed them. Barbie dolls—wearing red lipstick, gold high heels, and sequined dresses—had taken nails through their bellies. Like fashionable plastic crucifixes, they were tacked up high on the walls of the classroom for decoration, but the effect was surreal, as if I'd entered a Toys "R" Us cathedral.

Lee sat down on the wide, sunny cement steps outside Haregewoin's rooms. Around the courtyard, children froze in their actions to look: a white teenage boy was not something you saw around here every day; in fact, the children had never seen one before. Curiosity compelled them to approach, cautiously. A few came tiptoeing, and a few circled behind him on the porch, and a few little ones came jumping, until they all stood before him. He cocked his head at them and offered, "Hi!" They giggled. He propped his arms across his raised knees, palms up. A brave little girl of about four was the first to make physical contact: she reached out her finger and began to give Lee an almost imperceptible delicate tickle on his palm, and when he zoomed in to look at her and wiggled a finger to tickle her back, she fled, shrieking with terror and excitement across the courtyard, and crashed into an outdoor garbage bin. Others then drew bravely closer to sit below Lee on the steps and gaze up at him. A toddler wiggled up between his knees, and a five-year-old wrapped his arms around Lee's neck in order to hang down his back, and others began to fiddle with Lee's ankles, others to untie his shoelaces, and others to examine his soft hair, and more little girls inched closer to put themselves at risk of a tickle in order to shriek and run away and hide and look out from their hiding places to see if he was pursuing. Under the increasing soft barrage of shy attentions, Lee leaned back and laughed aloud in happiness.

For the children, having Lee sit on their steps was the peak of novelty and fun. But he stood up, shedding them, stepped back into Haregewoin's room, asked me for a soft rubber ball from our duffle bag of supplies and gifts, and then walked to the middle of the courtyard while tossing up and catching the ball. Children followed him like iron shavings around a magnet. He began to teach them his favorite version of dodgeball. "When you are hit, you're out," he explained. "You will sit there, on the steps, and wait. *But* when the kid who hit *you* gets hit, *you* come back in!" The orphanage's oldest child, Hailegabriel—a toothy, eager, and supersmart teenager not much younger than Lee—translated. The game began. The cycling in and out of players, the swift throws growing in velocity, the agile dodges, the rotating alliances, the cheers from the "out" kids on the steps—"Lee! Pinllin *mettow*! [Hit Pinl!] Yo-seffin *mettow* [Hit Yosef!]"—kindled pell-mell hilarity in the courtyard. Lee swooped up a small child and played one-handed so that the little boy could enjoy the frantic zigzagging, too, his eyes wide and head bob-bing. "I forgot: if you *catch* the ball when someone tries to hit you, that kid is out," yelled Lee above the mob, and Hailegabriel yelled his trans-lation.

A championship dodgeball game without end was launched; and from that day on, whenever Lee arrived, the children ran to their places—remembering who was in, who was out, and who had hit whom—and began yelling and running.

Then one afternoon, at the height of the ecstatic roughhousing, *W/o* (*Waizero*) Haregewoin stepped onto her porch. She surveyed the battle scene, clapped her hands, and shouted for attention. She was canceling the sport, *permanently.* Running around made the children wild, she told Lee, and destroyed their already tattered school uniforms. Before she could confiscate the ball, someone's shirt swallowed it. Haregewoin told Lee to set up a study hall instead and tutor the children. For two weeks Lee suffered from the imposed boredom as much as the kids did.

But *W/o* Haregewoin did her hair one day, put on her work shoes, took her purse, called for the driver, and left to do business in town. In the hot, still rooms, the children studied, then drifted out to the cement courtyard. Somehow Lee's rubber ball reappeared from its hiding place. Some minor scuffling and a few tosses began, and before anyone really planned it or agreed on it, a great and vigorous game of dodgeball began! Children sprinted out of every door to join it. Caregivers and cooks saw what was happening, raised their eyebrows in amused concern, and said nothing. They wanted the children to have fun but didn't want to be blamed.

In Haregewoin's absence the forbidden game got wilder, faster, and louder than ever before. The children and Lee pelted one another with the ball as hard as they could, the sound of the wallops echoing off the buildings. Children on the sidelines begged Lee to hit their attackers and free them; whenever he pegged one of the big boys—Daniel, or another Daniel, or Hailegabriel—a whole row of little kids cheered and ran back into the game. If Lee got hit and went to sit on the sidelines, the children cried, "Lee!" and ran to pet and console him. It was tumultuously great until the ball flew through the air for a direct hit onto the glass-covered poster of Haregewoin's late daughter, Atetegeb, which dropped from its hook and smashed onto the pavement.

In an instant the courtyard emptied. Every child disappeared. They hid in their beds and under them, behind the garbage cans, behind a mountain of laundry in the washroom, and under the skirts of the cooks. Lee disappeared, too. He hid under Hailegabriel's bed with many other boys, some of whom tried to hide under Lee as well for an extra layer of protection. Silence descended upon the orphanage. In the cool, dusty twilight on the cement floors under beds and tables, children dozed. The afternoon waned. Then, as if the giant from "Jack and the Beanstalk" approached, powerful footsteps shook the ground. W/o Haregewoin had come home. In their hiding places, children awoke, vigilant. She called out a general greeting but stopped when she saw the disaster. She strode rapidly toward the mess with a face already twisting with rage, and she stood above it covering her mouth with her hands in renewed grief, as if they had killed Atetegeb again. Children who peeked out from the windows slid back under the beds to whisper their reports: "She has seen what has happened!"

With a groan, Lee dragged himself out from under Hailegabriel's bed, anxiously tucked his hands in his pockets, and exited the dormitory. Children buried their faces in their arms, too scared to watch. At the scene of the accident, Lee dropped to his knees and began picking up the pieces of glass. "Haregewoin, I am so so sorry, I am so sorry. I'll get it fixed. It was my fault, I'm sorry. It was me, not the kids."

He glanced up at her with a face full of remorse and sincerity, but that other element, the boyish mischief-maker, flickered. She surveyed him silently while he picked up the glass, then asked, "You break a lot of things at your house in America?"

"Yes. I guess I've broken a certain number of windows with baseballs."

"Your mother is happy about this?"

"No. I might have dented my father's car a couple of times, too."

"Clean it up," she said crisply.

He returned to the task as she lumbered back across the courtyard. Her chest was going up and down in suppressed laughter.

After she returned to her room and loudly closed her door, the children, like little mice scattered by a cat, crept out of hiding. Their small fingers flew over the pavement, gathering the fragments of glass until the courtyard was clean and the pale cardboard poster of Atetegeb stood leaning against Haregewoin's door.

37

An Orphanage League

Lee also volunteered at two orphanages for HIV-positive children: Haregewoin's Little Atetegeb, a wooded compound that included a big house, a barn, and a cow; and AHOPE, an American-Ethiopian NGO. The children at both houses sensed that this tall but young person had not come to give them shots, take their temperatures, or scold them. He had come, it seemed, simply to sprawl on a kitchen chair in the smattering of sunlight in a dirt courtyard so children could climb up one of his legs and slide down the other.

Worldwide Orphans had taught him about the ways a person does, and does not, contract and spread HIV/AIDS; he was careful not to get infected, and he was especially careful not to infect the immunocompromised children with his own germs. But he wasn't scared of them. With the children who were losing their hair, or whose faces were covered with vicious warts and growths, or whose arms and legs were as thin and fragile as twigs, or whose bald heads were too big for their frail bodies, he played gently. They played a walking version of duck, duck, goose, and they colored with crayons, and they played hide-and-seek. But the children didn't want to be separated from Lee, even for the duration of hide-and-seek, so, once a child volunteered to be "it" and covered his or her eyes, thirty children waited to see where *Lee* would hide, and then they hurried as fast as they could to hide with him.

But his name confused the children at AHOPE. "Lee? *Lee?*" they asked again and again. It seemed something was missing—there had to be more to it. Lee had reproached me over the years with the same complaint! "I don't have an ending consonant!" he said. "When someone asks my name and I say, Lee, there's no natural stopping place; it just goes on and on: Leee . . . eee . . . eee."

Thinking he wasn't being truthful about his name, the children guessed that his name must be Aklilu. This was funny because Lee's baby nickname was Lee-loo. Now, at AHOPE, he was Aklilu.

AHOPE asked Lee to create a beginning English class, a kindergarten. The impossible was happening: as a result of the medicines, the children were going to have futures. So let them study and learn! Maybe they would reach high school someday! Let them (could they live *that* long? No one knew yet!) go to university, pursue careers.

"This is *A*," said Lee at the blackboard one morning. "It says *ah*. Bring me something that starts with *A*." Children fanned out across the AHOPE compound; they tore around the little plots of flowers lined with stones, dodged under the clothes dripping from the lines, and ran in and out of the freshly mopped buildings. Some children grasped the assignment while others ran in excited circles. The first winner returned with an *ant* walking across his wrist. "*A*. Ant!" announced Lee. "Great one!" The second brought a scarf with an embroidered image of the Ethiopian Lion of Judah. Lee was confused. "*Ambessa!*" shouted the children. *Ambessa* meant lion. "*A. Ambessa!*" they yelled.

"English! I need English words," said Lee.

An older girl shyly pointed at Lee: "American?"

Every day they learned a few more letters, and at the start of the following week they reached *X*, which stumped them. Children wandered dazed across the landscape like people lost in the desert. "Lee needs an *X*!" they wailed, but there was no *X* for Lee. Then a shriek of excitement rose from behind the washhouse, and a little girl tore across the compound waving twigs torn from a small pine tree.

"Yes?" said Lee.

"*X*," she pronounced. "X . . . mas . . . tree?"

"We have a winner!" yelled Lee, and everyone hopped up and down.

Z took a long time, too. "Z is too hard," the children commiserated with one another, walking slowly and without hope. Gradually they all seemed to gravitate to the nursery, so Lee returned to his classroom to tidy up, thinking the game was over. It was almost lunchtime anyway. Then he heard the rumble of a mob coming his way, and through the open window he beheld a crowd of trotting children bearing aloft a toddler, who was confused and weepy at having been roughly stolen out of her nap. The children burst into the classroom, set the whimpering eighteen-month-old girl on Lee's desk, and stood back in triumph while he sprang forward to make sure the baby didn't topple off.

"What's going on?" he asked.

They answered him in one big chorus, all pointing at the tiny girl, who burst into loud tears. "Zinash!" they yelled. "Her name is Zinash!"

The ill children at AHOPE and Little Atetegeb were regaining strength quickly as a result of WWO's medical treatment. Every day, at AHOPE in the morning and at Little Atetegeb in the afternoon, they ran to embrace Lee with new vigor. He'd never kicked a ball to these fragile children or organized races; suddenly, with flashing eyes, they challenged *him* to races, to soccer, to tag, and it turned out that there were athletes among them.

"They're killing me on the soccer field!" Lee e-mailed the family a couple of weeks after my return to Atlanta. "I'm pathetic. Little tiny kids are dribbling circles around me. The Ethiopian caregivers and drivers and guards stand on the sidelines and laugh." If Lee slipped and fell in the dirt, the children stopped the game. They ran to help him get up, brush him off, and ask if he was okay. One day Zemedikun punched Abel in the face, bloodying his nose. The caregivers grabbed Zemedikun off the field. "Why did you do that?" they scolded, yanking him toward the dorm for time-out. "Because," yelled Zemedikun, "Abel made Lee fall down!" Back in the game, children gently tipped the ball to Lee or pretended to lose possession so he could have a chance. "Let Lee SCORE!" children on both teams screamed in Amharic at the goalkeeper.

Lee wrote to us: "I worried about the wrong thing. I was afraid I would get attached to children who were really sick and were going to die. I forgot to worry, 'What if the kids are better athletes than I am?'"

Time to break out the baseball supplies! "I'm introducing baseball now at all three houses," he wrote to us. "The point is for the kids to learn a sport in which I can beat them handily. My already bottomed-out self-esteem can't take any more soccer debacles." At Big Atetegeb, Lee unzipped his duffle bag and handed out the plastic bats. Instantly the children began whacking one another with loud smacks. Lee collected the baseball bats and put them back in the duffle bag. He handed out little mitts and Wiffle balls. Children fought one another to receive a prize, then ran to hide their gifts. They weren't hiding them from one another—they were hiding them from *W/o* Haregewoin. She maintained that toys spoiled children and she knew children spoiled toys. The moment she saw these baseball mitts, everyone feared, she'd be nailing them up in between the riveted Barbies.

The children knew nothing of baseball. Lee had his laptop computer with him, and it was loaded with baseball movies. Haregewoin allowed Lee to sleep over in the boys' dormitory one or two nights a week, so he launched a baseball film festival after lights-out. Kids piled onto a bottom bunk beside him and on top of him and they scooted close on the floor and they hung down from the upper bunk, and the older girls snuck in from their dorm. Lee, with a few words of introduction, presented *The Sandlot, Major League, Rookie of the Year, Angels in the Outfield, Little Big League, Field of Dreams, The Natural* . . . The film festival was a success because the children adored having Lee sleep over! They loved secretly watching movies with him until all hours, even movies in a language they didn't speak about a sport they didn't comprehend. But the film festival was also a failure because the children's takeaway was: Baseball is stupid. These children were die-hard soccer fans, as Lee would have been if he'd been born outside the United States; they followed the British Premier League on games broadcast through a static storm on Haregewoin's portable black-and-white TV. The only decorations on the cinder block walls of the boys' dormitory were magazine cutouts and posters of Arsenal and Manchester United players.

"Lee!" they demanded. "Why man throw ball and, after that, nothing happen?"

"Lee! Why man run small small, and then he must rest?"

(They'd been similarly unimpressed with America's Olympic events: "Lee, why American runners only can go for ten seconds?")

"Why," they now asked, with pleading tones, "why we cannot play soccer?"

He surrendered and gave away the baseball equipment. The children ran to hide the gloves and bats. They would treasure them as gifts from Lee, whom they demolished at soccer.

Lee and the WWO driver, Baby, took the children on outings around the city. "On our van outing today, the kids gave me a full tour of Addis Ababa," Lee wrote to us. "'There is bank!' 'There is goats!' 'There is dying man with no legs!' Also, the kids are always quick to point out every *ferange* [white person] to me. (I can't help but think that *ferange* really just means 'Crackah'.) 'LEE!!! *FERANGE!*' they yell. I think they want to assure me that I am not the only white person on the continent."

I received an e-mail one day from an American nurse volunteering at AHOPE: "We were having a meeting in the dining hall this morning when suddenly there was a huge tumult of children screaming and jumping up and running out of all the doors and overturning their chairs. It scared me and I asked, 'What's happening? What's wrong?' 'Don't worry,' the director said. 'It must be that Lee has arrived.'"

Dear Family:

Last night I slept over at Haregewoin's bigger orphanage with the kids. We played dodgeball all afternoon, had a dinner of injera and kikwat, and then stayed up until 5 a.m. playing Go Fish and watching Arab television.

Thanks to dinners such as injera and kikwat, I am quickly running out of my Maximum Strength Pepto-Bismol. In addition to immediately following every meal, it has become a staple of my diet: a Coke and some Pepto make for a delicious lunch. My driver, Baby, is trying to convince me to try his favorite Ethiopian delicacy: raw meat. He tells me that it gives you tapeworm about 15% of the time, but my contracting intestinal parasites is a risk he is willing to take.

Speaking of raw meat, this morning I was witness to one of the most fantastic cultural clashes of all time. Around 11 a.m., while I was still playing at the orphanage, a group of about 30 blonde blue-eyed Evangelical Christian Norwegians came to see the kids.

They and the children stood on opposite sides of the compound staring at each other until a Norwegian woman broke the ice by announcing in accented English: "Jesus died on the cross not just for white people, but for you all too."

Here's how this story is related to raw meat. This week, a two-month fast (no meat, no dairy) begins in Ethiopia. For the big pre-fast feast, the compound had two sheep delivered early this morning. I was excited to have some new playmates. Sadly, halfway through the Norwegians' rendition of "Jesus Loves You," a man in the back began slaughtering the first sheep. Unfortunately, it took 4 or 5 hacks to fully kill it, so it was loudly squealing/moaning right in the middle of the Christian hymns. It kind of sounded like this: "Jesus loves you this I know. For the ERRRRRGAAAACCCHHHHHHH . . . Bible tells me UMMMMMBLACCCCCHH . . . so."

It only got worse as the sheep's blood began trickling across the compound and puddling at the feet of the horrified Norwegians. They quickly said, "Thanks for having us," and sprinted out of there while the kids alternately jumped on me and on the dirt/blood of the compound. I have sheep blood in my hair right now. I love Norway.

—Lee

Seeing that Ethiopian Little League wasn't going to happen, Lee wondered about organizing an orphanage *soccer* league instead. Dr. Aronson, in New York, loved the idea. Lee spoke with directors of several orphanages, drew up rosters and schedules, and held tryouts in order to assign positions. To the astonishment of all, he organized girls' teams, too.

At AHOPE he hesitated, unsure whether the HIV-positive children would have the strength and stamina to face teams of HIV-negative kids. He asked his AHOPE players what they'd like to do; maybe they'd sub into Big Atetegeb's team.

"No!" the children protested. "We will represent our house!"

At each orphanage the children designed their own uniforms; everyone chose English Premier League team uniforms to copy: the Atetegeb players preferred Manchester United, while at AHOPE they went with Arsenal. At the Mercato, Lee bought a cheap stack of cotton T-shirts and a bunch of permanent Magic Markers. The kids colored their uniforms and numbers by hand. The date of the first match approached.

Lee had met an American teacher at the American private school in Addis and knew that the school sat on a beautiful green landscape, with a soccer field. His kids had never kicked a ball across anything other than dirt and cement. In fact, they'd rarely kicked a ball at all—usually they played with a round thing made of old plastic bags and string, or balled-up rags and twine. He contacted the American teacher and gained permission for the new league's first game to be held at the American school. He bought a few real soccer balls with which to practice. The children turned out for practice, however, in flip-flops, snow boots, Mary Janes, high-heeled sandals, the most battered of the already used detritus landing by the ton as donations on Africa's shores. This was a problem Lee didn't have the money to remedy. The kids would play in the shoes they had.

One of the AHOPE children gaining strength as a result of medical treatment was Ermias (*URR-me-us*), a boy from the deep countryside who had blue-black skin, bloodshot eyes, and the sad history of having seen his whole family wiped out by disease. The children had a special nickname for Ermias: "Barrio." So Lee called the melancholy boy Barrio, too. "What does Barrio mean?" Lee asked him one day, just to make conversation.

Ermias replied, "Slave."

"No! What?" cried Lee, shocked that he'd taken up the name, too.

"Also," continued Ermias, "this have other meaning. This mean Midnight Face."

Lee hugged him and said, "I think I'll just call you Ermias."

Ermias didn't have the stamina yet to sprint down the soccer field, so Lee tried him out in the goal.

"Ermias," Lee e-mailed home, "is the single greatest, most natural goalkeeper I have ever seen in my life. AHOPE is seriously going to win some games."

The big day arrived. For the first game, AHOPE met Adoption Advocates International (AAI) on the field of play. Caregivers and workers from both houses came to cheer, lugging along tall leather-bound standing drums; they pounded the drums and waved colorful scarves and ululated on behalf of their children. Teachers from the American school wandered down to the field to watch. The play was skilled and joyful, children kicking up their heels, frolicking like goats. When players collided, they laughed and helped each other up. Many discarded their ridiculous ill-fitting shoes and continued barefoot. Ermias was a standout, springing around within the goal like a canary in a cage. A British teacher told Lee: "Your keeper is quite something."

The AHOPE boys lost, but not by much, thanks to Ermias. The AHOPE girls won! (By default, because the AAI girls began bickering over who should play which position and the arguments lasted so long, they had to forfeit.)

Lee rode back to AHOPE on a van rocking with drumbeats, foot stomping, whistles, and victory songs. He asked the driver to let him out for a moment at a small grocery, and he dashed inside with a few big kids and emerged with forty bottles of Coca-Cola for a celebration back at the orphanage. When the children disembarked in the AHOPE compound, they ran yelling up the walk and burst into the dining hall, where the younger children sat at long tables. The soccer players drummed their hands against the walls and along the tables, whooping in joy. The younger children began pounding the tables, too, and the cooks came out of the kitchen and the caregivers came out of the dorms to cheer for the returning heroes.

38

Room for Two More?

The American school in Addis hosted an American-style spring carnival. A few teachers invited Lee to return and bring a few of his kids. He took along five of the oldest children—three boys and two girls—from Big Atetegeb:

Dear Family:
  Yesterday I took Pinl, Hailegabriel, Betti, Mekdes, and Daniel on a field trip to the super-rich exclusive American private school to attend their spring carnival. The place was so decidedly un-Ethiopian, in fact, that nobody there was able to communicate with the five Ethiopian children I had brought. There was also no food there that the kids could eat during the Ethiopian fast months (no meat, no dairy) except cotton candy. However, there was a dunking booth, a video game room, a movie room, and a dodgeball field. The kids instantly ran to play dodgeball (which they learned from me) and they beat the crap out of dozens of ambassadors' kids. Seeing the Swedish ambassador's son get knocked out by Daniel and run off crying was a proud moment in orphanage history.
  Later in the afternoon, I took Pinl (age 8) and Daniel (age 11) to

the bathroom. This basic school bathroom was the most magical and fantastic place the boys had ever seen. First, they spent five minutes washing their hands in the miraculously hot water. Then Pinl experimented with the box on the wall and discovered that it automatically dispensed soap when you put your hand under it. This was spectacular. The two of them emptied the two boxes of soap and then tried to run out the door to alert Hailegabriel about this unbelievable place, but their hands were too slippery to open the door, so they had to run back and play with the hot water some more.

Then they spotted the urinals and asked me what they were. I told them that they were toilets, so Pinl turned around, dropped his pants, and sat in one. I quickly showed him how it is meant to be used, but he didn't approve, so he went into a stall. In there, the automatic flusher scared him and he came jumping back out. Meanwhile, Daniel discovered the automatic hand dryer and was heating up his whole body with it, even taking off his shirt and pants to better feel the warmth. After recovering from the shock of Auto-Flush, Pinl brightened up and joined Daniel, completely undressing under the hand dryer. Finally, they both successfully used the bathroom, but then walked out without washing or drying their hands.

After the toilet episode, I took the kids to the video game room, which was too mind-blowing to even be comprehended. They gaped at the screens for ten minutes before mustering up enough courage to try to play. Daniel, Mekdes, and Pinl were very interested in the blood and gore of Mortal Kombat, while Betti liked Lord of the Rings better. After a few fights (with me doing most of the controlling), Daniel got the hang of Mortal Kombat and began beating some white people. His strategy was to constantly walk his character forward and hit the triangle button over and over again, disabling his opponent from ever blocking or fighting back. He actually won a number of matches that way and made the Swedish ambassador's son cry again.

While we were in the video room, Betti wandered off and ended up getting dunked at the dunking booth, fully clothed. She ran back to me, soaked, and seeming really shocked and hurt from the experience. Seeing how upset she was, Daniel walked over and grabbed her hand, talked to her in Amharic for a minute, and then led her away to the boys' bathroom. I ran after them and found Daniel instructing Betti

to undress and dry herself off under the automatic hand dryer. Never again will I take our American bathrooms for granted.
  —Lee

Daniel, who went with Lee to the American school carnival, had a look-alike little brother named Yosef. Daniel, at eleven, carried the burden of what had happened to them—the deaths of their mother, father, and younger brothers; displacement from the semi-mountainous southwestern countryside where they'd lived in a round hut with their grandmother and older brother; the loss of their first two Gurage languages. The boys belonged to the Gurage ethnic group, which made up less than three percent of the population of Ethiopia. Yosef, by contrast, was a comedian, a goofball whose greatest joy was to torment Daniel. He was a superb soccer player who took losses hard. Lee, with growing Amharic fluency, overheard Daniel talking to Yosef on the field one day as Yosef sulked. "Yosef," said the older brother. "Think of our history. This is not the thing to be sad about."

On Friday nights Lee had Shabbat dinners at the home of a Jewish doctor, Rick Hodes, who'd lived in Ethiopia for nearly twenty years; then he usually headed to Big Atetegeb for a sleepover. One Friday night Lee lingered longer than usual after dinner with Rick's family and didn't reach the orphanage until after 11:00 p.m. It was dark and quiet. He regretted having disappointed the children, who so looked forward to his weekly sleepover, but at least they'd find him there in a bunk bed in the boys' dorm in the morning. He let himself silently into the courtyard and cracked open the door to the boys' dorm, at which point he was tackled with hugs and kisses by Daniel and Yosef, who had waited up for him. They were irrepressible in their happiness at his arrival, regardless of the hour; their twin faces in the darkness radiated joy.

At that moment of headlocks and scuffle, a new thought crossed Lee's mind.

Were Donny and I surprised when he phoned home to ask, "Do you think we could adopt again?"

No, we were not surprised. "We weren't really planning on it," I said. "Why, do you have someone in mind?"

"Well . . . two, actually. They're brothers."

"Wait . . . what?"

"Daniel and Yosef Gizaw. Daniel is the second-oldest after Hailega-briel, but Hailegabriel is being adopted. He's going to France! They've been waiting so long. No one is going to adopt them!"

Donny, having caught wind of my end of the conversation, watched me and waited to learn the name and gender of our new child. When I held up two fingers, he guffawed.

"They've got nothing, they've got no one," Lee was saying. "They're wonderful boys. They're with me all the time. It's like they're my brothers already. They'd be perfect for our family. What will happen to them if we don't adopt them? They'll end up on the streets."

Spring 2007, Addis Ababa. Yosef and Daniel Gizaw with Lee

"How old are they?" I asked, but it didn't really matter. Issues of too few bedrooms, too few seats in the car, and too little money were overshadowed by the likely fate of a pair of orphaned brothers whom Lee loved.

"They're about eleven and eight," he said. *"Please."*

"Here's the thing. I've known all of Haregewoin's children for years. How will the others feel if we suddenly adopt two? They'll say they never *knew* I was look-ing for more children. I'm afraid they'll feel that I don't love them."

"I'll explain to them," Lee said. "Daniel's the oldest kid here without a family. I'll tell the other kids it's Daniel and Yosef's *turn.*"

"Sweetheart. Let us think about it."

"Really?" he cried. "You'll think about it?? Oh my God, really?? Thank you so much!"

Lee's clarity, Lee's certainty, carried the day. We trusted his judgment. We believed him that these were two great boys, and that our family would be a perfect match for them. Too late I realized that I *could* have said—he'd *expected* me to say—NO.

I e-mailed Molly, who was working for ForestEthics in San Francisco, and Seth at the Oberlin Conservatory, and copied Lee: "Lee wants to bring home two brothers from Ethiopia."

"How old are they?" Seth asked.

"Eight and eleven," I replied.

"Don't we have those ages already?" he said.

Later he e-mailed, "Just wait one minute. I don't want to go from being the fastest runner in the family to being the fourth-fastest, outrun by Fisseha and two new Ethiopians."

"You're already not in the top three," Lee e-mailed from an Internet café in Addis Ababa. "I'm first, then Fisseha, then Jesse."

"I'm first," replied Seth. "Ask anyone."

"Hey, am I good at anything?" typed Molly from San Francisco.

That night at dinner I asked the four children at home: "Who's the fastest runner in the family?"

"Seth!" all the kids agreed.

"Okay, another question: What is Molly best at?"

Because they were focusing on athletics, this gave them pause. Lily, Helen, Sol, and Jesse stopped eating to consider this important question. Not soccer, not baseball, not basketball, not swimming. She jogged and she biked, but was she the best? (This conversation reminded me of one that had occurred on the night of July 3, 2000. Jesse, age five, had been in America for nine months. Donny was preparing to run in the 10K Peachtree Road Race the next morning and Jesse grasped that Daddy was entering a race. "Daddy, you going win!!" shouted the small boy. "Daddy, you be fastest! You beat *everybody*!!" What lovely encouragement! What filial pride. We all continued to eat. Donny finished his meal first, got seconds, and cleaned his plate again, as was his wont. I raised my eyebrows at him. "Carbo-loading," he explained. But then Jesse suddenly gleaned that we were talking about a *footrace*.

"You running, Daddy?" he yelped.

"Yep."

"Oh, Daddy," he cried, now forlorn. "Daddy, you going lose! You not fast running, Daddy! You too fat, Daddy! Daddy, you coming last!"

"Well, Jesse," I said, perplexed by the abrupt halt in cheerleading. "We told you Daddy was in a race. What kind of race did you *think* it was?"

And he was not kidding when he earnestly replied, "A eating race.")

So it was well established that Seth was the fastest runner in the family and Donny was the fastest eater. But Molly needed a superlative.

"I thought of something!" piped up Helen, eager not to hurt Molly's feelings. "Molly has the cutest car!"

I e-mailed Molly in San Francisco that her siblings had voted her 2004 red Toyota Corolla to be the Family's Cutest Car, and she made her peace with that. But then she and I realized that on her trip to Ethiopia with me the previous October, she'd *met* Yosef and Daniel; we had pictures of them together!

But now the younger ones were protesting: "Wait a minute, wait a minute! We've been asking for *years* if we could have a ferret for a pet, and you always say, *'No. Too much responsibility.'* And now Lee calls from Africa to ask for two more brothers and you say, 'Yes. Fine!' Is that fair?"

"You're right," I agreed. "That is completely ridiculous and unfair."

"So, CAN we have a ferret?"

"No," I said. "It's too much responsibility."

In July 2006, I flew to Addis Ababa with twenty-one-year-old Seth, and we joined Lee. Sitting in the orphanage van outside the gates of Big Atetegeb, I told Daniel, while our old friend Selamneh translated, that our family was interested in adopting him and Yosef. He closed his eyes and dropped his head in gratitude. "There's something I need you to understand and to think about," I added quickly. "This is important. Our family is Jewish."

Yosef and Daniel had been raised as Ethiopian Orthodox Christians. Yosef wore a wooden crucifix on a string around his neck; Daniel fasted for Lent.

"*Ishii ishi ishi,*" Daniel said, meaning okay, okay, good, good.

"That's different from your religion," I insisted. "We believe in God, but we don't worship Jesus."

"*Ishii ishi ishi.*"

"Or Mary."

"Okay, okay, *ishi.*"

"We're not Christian."

"*Amesegenalo,*" he said. Thank you.

"We don't go to a *church*," I emphasized—Yosef had joined us now—but the boys were grabbing my hands and kissing them and kissing them.

These children just really wanted a new family.

With the religion question cleared up, the look-alike brothers—long and lean, dark-skinned, with smooth, narrow faces, huge smiles, and gentle natures—moved with us into the little Yilma Hotel. When they stood side by side, I knew the shorter one was Yosef. But if I confronted one of them alone, I had to look for the telltale sign: Daniel's hairline was smooth above his face, while Yosef had one tiny curl at the top of his forehead. In the hotel, I took a single room and the four boys moved into a double next door. Yosef's and Daniel's shoes were so small on them that the boys' toenails had been rubbed off. Their clothes were filthy; they themselves were dusty and unwashed.

I knocked on their door, handed Seth a fresh set of boy's clothes from my suitcase, and said, "Yosef." Seth handed the clothes to Yosef, herded him into the bathroom, reached over and turned on the shower, pantomimed what needed to happen here, put a bar of soap in his hand, and withdrew.

A minute later Yosef came dancing out of the bathroom dripping wet and naked.

Seth shooed him back into the bathroom and closed the door. Yosef sprang back into the room, still naked, gleaming wet, and wearing his brand-new boxer shorts on his head. He shouted two of the only English words he knew: "YOU *READY*?"

Seth chased him back into the bathroom and held the door closed until Yosef made himself more presentable while Daniel collapsed in laughter on one of the beds.

The five of us, plus Hailegabriel, walked to a small Italian restaurant for dinner. All three Ethiopian boys now looked clean and sharp, but dining at a European restaurant with white tablecloths, candlelight, menus, and waiters wasn't really within their skill set. Meatballs rolled off their plates. Yosef held the saltshaker upside down to figure it out and gazed with growing admiration at the accumulating crystal hill. A water glass spilled and ice cubes skittered across the wood floor, and the boys dove after them, pursuing them like kittens after a ball. Among the many things they'd never experienced, ice cubes were near the top of the list of the most mysterious.

"Calm down!" I hissed. "Really, you have got to *calm down*. This is a nice restaurant!" The restaurant was full of well-off Ethiopians, Japanese, and Europeans.

Over went another water glass.

"Yosef, I mean it!" I snarled sotto voce.

"Okay, Crotch, I calm down," Yosef said to Seth, beside whom he sat at the foot of the table. He and Daniel thought Seth looked like the six-foot-seven-inch-tall Tottenham Hotspur soccer star Peter Crouch. So they called Seth Crouch. Except they pronounced it "Crotch."

"Well, actually, that's another thing," said Seth. "It's 'Crouch.' As I've mentioned."

"Okay, Crotch!" said Yosef cheerily, rolling the *r*.

"Yosef, do you know what 'crotch' means?" asked Seth.

"What mean?"

This required a conference between Seth and Lee. They hated just to *point*, right there in the nice restaurant. But even working with Hailegabriel, whose English was excellent, they failed to come up with the word.

"Does the word 'scrotum' mean anything to you?" asked Seth.

It did not.

So Lee and Hailegabriel grabbed themselves in the vicinity referred to by Seth's nickname.

Yosef had calmed down for a minute and was trying to eat his spaghetti with a fork, but when he learned what he'd been calling his new big brother, he exploded with mouth-filled laughter, shared the news with Daniel, and the two of them laughed so long and hard they had to push aside their plates and their stranded meatballs and their loose ice cubes and lay their heads on the wet tablecloth and laugh until they cried. I abandoned all attempts at decorum, gestured for the bill, and herded the hysterical boys out of the nice restaurant as quickly as possible.

Later that night Seth said, "These are the two happiest human beings I've ever seen in my life."

39

Their Histories

As often happens in international adoption, Daniel and Yosef's adoption was delayed by every conceivable slowdown. Their facts were clear: both parents were deceased, their uncle was too poor to raise them, and their uncle wished for them to be adopted. Legally, they would be free to go, once all their documents were gathered and signed. But their documents got stranded in cubbyholes and waylaid in in-boxes, birth certificates were misplaced, names were misspelled, and the process slowed to a halt. Seth returned to Oberlin; Lee flew to Israel for Young Judea Year Course, a gap year of work and study; Molly was in San Francisco; the rest of us were in Atlanta; and Daniel and Yosef continued to grow up in Haregewoin's orphanage, their fifth year there.

From afar, I hired a tutor to teach them English. I asked the young man if he'd encourage them to write their autobiographies in Amharic and English and then share them with us. A few weeks later, by e-mail, these stories arrived:

A message from Yosef
I was born at the place called Woliso. It was a rural area. When I was a kid Daniel was a shepherd. Because he was two years older than me. After I grown up I start helping him with looking after the cattles. I had

best friend called Birhanu. He is the only person that I remember. He was a shepherd for his family too. We always look after the cattles together. We go to the field early in the morning. And we came back at the evening. I do remember, the day that I feel sad, the first one was like this: We had two oxen and three cows. I had a great love to them. Mama told me that she is going to sale one of the cows. When I heard that immediately I start crying. I ask her why she does this thing. She told me with dad that they have got a financial problem.

One day Mama asked me why I am crying. I told her that it is because of the cow she sold. Then she remind me not to cry and she promised me that she won't sell any more. She also promised me that she is going to buy sheep for me instead of the cow she sold. Then she did what she said. Finally I stop crying.

The second one is when our father has died. It was like this. One day Dad felt sick. He was on a bed. I was at the field with Birhanu. I was thinking about Dad while playing with Birhanu. Immediately I told to Birhanu look after the cattle and I go home to Dad. Mama asked me why I come back home and to whom I left the cattle. I respond to her that Birhanu is looking after them and I want to see Dad. Then she told me that he is feeling good and she want me to go back there. But I said no. Immediately I go to Dad when I saw him he looks dead. When I talk to him he told me that he is glad and he reminds me to go and stay with Birhanu to look after the cattle. After that I go back. At the evening when I came back in the house there were lots of people crying. I run to Mama and ask her what happens to her. Immediately she told me that Dad has died. I start crying. I felt so Sad. On that day Mama fall on a big stone. She had been hurt badly. Since that day she was not glad. Day to day she became sick. At the end she asked to her brother to take us to Addis Ababa and to take care of us (me and Daniel). She told us that we are going to live with him in Addis but Wogene our elder brother will stay with her because no one will look after her. Finally we came to Addis, at place called Mercato. After staying one week, he heard that our mother has died. Then our uncle try to find an organization which can help us to fulfill our basic needs. At the end, he has got *Waizero* Haregewin.

A message from Daniel
I was born in 1986 Ethiopian Calendar (1994) at the place called Woliso which is out of Addis. Our mother name is Amarech and our father's is

Gizaw. By the time we were born my father had a job our mother was housewife. We had great love to each other. They worried so much about us. We had three animals three of them were cows, two oxen, one calf and a horse but the horse has been eaten by hyena. At that time Yosef was too young. So I use to be a shepherd but when he became four years old he also start to look after the cattle with me. I was six. When I became nine year old I start attending school. Instead Yosef take the whole responsibility about the cattles. I didn't remember any of our neighbors but I used to sing holy songs. Also our mother used to tell us interesting story. We had no sister but we were five brother. Two of them died we remain three: we, Yosef and the third one called Wegene. He is living there in Woliso. Our father has died when I was seven. When we came to Addis I was attending the second semester class by the time I was nine year old. After one week we heard that our mother has died. We stay for one month in our uncle's house after one month we got w/o Haregewin. I had a best friend his name is Birhanu when we were at Woliso. We were so happy at Woliso.

In the fall of 2006 my book about Mrs. Haregewoin Teferra and her foster children, *There Is No Me Without You: One Woman's Odyssey to Rescue Africa's Children*, was published here and in fifteen other countries; my book tour took me to England and Ireland. In the London BBC radio studio, I was interviewed, and then the producer asked if I'd like to step into the sound booth to hear an interview recorded a few weeks earlier in Addis Ababa by a BBC reporter who'd visited Mrs. Haregewoin to gather her words and ambient sounds for the story.

I sat transfixed in the high-tech chamber, its thick glass window opening only into another dimly lit room. Red and green lights blinked on the polished black soundboards as the studio filled with the voices of faraway people I knew. A door opened, and then Haregewoin whispered to the reporter, "Here are the very, very small ones." I could picture the nursery and the sleeping terry-cloth-clad babies snoozing in the rows of cribs.

"How do you feel about foreign adoption?" the Englishwoman asked Haregewoin after they stepped outside. (Madonna and her controversial adoption of a Malawian toddler was the top story in the British press that month.)

"Very sad. I feel very sad for them to leave," Haregewoin said.

"Will the children still be Ethiopian if they grow up in foreign countries?" asked the reporter.

"No, they will not. They will become like the people of that country. They will not be Ethiopian."

"Would it be better then for the children to stay here?" the reporter asked.

"No. Look around." Haregewoin sighed bitterly. "What can I give them here? No, they are too many. They must go. No one person in Ethiopia will adopt them. We are a poor country and we have too, too many orphaned children. Look at them. They need parents."

Now the BBC reporter and Haregewoin moved to a different scene. They stood on the sidelines of a soccer game. The shouts of children rocketed across the field. I knew this rocky, muddy soccer field very well. I gleaned quickly that this was a game in the still-thriving orphanage league organized by Lee earlier that year.

Wind hit the microphone and there were muffled voices before it appeared that two boys were being waved off the field. This was a surprise that had been prepared for me. Extra BBC staffers entered the studio to listen. "She is going to hear her own children!" they whispered to each other.

Two boys jogged over to be introduced to the reporter by Haregewoin. They had been pulled out of the thick of play and were huffing for breath. It was Yosef and Daniel.

"Do you feel happy about going to America?" the BBC reporter asked them.

Haregewoin translated the question for them.

The boys replied, *"Ow, ow."* (Yes, yes.)

"Why do you feel happy?"

The question was translated. Daniel replied, and Haregewoin translated: "Now we live in an orphanage. That is rather a sad thing for us. In America we will have a family."

Everyone in the BBC studio in London looked at me.

The entire world suddenly felt about the size of three city blocks. Down the street stood my Atlanta house; here was BBC's global broadcast studio in London; and just over there, just around the corner, were two handsome boys, panting and sweaty and happy, who were going to be my sons. Unconsciously I had rolled my chair closer to the speakers, from which the boys' voices called *"Ciao!"* to the reporter as they jogged back to the field. I was like Tsehai squinting through a camera lens to see all the way to America. The boys were right there, just on the other side of the soundboard; but their adoption was delayed; we could not bring them home.

40

Homeland Tour

We approached the one-year anniversary of the day I sat in the van out-side the orphanage with Daniel and Yosef trying to explain that our fam-ily was Jewish while they bowed their heads and covered my hands with kisses and murmurs of *Ishi, Ishi,* it's fine, it's fine. The Great Recession hadn't yet descended on America; there's no other explanation for the fact that Donny and I bought round-trip plane tickets to and from Addis Ababa for ourselves and for everyone in the family who was free to travel—Lily, Sol, Jesse, and Helen from Atlanta, and Lee from Israel—to spend spring break with the waylaid brothers. I feared that Daniel and Yosef no longer believed we were coming for them and that the children at home had lost sight of the fact that our family was still growing. For Helen and Sol it would be a homeland tour. So we packed for a vacation with Daniel and Yosef, though they would not be legally free to return to Atlanta with us at its conclusion.

With the help of their English tutor, the boys e-mailed a letter to us:

Dear our family how are you I am too glad.
  How is everyone. We have been so excited hearing that you
  Would come sooner to
  Visit us.

we hope that it will be a great visit
here with us.
Your lovely kids
      Yosef   Daniel

Helen, ten, was in the spring of her marvelous fourth-grade year. She held schoolwide elective office and had taken the gold medal in the Fun Run and the blue ribbon in the science fair. She was a flutist, a jazz dance student, and a soccer player. She could read and understand Amharic (though she'd grown too shy to reply aloud to Ethiopian American adults), and our Ethiopian babysitter, Azeb, prepared traditional foods every day for her. Spring break in Ethiopia, Helen hoped, would refresh her Amharic and give her limitless access to Ethiopian food. She also looked forward to shopping.

"Addis is not exactly a shopping mecca," I warned my stylish daughter. "There's no Target in Addis. There's no Limited Too."

But she reminded me that on the day we'd met, I'd taken her shopping. In dusty overalls and outsized rubber flip-flops, she had stepped into a clothing boutique and, within the hour, had been transformed into an upper-middle-class child in red plastic sandals, lacy white socks, and a blue wool dress dotted with fluffy sheep. If there were no Gap or Target, she was more than willing to shop *there* again.

Sol, thirteen, was excitedly preparing, too. The distance from Addis Ababa to his Atlanta life was the distance between the past and the present. It seemed inconceivable that a plane ticket could bridge the gap, but here he was packing as if it were really true, as if he *could* travel back in time. Remembering the ill-fated wedding cake, I asked him, "Shall we take a present to your grandmother?" He looked up and said "Yes!" with great warmth. What do you buy for a person who has *nothing*? I wandered the aisles of Burlington Coat Factory. A down jacket? Not a popular item in sub-Saharan Africa. Curtains? Her mud hut had one carved-out hole and a piece of corrugated metal as a shutter. African wooden sculptures? Available locally. Blender? No electricity. Bedding? I recalled that Tsehai's bed was made of a dry dirt mixture (mud, cow manure, and straw). She covered it with newspapers. A soft queen-sized bedspread might be a welcome addition on chilly mountain nights. I brought a big, thick velour bedspread made of brightly colored squares, and matching bolsters. The rich feel and bright colors and large size pleased Sol greatly. He even liked the zippered see-through plastic packaging. He unpacked most of his suitcase to make room for it.

I flew over a week ahead of the family to do some reporting; Lee flew over early, too, and stayed at Big Atetegeb. Then we, with Yosef and Daniel, checked into the Hilton Hotel the night before the family was due to arrive.

The boys were ecstatic to be with Lee and me, and to be staying in the most luxurious and elegant place they'd ever seen, and to know they'd meet their new family the next day. I don't know if they slept at all. Lee and I were awakened at 5:00 a.m. by a commotion in the bathroom. We groggily opened the bathroom door to discover the shower blasting hot water, the tub sloshing over, water pouring into the sink, the sunlamp beaming, the overhead fan rattling, and the hair dryer—dangling from its cord—emitting gales of hot air. The brothers were wet, bright-eyed, and stark naked. I withdrew while Lee dove into the steam, helped them knot towels around their waists, and turned off faucets. I returned to discover they'd opened my cosmetic bag and experimented with every item, from dental floss to contact lens supplies. In Lee's shaving kit they'd discovered an electric shaver and plugged it in. Fortunately, they hadn't electrocuted themselves, but each had mowed a short, baldish track in his hair. Lee and I mopped up the standing water and tried to calm down the anxious, eager fellows who smelled vibrantly of peach skin lotion, Old Spice aftershave, powder-fresh deodorant, honeysuckle shampoo, and mint toothpaste. They desperately hoped to make an excellent impression on their new family.

Selamneh's friend Ketema came to the hotel to pick us up. As the boys' fragrances preceded them into the van, Ketema raised his eyebrows in a smiling question but refrained from saying anything other than "Very nice boys." At the airport, we joined the crowd in front of a glass barrier at baggage claim. Daniel asked Ketema for coins; as recent arrivals poured into the lobby, he ran to buy two bouquets of flowers for the new sisters. We saw Helen first. She wheeled her pink-flowered black suitcase, her headphones were draped around her neck, and she was chatting with an Ethiopian woman from the airplane. Someone had already given Helen the traditional flower bouquet that is offered to returning Ethiopians. When Yosef ran to shyly present his flowers to Lily, her eyes darkened to instant compassion and tenderness.

Daniel, overwhelmed with the greatness and importance of the moment, thrust his flowers at Donny. As we exited the airport, the tall, shy boy wheeled Helen's suitcase and impulsively took Donny's hand; they walked hand in hand through the parking lot, an unusual position for Donny to be in, but one he enjoyed.

We descended by van into the tumultuous city. At the first red light, a hungry man suddenly appeared at Helen and Lily's window. His face loomed close, and then he pressed a congenitally disfigured bent-back arm, sprinkled with dislocated fingertips and fingernails, against the glass. Helen screamed and fell backward against Lily. She covered her eyes and couldn't look. Lily, looking to me for guidance, shakily guided a worn white paper birr (11 cents) through the window. The man grabbed it and leered his thanks with yellow and missing teeth. At the next intersection, street children mobbed the van, reached up high, and tapped on our windows. Some tried to sell us packets of tissue, one birr apiece. "'Allo! Tissue!" called the young voices. "'Allo! Soft!" A tall boy leaned close to the glass and said, "Stomach   hurt."

"Give! Mommy, give!" cried Helen, ransacking her backpack in search of money. "I don't like this! They scare me."

Although my chief concern about this trip was the children's face-to-face confrontation with the worst poverty on earth, I failed to prepare them for it. "There's no Limited Too" had been the closest I got to trying to remind Helen of what she knew of Addis Ababa from earliest childhood. I wanted her to feel proud of Ethiopia for its magnificent culture and history and literature, its wealth of languages and diversity of peoples, so I'd kind of skimped on details of violent modern regimes, and I'd failed to mention the country's global ranking at the bottom of every socioeconomic ladder.

Had five years of happy American family life in a treelined upper-middle-class Atlanta neighborhood displaced Helen's memories of bitter and life-eroding poverty?

They had.

"I don't remember this," she murmured, gazing in awe through the van windows at the dusty throngs. "I don't feel like I came from here."

The failure of Ethiopia's economy, health care, and education was everywhere on display. Lily and Helen sat beside me; in the row behind us, Jesse leaned against Sol/Fisseha. Yosef and Daniel were in the back, and Donny sat up front with Ketema. We all gazed through the smudged windows at the panorama of suffering. Unemployed, sick, handicapped, congenitally disfigured, blind, leprous, tubercular, AIDS-infected people limped or crawled down the sidewalks or stood on the median strips or stretched out defeated in the gutters. Indigent children dashed into the heavy traffic. Two-thirds of school-age children were not in school in this country, and more than a million children had been orphaned by HIV/AIDS. There was great beauty in this hilltop city perfumed by eucalyptus trees. There was history here so ancient it reached beyond biblical epochs to touch the dawn of human life. There was evidence of financial wealth and of education: professionals steering Mercedes with tinted windows, marble mansions with satellite dishes, law schools and medical schools, bookstores and art galleries, folklorists and poets, economists and dissidents.

But at eye level, for tenderhearted children, there were people begging for help, including homeless, ragged, and ravenous children.

Helen and Lily rooted in their backpacks and found a bag of bite-sized Milky Ways. When the van stopped again, blocked by a herd of raggedy sheep, a barefoot boy approached. Helen gingerly served him a gold-wrapped candy through the narrow open space at the top of her window. He examined it suspiciously, peeled it open, sniffed it, popped it into his mouth, and looked up with a happy smile. He held out his hand for another one. "For brother!" he called through the glass. The herd of sheep departed the roadway and the van accelerated. "His brother!" cried Helen. "He needs a candy for his brother!" But we were already jerking and honking our way down the street. She burst into tears. "Please, please, go back!" she begged Ketema. "Let me out, I'll run back, please!" But there was no turning around. She fell into Lily's arms, crying.

A few minutes later she raised her face to ask, "What *makes* a country rich or poor?"

Feeling unequal to the task of outlining global injustice and autocracy, I tried to draw her attention to occasional bursts of progress—the sudden office tower rising above the hovels, the unfinished glass-and-neon shopping strip half buried in the dust of construction. "I know, I see it," Helen said, "but did that beggar have eight fingers on his hand? Was he born like that?"

41

Class Differences

Our American children were relieved to enter the leafy grounds of the Hilton Hotel and to stroll across the elegant lobby wheeling their luggage. Helen attracted attention from the hotel staff: she was obviously a stylish and confident American girl, and yet she was also, obviously, a beautiful Ethiopian girl. Few adopted Ethiopian children had returned from the West to Addis. For the desk clerks attempting to converse with her, Helen seemed a sparkly and happy result of an intriguing social experiment. She was the "after" picture; previously they'd only seen the "before." Pretty Lily, in tight jeans, tossing long brown curls, drew their gaze, too, and when the two girls entwined their arms and whispered and laughed together or one took a moment to adjust the other one's earring, everyone marveled again: obviously not sisters and yet obviously . . . sisters.

We seated ourselves at a long table on the outside patio for lunch. In the canopy of leaves overhead, colorful birds whistled; children splashed in the swimming pool nearby. "Can we swim after lunch?" asked Fisseha. "We're going to the orphanage then, but we'll swim tonight," I said. As our kids relaxed, browsed the menus, ordered Cokes, wondered whether the hamburger came with french fries, asked for catsup, and blew spitballs while waiting for their lunch platters, Yosef and Daniel dropped into a painfully shy silence, unsure what they were even allowed to touch or to ask, incapable of participating in our American banter. "Talk to them in Amharic," Donny urged Fisseha, but Fisseha felt shy about his rusty Amharic. Yosef appeared at my side and whispered, "Stomach hurt." I led him from the table and sought help from the patio hostess. She spoke to him in Amharic and took us to the office of the hotel doctor in a small office next door to the weight room.

"You are staying here?" the doctor asked, perusing Yosef skeptically. "The food here is too rich for him. He is fine, but he is not accustom." He gave Yosef antacid tablets and we returned to our table. Yosef looked chastened and scared. The class difference among our children was at no time greater than at that lunch on the patio of the Addis Hilton.

First meal together at the Addis Ababa Hilton. Left to right: Daniel, Lee, Fisseha, Jesse, Yosef

The question of who felt at home in which venue was answered differently after lunch, when we traveled by van across the city to Big Atetegeb. The orphans welcomed us all excitedly while Yosef and Daniel melted away to rejoin their friends. Lily, Fisseha, Jesse, and Helen were mobbed by children. Toddlers in need of being carried—who, since the deaths of their parents, had not been held enough—lifted up their arms in inchoate longing. Helen hoisted a two-year-old boy named Binyam, who had a close-shaved head and wore a pink jacket; he wrapped his legs around her waist and his arms around her neck and claimed her. He kicked out at other children who approached. From that moment on, Helen belonged to Binyam.

The older girls—about eight to thirteen years of age—surrounded Helen with curiosity. They devoured her with their eyes, familiarly examined her wristwatch and earrings, and then led her, with Binyam, to their dorm room, where they drew her into a circle on the floor. "I don't really understand what you're saying," she protested in English, but they didn't believe her. They held up her purse, and when she nodded, they dumped it out and plunged their hands through the treasures. They held up a few stray nickels and dimes. They looked through her pocket camera. They borrowed her hairbrush and used it. They applied her lip gloss. When they tried tickling her, she collapsed in giggles and tickled them back, and then they braided her hair.

Outside on the courtyard, Jesse made the acquaintance of a yellow, long-feathered chicken. Always good with animals, he seemed to sense the wandering chicken's disorientation (the chicken had just been acquired for the upcoming Sunday dinner). Jesse sat cross-legged on the ground, brought the chicken into his lap, and soothed it. A passing boy stopped, looked, kicked the chicken in the side, and walked off. "Hey, watch out!" yelled Jesse, cradling the chicken.

Haregewoin, watching Jesse from her porch, nearly split her side laughing; she had to sit down. In all the years I knew Haregewoin, this was the hardest I ever saw her laugh, watching Jesse with that chicken. The notion of a boy bonding with a food product undid her! She crossed the courtyard to him. "You like this?"

"Yes," he said tenderly, smoothing the chicken's head.

"You may have it!" she announced.

"Really?" he cried. "Really? Mommy, can I?"

"If you're asking if we're bringing this chicken home to Atlanta, the answer would be no," I said.

"But can we at least bring her to the *hotel*?"

"Jess, no, sorry."

Haregewoin staggered back to the steps and sat on the top one to jiggle with laughter and wipe her eyes with the tip of her apron. "Let him take it! It is his!" she called, flinging out both arms. Vexation was a frequent emotion for Haregewoin, as was worry; severity was her mode; it was rare that she got to make a joke. "Where is your chicken?" she would ask Jesse every day during our visit, until we reached the hour for Sunday dinner, at which point she realized it would be kindest to abandon the gag.

———

Helen came to me with the girls' shopping list. "They each need a bottle of shampoo and a bottle of conditioner. And a watch. And a purse. But what they need right away is Crocs. Like mine!" They'd taken turns skipping about the room in Helen's green Crocs.

I knew they needed shoes. Their desire for Crocs was an easy one to answer, as there were street merchants everywhere offering Croc knock-offs from China for a dollar a pair. I asked Haregewoin's permission for Lee and Lily to lead an outing to a nearby shoe kiosk. Normally she would have disapproved of a request like this—such extravagance! Such spoiling of the children! But she felt particularly honored to have Donny as a guest, and she was always delighted to have Lee, whom she loved and for whom she broke the rules, and it couldn't be denied that the children needed shoes, so she gave Lee and Lily her blessing and I gave Lee the money.

Lee led the way, and Lily took up the rear, holding the hands of two little boys. Helen's new friends angrily shouldered each other aside in their attempts to be the ones closest to her, and out they all went. It was a dazzling moment for fourteen-year-old Lily, to be trusted to take the children down the road. The brightness of the East African day, and the sweet children, and the racks of colorful shoes, and how it felt to match a longing child with his or her first-ever new pair of shoes—to kneel and measure, to help a child try on a pair, to swap that pair for a smaller or larger size, to lean back and nod to a child that this was the right fit (because how would he know what it meant to have shoes that fit?)—was confusing, daunting, and exhilarating. The children hugged and thanked her again and again, then all marched back to the orphanage with colorful rubberized feet.

Daniel and Yosef quietly returned with us to the hotel in the late afternoon. They alone were silent during the van ride, and silent again during dinner at a Chinese restaurant near the Hilton. Lee and two friends from Year Course—Sam Schiff and David Nagel—moved into one room; Lily and Helen into another; Donny and I into a third; and the four younger boys into a fourth. Jesse and Fisseha threw clothes around the room, turned on the TV loudly, and wrestled, but Yosef and Daniel sat primly side by side on a bed, their hands in their laps. The next morning I said to Lee, "I feel bad for Daniel and Yosef; they seem petrified, don't you think?"

"WHAT? No way! They were wild last night! We had pillow fights, wrestling matches, group showers. They ran back and forth visiting my room and the girls' room. They're having a *blast*." I realized then that Yosef and Daniel maintained their public decorum in deference to Donny, in their mistaken fear that he wouldn't accept them.

42

Swim Party

We organized a field trip. Cramming thirty children into two vans, we brought the oldest children from Haregewoin's two houses to the Hilton Hotel for a swim party. As I paid the prearranged entrance fee, the boys trotted behind Lee to the locker room, quickly changed out of shorts into swimsuits, and ran to the warm, shallow water. Girls are more complicated creatures. I got trapped for forty-five minutes in the steamy locker room trying to get twenty girls outfitted in swimwear. I knelt on the tile floor to root through the duffle bag of used and donated clothing I'd brought from home. The biggest girls pushed me aside and began grabbing and tugging within the duffle bag like Cinderella's greedy stepsisters. Everyone was unhappy. "Melissa [May-leese-ah]," said the older girls reproachfully, showing me that a two-piece top didn't match the bottom, or that the bust was too baggy. Just because they were destitute AIDS orphans didn't mean they were without all fashion sense! Lily and Helen helped them to piece outfits together, relying on sports bras and flowery underpants to complete a few bathing ensembles. Reluctant, distrustful, the girls modeled for one another and then posed, hands on hips, angling their faces, in front of the bathroom's floor-length mirror. They pursed their lips, sucked in their figures, turned this way and that, and asked one another, Lily, and Helen for compliments and reassurances before they were willing to toss their braids, square their shoulders, and saunter to the pool.

A scrawny six-year-old boy with a recently shaved head waited patiently for my attention. I knew he was HIV-positive—he'd come from Little Atetegeb. He was skinny and barefoot, and his face was disfigured by outbursts of wartlike molloscum, a viral skin infection that can savagely colonize the face of a person with HIV/AIDS. I shooed the scrawny little fellow repeatedly out the door toward the boy's locker room. "Lee! Donny! Help this kid!" I yelled. But the child slipped away from them every time and reappeared beyond the circle of girls, last in line again, waiting for a turn with me.

"What?" I asked him. "Go swim!"

He gestured hopefully toward the duffle bag.

"These are for *girls*," I said in English to the non-English-speaking child.

He inched closer to look into the duffle bag himself. He looked crestfallen at its emptiness and raised huge, sad eyes to me.

"Oh my God," I said to the bald child. "You are a girl. *Simish man naw?* [What is your name?]"

"May-leese-ah!" she said reproachfully, for how could I not remember her name when I'd known her for years? "Feven."

"*Nay, Feven* [Come, Feven]," I said. I hadn't recognized her. I looped my arms around her waist and we peered deep into the empty duffle bag together.

No swimsuits remained.

She looked as if she was about to cry. I'd have ripped off my own swimsuit and given it to her if there were any chance of it fitting. "*Koi, koi* [Wait, wait]," I said. I ran to find the cleaning lady to learn if there was a lost-and-found here, from which I could borrow a girl's swimsuit. There was not. I asked the few other women in the locker room—Ethiopian and European—whether anyone had a spare girl's swimsuit. No one did. Nor did they seem pleased with our field trip. Feven watched me with plummeting hopes, her special day spoiled. I dug into the mountain of sweaty clothes abandoned by the older girls, found a pair of white soccer shorts, and offered them to her. Success! She dropped her overalls and pulled on the shorts. Digging deeper through our discard pile, I found someone's white cotton camisole with spaghetti straps. I slipped it over Feven's bony torso and tied the straps together in back.

"*Gonjo!* [Pretty!]," I said. I pulled her over to the mirror to look. She covered her face with her hands, not wanting to see the red and white nodules encroaching on her mouth and eyes. But she peeked out through her fingers at the cami and then turned to me with a huge, excited smile. She scampered off to the pool happily. All afternoon she called my name and waved to me from the water or from the lawn. She was a feminine little girl, and I had made her feel pretty.

When we returned with the children to the orphanage, Binyam—who'd been too small to go on the pool outing—screamed Helen's name. He squatted down and made his fierce smile. When she picked him up, he laid his head on her shoulder. He was solid and heavy; she sat on the steps, and he fell asleep in the sunshine, cradled in her arms. She kissed his warm head. "We have to adopt him," she said.

"You know we can't, sweetheart."

"Please, Mommy, please. Please. I'm not kidding." Her voice was flat, intense.

"We're already adopting Daniel and Yosef; that will give us nine children."

"Mommy, Binyam needs me."

Lamely I offered, "I hope someday you and your husband will come back to Ethiopia to adopt."

"No! Binyam will be too old then. I can't leave him, Mommy."

"Sweetheart, he's *two*. I'm too old to be the mother of a two-year-old."

"You're not, Mommy. You have lots of energy! I'll help you! I'll do all the work!"

Binyam woke up and seemed to follow our conversation. Putting in his vote, he snuggled even closer to Helen, then looked up at her with adoring eyes.

Outside the orphanage, Helen soaked up Ethiopia. We visited her old orphanage, which was also Fisseha's; teachers remembered them, and marveled over how they'd grown. In public, at restaurants or shops, Helen lowered her eyes and smiled at the many compliments from strangers. She feasted on the spicy stews; she swayed and clapped at a dance performance; and she tore up the field in orphanage soccer games—nothing white-bread American about *those* skills. She still wanted to shop, but not for herself: she wanted to shop for the girls at Atetegeb, and for Binyam. And she struggled toward a new concept for her future—maybe not a gymnast or a fashion designer after all. Was it possible, she wondered, to create a beautiful place for all the homeless people to live? With clean bedrooms and beautiful paintings and free doctors and wonderful teachers?

As we crossed the city in the van, Helen sat up straight and alert. She held birr notes in one hand, candy in the other. If, at a red light, destitute adults and children didn't jog toward us at the sight of white faces among the passengers, Helen tapped on the glass to catch their attention, unusual behavior for a tourist.

Squeezing our way through the stalls in the vast open-air Mercato one day, Helen asked, "Why is everyone staring at me?"

"If I may reply in my role as a white foreigner in sunglasses, they're staring at *you* because you're holding *my* hand."

"Oh!" she cried. She released my hand, skipped ahead, and blended into the market crowd. With a giggling voice, she called over her shoulder, "No offense, Mommy!"

43

Reunion

The great day arrived for our surprise visit to Tsehai the Chickenless.

All visits to Tsehai were surprise visits because no mail service, electricity, or phone lines reached her community. Eleven of us—Donny, Fisseha, Lee, Lee's friends Sam and David, Lily, Helen, Jesse, Yosef, Daniel, and I—stuffed ourselves into the beaten-up minibus with ripped seats rented by Selamneh. We rode into the eastern outskirts of the city, past new construction projects, modern condominiums, truck stops, fields of goats, and a brick factory. Tsehai lived in a rustic village of squatters in the foothills of the Entoto Mountains. To find the hidden community, we parked on the shoulder of a country road, clambered over a stone wall, and hiked up a mud path through a steep cow pasture, steering clear of the grazing cattle.

At the top of the slanting field we climbed over a fence made of hand-turned wooden posts and rough twine, and we stepped down onto the main mud path leading into the community. Rough fences separated one dwelling place from the next; the greenery through which we hiked was high and coarse.

We walked up the path single and double file, and reached Tsehai's compound. Molly and I had been here before, as had Lee with Seth, but it was new for everyone else. We called Tsehai's name, but she wasn't

home. We let ourselves into her yard. I'd brought a plastic bag of bananas and a paper sack of bakery rolls, and I set them on a wood stool
outside her door. Tsehai's house (built with our contributions) had a tin
roof above thick mud-and-straw walls. It was a duplex: two side-by-side
rooms, two front doors. The right side, where Tsehai lived, was painted
white; the left side—where her son Birhanu and his wife and baby lived—
was the natural mud color. Two uneven corrugated metal doors had
been painted bright blue. Two skinny branches held up a tin canopy. A
latrine made of vertical branches stood across the yard. There was an
outdoor fire ring and an indoor brazier. There was no electricity or
plumbing. The family walked to a communal pump for water and carried it home in plastic jugs.

Suddenly there was the sound of a tiny, ebullient little lady trumpeting and skipping down the path. I stepped into the lane and received the
initial barrage of chortles and tears as she rained down blessings on my
head and kissed this cheek and that one, and this cheek and that one,
back and forth many more times than is traditional. Before I could prepare her for the rest of the surprise, ten more visitors emerged from the
compound. Yelling, shouting, and praying, clapping her hands together
and clapping her hands against her cheeks, Tsehai ran from person to
person, blessing and kissing. The mud lane filled with her neighbors.
Tsehai herded all of us back into her uneven, rocky mud yard. I noted
that her reception of Fisseha seemed identical to her embrace of everyone else. I'd expected something like a nuclear detonation when she beheld her grandson, but it seemed that the specific joy of her reunion
with him was engulfed by her exultation in having so many important
visitors from afar. "That was actually a milder reunion than I'd expected
with Fisseha," I mentioned to Lee, and he'd had the same thought, but
then we both laughed at the notion that this testifying, screeching, tap-
dancing performance was "mild."

I liked it here, high on the hillside; the air was fresh and clean and
fragrant; wildflowers grew in the woods, and donkeys meandered unac-
companied down the mud lane outside the gate. *Fisseha can visit here in
the summers, herd goats, and sleep under the stars,* I thought. *It will be
like Heidi, visiting Grandfather. Maybe Jesse can come, too.*

No matter how humble the hut or *tukul* I visited in this country, the
homeowner dashed ahead to tidy up, apologizing for the mess, just as I
did at home. Crumbs needed to be swept from the rough-hewn table onto

the dirt floor; the thin blanket over the plywood or mud bed had to be smoothed. Tsehai shooed us away from her door to give her a chance to straighten up. A male relative entered the compound carrying a long plank bench in his arms; he ducked into the little house with it. Then they called us inside. It was dark in the interior. We squished together, the kids in two rows on Tsehai's bed, the rest of us on the plank bench. As if we'd come here specifically for lunch, Tsehai commenced to feed us. She quickly cut up the bananas and bread into bite-sized pieces and passed them around on a plastic plate. Then, though we protested and said we weren't hungry, she squatted above the brazier on the floor to heat up a cast-iron pot of *shiro* (chickpea mash). She poured it over a platter of *injera* and shouted at us that we must eat and not be shy. The sauce was so spicy that everyone other than the Ethiopian children began to cry.

Fisseha had squeezed in among the boys on the back row of the bed, leaning against the mud-and-straw wall. With a contented smile he watched his grandmother's bossy comings-and-goings, barking and clanging. Suddenly Tsehai grew attentive—a familiar word had flown by her ear in the midst of the incomprehensible streams of English passing among us. "Fisseha?" she repeated. Had someone said the name Fisseha? "Fisseha?" she asked again. She stopped banging and serving; she carefully scanned the crowd in her hot, dark interior. "Fisseha?"

She looked into the face of each of us, one by one, and then elbowed across the bed to squint into the face of the last candidate. "FISSEHA???" she cried. She attacked the boy with arms, palms, prayers, shouts, and tears; she yanked him to his feet and pulled him outside into the bright sun so she could look at him more closely and be sure. She threw up her arms. It was Fisseha! She hadn't recognized him! He had grown tall! He had a young man's handsome face. His long hair was rounded into a smooth Afro. He wore a Brazil soccer jersey and Nike running shoes. She'd greeted him as part of this tall, bewildering, thrilling group of rich foreigners without seeing that it was her beloved grandson.

"Fisseha, Fisseha," she wept. The rest of us squeezed out the door to witness their reunion. Like a honeybee she buzzed from him to each one of us, kissing and thanking. Then she zipped back to Fisseha to pat him all over his face. She couldn't believe it! She hadn't known that God would permit her to reach this day, that God would shower her with such blessings. Fisseha wore a sweet, sleepy half smile as she clamored all over him, but tears brightened his eyes when she held him close. Then Tsehai shouted not to God but over the fences and hedges and stalks to her neighbors and relatives to hear the news: Fisseha had returned to Ethiopia! People came running down the dirt lane and dashed into the yard. We met Tsehai's adult son Birhanu and his round-faced, pretty freckled wife, and Fisseha's half brothers and half uncles, and Fisseha's full biological sister, Haptom, sixteen, whom we knew and whom we helped to attend school. Runners were dispatched to spread the word and bring more people. A little boy was taken out of school. He showed up looking very handsome with a buzz haircut, wearing a school uniform, a blue button-down shirt and blue shorts. His name was also Fisseha. He was our Fisseha's half nephew. He came and shook big Fisseha's hand.

We unzipped the duffle bag full of gifts we'd brought for the family. Fisseha presented to Tsehai the bright queen-sized fuzzy comforter and bolsters from Burlington Coat Factory. Lily and Helen assumed the task of making and fluffing up Tsehai's mud bed for her while she marveled at miracle upon miracle and called out for God to come see for Himself what a lucky and happy woman she was.

44

A Family Feast

Two days later Selamneh drove Lee, Fisseha, and Jesse back to the hillside community to see Tsehai. She had promised to braid a twine bullwhip for Jesse if he came back. He wanted to go anyway. Jesse was not in contact with anyone from his birth family, and he was thrilled to be included in the general enthusiasm by Fisseha's grandmother (as he basked in the love of his two American grandmothers).

I was out and about in the city with Donny, Lily, and Helen, escorted by Ketema. We were deep in a basket shop, selecting gifts, when Ketema's cell phone rang. It was Lee, calling for me from Tsehai's house.

"Hi, sweetie."

"His mom is here."

"Whose mom?"

"Fisseha's. His mother is here."

"WHAT? No. That can't be; she's not alive."

"Well . . . she's here."

"This can't be true. We were told that both his parents were dead. Even Tsehai told me his mother had died."

"The minute we walked into Tsehai's house, Fisseha said, 'That's my mom.'"

"Is he . . . well, how is he? Upset? Excited?"

"Not much of a reaction. I think it's been eight or nine years since he last saw her."

My hands began to shake, and my legs began to shake, and I think my heart began to shake, so I kind of tossed the phone to Donny before dropping it.

I was familiar with this situation in *other* families. I always reassured adoptive parents who e-mailed or phoned me in panic upon receipt of the news that their child had a living birth mother or father in Ethiopia. "*Most* adoptive children in the world have one or two living birth parents," I told these parents. "Think about domestic American adoptions of newborns, or of foster care kids. Those children aren't 'true orphans,' with both parents deceased. It's as old as humankind for birth parents to find better situations if they can't raise their children."

Those were the things I said, to other people.

Now, to Donny, I said, "What do we *do*???"

"Let's go meet her."

"What do we say? What should we take? We should take her a present! What should we buy?" Now my brain was shaking along with the rest of my body.

Ketema's phone rang again. He handed it to me. It was Lee.

"Wait, let me guess: his *father's* there."

"No, his father is dead."

"What, then?"

"He has a little sister. She's ten."

"Oh my God. How *is* he? How's Fisseha?"

"Oh, he's fine. Jesse's a mess."

"What's wrong with Jesse?"

"He's so happy for Fisseha he can't stop crying."

With shaking hands I chose a dress for my son's mother from a nearby dress shop, and a purse and some hair ribbons for my son's little sister. Selamneh and Ketema conferred by phone and agreed that we should all meet for lunch at an open-air restaurant and banquet hall halfway between the city and Tsehai's village. We swung by Atetegeb to pick up Yosef and Daniel. As we jolted over the roads, I held the tissue-wrapped gifts in my lap. What if his mother wanted him back? What if Tsehai had made a mistake in taking him to the orphanage and none of this was meant to happen? What if he wanted to return to his village with his mother and sister and pick up the threads of his former life?

A big crowd waited for us on the gravel parking lot of the restaurant. It had rained hard that morning, but the dark clouds were receding now, revealing a pale blue undercoat. On a brick courtyard beside the restaurant, potted trees encircled wet tables; rain had fallen on stacks of stored folding chairs, too. I spotted Selamneh, Fisseha, Jesse, Tsehai and her son Birhanu, other half brothers and sisters-in-law and sisters of Fisseha . . . and a small-faced, dark-skinned woman wearing a flowered dress and a traditional cotton shawl. Her hair was concealed by a knotted blue kerchief. As we got out of the van, this slight woman hurried toward me and threw herself onto the gravel to kiss my feet! It was just like my first meeting with Tsehai!

"No, please, no, no," I said, helping her up. We shook hands and kissed on each cheek, and again on each cheek, and across her face traveled waves of shyness, incredulity, and happiness. Her name was Waganesh. She barely reached my shoulder. The youngest of her three children (the older two were Haptom and Fisseha) was a little girl named Azmara, who shook my hand politely. Azmara, like Haptom, wore a blue crucifix tattoo in the middle of her forehead. Donny introduced himself, supporting Waganesh by the elbow lest the diminutive woman throw herself upon his feet, too. Jesse ran to me and said, "That's Fisseha's *mother*!!!"

Fisseha's half brothers, mustachioed uncles, whatever they were—the rest of the clan—greeted all of us with many handshakes and bows. We were escorted to the outdoor patio, which was being opened and prepared for our group of twenty-five. Waiters pushed tables together and dabbed them dry and snapped open the chairs and distributed menus. I saw that half our number was fasting for Lent and the other half for Passover. The vegan "fasting menu" worked for all. As we found seats, Selamneh explained to Donny and me how this had come about: two days earlier, after we departed from Tsehai's house, she visited the only person in her community who owned a cell phone and she purchased a phone call. Tsehai's neighbor called the only man with a cell phone living in the village of Fisseha's birth in southwest Ethiopia; the neighbor asked that man to relay to Waganesh the news that her son Fisseha had returned to the country.

Waganesh had never left the village before. She'd never ridden a bus or visited the capital. She'd barely ever used currency. She and Azmara walked for three hours to reach a paved road, squatted most of a day on the shoulder of the road, waiting for a bus, rode the bus for ten hours, and arrived in Addis Ababa this morning. The moods crisscrossing her face must have included the fact that she'd never before seen a modern metropolis, ridden in a bus or a van, eaten in a restaurant, or met white people.

Tsehai was not Waganesh's mother or mother-in-law . . . it was complicated. Still, Tsehai called Waganesh "my daughter" and Waganesh addressed Tsehai as "my mother." As we waited for platters and baskets of food to arrive, Fisseha remained serene. He wore a multicolored Zimbabwe soccer jacket, with a digital camera on a strap around his neck. He stood at one end of the porch while the middle generation of his relatives—people in their twenties and thirties—milled about him. With his cool half smile, he leaned against a porch railing and fielded questions. His Amharic came back rapidly.

Lily said, "Look at Fisseha. He's a rock star."

Our banquet was long and merry. Azmara wore her new purse hanging from her shoulder, and occasionally she stroked the strap and looked up at me with a smile. The tattooed crucifix on her forehead gleamed in turquoise ink. I found myself thinking, *Please do not offer us this girl to adopt, because what would I do with a child with a crucifix on her forehead? This would be a worse issue than someone's* butt *not being Jewish.*

With Selamneh and Ketema translating, sensing an eagerness around the table for this sort of thing, I told the assembled relatives stories about Fisseha in America. I told them what a good and polite student he was, and they made the *tseh-tseh* sound that is made by unsticking the tongue from the roof of the mouth, signifying pride and pleasure, or regret and empathy, in reaction to a bit of news. We told about the bullwhips he wove and snapped, amazing all his friends; and the Ethiopian men at the table all laughed, since this was the most basic of an Ethiopian country boy's skills.

"Are any of you athletes? Are there athletes in the family?" I asked. "Because Fisseha is an incredible athlete." This, when translated, prompted even more laughter. Tsehai's son Birhanu replied in Amharic, and Selamneh translated: "It is that the life of a country boy is very hard and makes his muscles very strong and his legs very fast."

Everyone laughed to hear that Fisseha built little wood huts in our backyard, as he had enjoyed doing that since early childhood. Mostly they loved hearing that an Ethiopian boy could land on America's shores with such success, that *their* boy was so widely admired and loved.

I told them about a recent meeting I'd had (at Shamrock Middle School) with Fisseha's teachers. One teacher complained about a very unruly class, in which students refused to listen to her. One day, aggravated, she announced, "I am going to go sit at the table under the windows. If anyone here actually wants to learn social studies, you can join me." She decamped to the far table. No one moved . . . except Fisseha. He picked up his backpack and moved to the far table with the teacher. The teacher had tears in her eyes when she told me this. Later, she said, one of the tough guys in class had said to Fisseha, "Don't you ever do anything wrong?" and Fisseha had shrugged and said, "Why should I?" And the fact that Fisseha was a superb athlete, famously strong, inspired the tough boy to step back and let him pass. Selamneh translated this story. Waganesh covered the lower half of her face as smile after smile burst from her.

"May we ask *you* something?" I said to Birhanu.

Selamneh translated his answer: "Of course, please."

There was so much about Fisseha's history we didn't know. We were unclear why he left his village in the first place; the fact that his mother was still alive made it even more confusing.

A year or two earlier he had told us about his early life, but it hadn't rung true with us.

"I had to leave my mother to save my life," he'd told us. "One of my older brothers accidentally killed a man in a fight. That gave the man's family the right to kill me. They sent me to my grandmother in Addis so I wouldn't be killed."

Oh, right, we'd thought. *They sent you away because they loved you so much. Well, it makes a good story.* We'd thought it more likely that his mother had sent him to his grandmother in the mistaken belief that Tsehai was better equipped to support him; and then, after he left, his mother had died. "Fisseha, I think your mother died after you left," I'd said.

"No, she didn't," he'd said in a matter-of-fact way.

"I'm so sorry, but I really think she did."

"No, she didn't."

I'd felt (having immersed myself in adoption literature) that these were Fantasies of the Adopted Child.

"Why did Fisseha leave the village?" we asked now, and Selamneh translated.

Alematu, a man in his late thirties—a half brother of Fisseha's, an older son of their late father, Mengistu—gave the answer. In Amharic he explained, and Selamneh translated, "In the village, we have the land that is our land, and it is inside a fence. There is a neighbor who allows his cows to eat on our land. Many times I tell this man no, this is our land, but the neighbor does not want to listen. One day he wants to fight over this land. We . . . unfortunately . . . got into a fight with sticks and . . . it has happened that . . . this man has died. Then we believe that the man's family will take revenge on our family. By our custom, he is entitle. If they plan to take the life of a male of our family, small Fisseha is the one. At this time we have sent him to Tsehai."

So much for our theory that Fisseha was engaging in an adopted child's fantasy of narrow escape and heroic rescue! Or in an adopted child's fantasy that his birth mother was out there somewhere looking for him. It was all true.

Now Birhanu, Tsehai's son, stood up at the end of the table and cleared his throat. Selamneh said, "He wishes to tell something to you and Donny."

We stopped eating and folded our hands to listen. It was like an after-dinner toast. Birhanu, looking down at the table, cleared his throat many times, trying to find the way to begin.

He spoke haltingly, and Selamneh translated every few lines: "We would like to make an apology to you, Mister Don and Missus May-leese-ah . . . We have said . . . we have done . . . a thing that is not true.

"We have told to the orphanage that Fisseha's father and mother are dead. We cannot care for him, we have not the money to care for him, so that is why we have said that he has no parent. His father is passed away when he is very small boy, but his mother is alive, as you see. This is the lie that we have told." He sat back down with his head bowed, waiting for our judgment.

No one stirred. Then a few family members glanced over at us, to see our reaction. I looked sideways at Donny to see if he was inclined to stand up and make a return announcement of some sort. He was not so inclined.

"Thank you for telling us," I finally said, and Selamneh translated. "I know the Ethiopian adoption law, and so I can tell you that this adoption did *not* break the law. A child is considered to be an orphan if both parents are dead *or* if one parent is dead and the family cannot care for the child. In that case, which is your case, the Ethiopian government considers the child to be an orphan. You could have told the orphanage the truth and nothing different would have happened. They still would have accepted Fisseha. We understand that you wanted a better life for him. You did not break the law. We are grateful that you have trusted us to raise him."

Everyone glanced back and forth between my face and Selamneh's as he translated my statement into Amharic. At the conclusion, a burden was lifted from Birhanu. He relayed his gratitude to me by meeting my eyes and placing his hand over his heart.

The platters and baskets were empty; we pushed back from the table. We posed for photographs in different constellations of past and current families and all together. As we said goodbye, Donny gave Waganesh enough money to help with her stay in Addis and her return trip to the village, and to sustain her for many months. Tsehai and Waganesh wiped their eyes after hugging Fisseha goodbye, and he blinked back tears.

Later, I asked him, "How are you feeling about seeing everyone?"

"I feel . . . like I want to see them again."

"What were they all asking you?"

"They were asking if I remembered them."

He had.

It was the end of our vacation in Addis Ababa. We returned Daniel and Yosef to the orphanage for the last time, promising to do everything in our power to speed the adoption along. It was a painful separation for everyone, but perhaps most of all for Helen and Binyam. She held the little boy until the last possible moment; he seemed to think he was going with us. He rode on Helen's hip with confidence, his hand lightly resting on her shoulder, stoutly preparing to say goodbye to W/o Haregewoin and everything and everyone he'd ever known. As we stood just inside the orphanage gates, with the van waiting outside with our suitcases, Binyam squeezed his little fist open and shut at the other children, in babyish waves of goodbye. Helen still hoped I would change my mind and say, *Okay, yes, let's bring him!*, as if one could simply pick up a child and stroll out of an orphanage with him. Finally, we couldn't delay any longer; Binyam had to be pulled from Helen's arms. Both children's faces crumpled with disappointment; both began to howl. A caregiver carried

Binyam briskly away across the courtyard, jiggling him and offering soothing words as he shrieked and reached his arms toward Helen, and we hustled Helen up into the van. "Mommy, please! *Please!*" she cried. She sobbed jaggedly all the way to the airport and looked back out the plane window toward Africa with desolate eyes.

Daniel later told his tutor: "When the family left, that almost killed me."

45

Daniel and Yosef in America

Two months later the wheels and documents of justice ratcheted forward a notch: Yosef and Daniel Gizaw, eight thousand miles away, became Yosef and Daniel Gizaw, Samuel, our sons. "You delivered our first seven children; I'll deliver these two," Donny said, and flew back to Addis. In the twenty-eight years of our marriage, it was his first international trip without me. Lee joined him from Israel, and they checked into the small Yilma Hotel with the boys.

"Daniel chuckles over Yosef like an amused grandfather," Donny e-mailed from an Internet café. "Last night, walking home from dinner, we bought heavy packs of bottled water. Yosef explained that he was not very strong and couldn't possibly take his turn carrying them. At that moment he stepped into a pothole up to his waist. Daniel said: 'Yosef not very strong. Also Yosef not very smart.'"

The night before their departure, the American horror movie *Snakes on a Plane* was broadcast. If I'd been there, I would have yanked the cord out of the wall and thrown a rug over the television set. But Lee and Donny fluffed up their pillows and leaned back for some light entertainment involving hundreds of poisonous snakes winding their way through a crowded airborne cabin to bite, poison, strangle, and terrorize

hundreds of hysterical passengers. At bedtime, Yosef asked: "I . . . take . . .
boat to America, yes?" while Daniel volunteered to walk.

Donny woke them at 3:30 a.m. for their 9:00 a.m. flight. Donny is an
advocate of arriving at an airport in time to enjoy at least one sit-down
full-service meal. The possible adoption and visa complications added
several more hours to his estimate of how much time they'd need; thus
he, Yosef, and Daniel arrived at their gate with a four-hour wait ahead of
them.

Three hours into their stay in the waiting area, about to perish from
boredom, Yosef asked Donny: "Dad, we almost in America?" Back
home, we were delighted to learn that—only forty-eight hours after becoming Donny's sons—the new brothers grasped the Arrive-at-the-
Airport-Four-Hours-Early element of their new father's character.

On June 10, 2007, they landed in Atlanta. The boys wore looks of
dazed happiness and bewilderment as miracle upon miracle flowed to
them, beginning with their very own suitcases popping out of a carousel
in the Atlanta airport. "*Mom* car?" they asked as we all shoved the luggage into my beige Honda Pilot. Such a big and fine car! It would be
weeks before they believed it belonged to our family. And far more as-
tonishing: "Mom . . . *drive?*" I lowered my electric window, stuck out my
elbow, and wheeled us carefully out of the airport parking lot so that
they could feel confident and impressed. At the house there were beds
for each of them, and dresser drawers (they'd never had those before),
bikes to ride (they didn't know how to ride bikes), basketballs to bounce
(they didn't know the game of basketball), and fruit bowls towering with
apples, bananas, plums, peaches, and cherries. They knew only a few
words of English, but offered them readily and emphatically. I had new
clothes ready for each of them, but Daniel had grown a couple of inches
since I'd seen him. When the bashful, gangly boy emerged from my office bathroom, his stiff new jeans stopped at his calves and the arms of
the long-sleeve T-shirt fell shy of his wrists.

"Nice!" he said in the up-down bark of a young teenage male.

"No, Daniel"—Lily, Helen, and I laughed—"the pants are too short,
the shirt is too small."

"No, Mom, NICE, I like. Very nice," he said, giving an Ethiopian roll
to the r in *very*.

I took the clothes away, and he looked crestfallen. I brought him
hand-me-downs from Seth and Lee instead. This time Daniel peeked

out worriedly in pants that reached the top of his shoes and a shirt that covered his wristbones. "Too big," he said with a shrug of resignation. He'd never worn clothes that fit before.

Around the house Daniel was cautious and quiet like a deer, as if he were about to dart away. He kept track of Yosef at all times, though Yosef didn't seem to be returning the favor. There was an air of melancholy about Daniel; I think he had been scared and worried for a long time. He had probably wondered what would become of him and his brother once they aged out of Haregewoin's foster home. They'd have no skills and no jobs. Where would they live? How would they find food? Somehow he'd sheltered Yosef from these concerns, giving Yosef a childhood. Yosef gleamed with pure joy and love of life. He was like a young seal, with a smooth, shining face, wide grin, and athletic exuberance.

One steamy morning Daniel came along with me to walk the dogs. Franny pulled me ahead, hot on the trail of a squirrel, but Theo lagged behind. When I looked back for Daniel, I saw that he was cradling the dachshund—with its old man's face, bushy brown eyebrows, and raggedy Fu Manchu mustache—in his arms like a baby.

"Very small, Mom. Very tired," Daniel explained.

Theo gave me a smug look that seemed to express *Finally you have a child who understands me.*

For three miles in the oppressive heat I urged Daniel to put the dog down. "Theo can walk," I told Daniel. "In fact, in English, this is called 'walking the dog.'" Every time I said this, Theo raised his head and glared at me from under those fierce eyebrows. When Daniel shook his head no, Theo gazed up at him adoringly.

Later I realized that Daniel's carrying Theo was the act of a shepherd boy who had been taught not to let a lamb fall too far behind the flock lest it fall prey to a wolf or hyena. Theo loves Daniel.

June 16 was Helen's eleventh birthday. Since the date that appeared on Yosef's documents as his birthday had come and gone a few weeks earlier, Helen shared her party. (Yosef did not know his actual birth date.) I rented a moonwalk (an inflatable bouncing place) and brought home balloons and water guns. Seth, twenty-two, had just graduated from the Oberlin Conservatory with a bachelor's degree in composition. He would move to New York in August to begin a master's program in film scoring at NYU. He stood at the kitchen sink filling up water balloons, knotting them, and gently depositing them in laundry baskets, while Helen ran back and forth, carrying the laundry baskets outside for strategic placements.

Dozens of kids—Helen's friends, and Jesse's and Sol's—arrived, met the new boys, and descended into the backyard, where the battle began. Our family has known many great water fights over the years, but this may have been our finest hour, our Battle of Midway. Children armed with bright yellow and orange Super Soakers roared lustily and lobbed water grenades. Attackers aimed streams of water through the mesh at the jump-

ers until the moonwalk sloshed with water like a sinking vessel. A small blond child, holding an enormous water balloon with both hands, backed Yosef against a wall and threatened him in a high, brave voice: "I am NOT afraid to use this." He gazed openmouthed between her flushed pink face and the yellow water balloon undulating like a live jellyfish in her hands, unable to decide which was the more fantastic. I glanced up to see that children in the kitchen had opened the second-story windows and were dumping cooking pots full of water onto the heads of children below. I ran in to put a stop to that.

I encountered Daniel tearing across the living room with baggy water balloons tied to his belt and a Super Soaker slung across his back—drenched, and ferocious with joy. Seth resumed his post at the kitchen sink to fill more balloons for Helen, though he could barely see through his dripping hair and fogged-over glasses. Lee, nineteen, was leading an assault from the driveway up onto the deck. "Ready, aim, fire!" yelled Lily, fifteen, mounting the deck defense with giggling girls in two-piece swimsuits.

Finally the last balloon exploded, the water guns were pumped dry, and I called a halt. In the quiet after the storm, water dripped from the roof, gutters, and eaves of the house, and a thousand colorful balloon fragments speckled the yard as if a ticker-tape parade had come through. Now crowds of soggy children piled into the kitchen for cake. They crowded around the table and sang first to Helen, then to Yosef, at the tops of their voices. Yosef watched how Helen blew out her candles, and then he did the same. When one remained lit, he plucked it from the cake, held it to his lips, and gave it a delicate puff. Everyone cheered.

I happened to spot Daniel at the fringe of the crowd. As everyone sang and shouted, "Happy Birthday, Dear Yosef!" he stood silently in the outer circle, not knowing the song, angling for a glimpse of his brother, and wearing a look of bewildered, poignant curiosity.

"YOUR birthday, NEXT month!" I shouted into his ear, over the noise of the crowd. "NEXT time, party for YOU!"

He furrowed his brow to try to understand. Then he waved that silliness away. He gestured toward Yosef, somewhere in the middle of the pack of children, with cake in front of him and presents piled around, to indicate *This, this for Yosef, is all I wanted.*

On paper, Yosef had turned ten two weeks earlier, not on Helen's birthday. We'd explained this to him, but something must have been lost in translation, for that night, sitting amid his gifts, he sighed happily, "Now I eleven."

The next day, a late birthday gift arrived for Yosef. As he eagerly tore into the wrapping paper, Daniel wryly offered, "Uh-oh. Now Yosef twelve."

In early August, when school starts in Georgia, Yosef entered fourth grade at Fernbank Elementary. But he protested: "I do fourth grade Ethiopia! Fifth grade me!"

"I want you to do fourth grade again. I want you to have an American fourth-grade year," I said.

Daniel started seventh grade at Shamrock Middle School. He protested: "I do fourth grade Ethiopia! Fifth grade me!"

"Unfortunately, American schools don't place you according to your level of schoolwork; here you go in based on your *age*. You're the age of the seventh-graders, so you go to seventh grade. With Sol."

Both began intensive classes in English for speakers of other languages (ESOL). Daniel returned from his first day of ESOL and reported, "Friend me yes! Many friend me. One French he speak Nepali; one Mexican he speak French; two African."

"What do they speak?" asked Donny eagerly.

"Mexican."

Donny roared in delight.

"Oh my God," said Daniel. Daniel often said this, slapping himself in the forehead when our conversations hit a wall, which they did several times a day. "Oh my God" signaled a throwing up of hands, a complete abandonment of the attempt. He walked off in his gangly, storklike way, his shoulders prematurely hunched.

The next day he had more happy news from ESOL: "New friend me. Good friend."

"Where is he from?"

"China."

"Nice," I said. Then, unable to resist, I asked, "And what does he speak?"

"Korean."

I burst out laughing.

"Oh'my God," said Daniel.

"Mom, this? This?" asked Daniel very late one Saturday night in August. He approached me with his hands shaping a circle. He showed me the circle. "This? This I like. Seth like."

"Hmmm . . . a *CD*?" I asked, speaking loudly and slowly, as to a foreigner. "Seth likes CDs. You want to hear some *music*?"

"No, Mom! This! This! Seth like!" He showed me the circle of his hands again.

"A DVD? You want to watch a *movie*? You want to watch one of *Seth's movies*?"

"Oh my God, Mom, THIS," he said again, showing me the circle.

"Daniel, I don't know. I don't understand. Seth's home; why don't you ask him?"

Daniel took the stairs three at a time. A few minutes later I heard the jingle of Seth's car keys in the front hall as he and Daniel headed out the door. "Be back in a bit!" called Seth. "Going to Krispy Kreme!"

My old friend Sue Kaufman visited from Boston. I bragged to her of the advanced work Daniel was doing in ESOL. When the tall young teenager hobbled in after school, I asked, "What did you learn today?"

"Mom!" barked Daniel. "Thirteen month! Name!"

"You learned the names of the thirteen months?"

"Yes!"

"That IS advanced work," commented Sue.

"Daniel, we only have twelve months in America."

"No, Mom. Thirteen. Teacher say."

"I'm pretty sure about this one, kiddo."

"Thirteen, Mom."

Jesse had come in and taken a seat. I said, "Jesse, how many months are there in a year?"

He looked up from his bowl of Froot Loops, thought for a moment, and said, "Four."

"Okay, Jess, that's the seasons. What about the months?"

"Sixteen?"

"*Thirteen*, Mom," insisted Daniel.

"You're going to have a long year," said Sue.

46

Strife

Our long year was just beginning. In August, when Seth moved to New York for graduate school. I helped him set up an apartment in Queens and to find his way to his first day of work at the David Black Literary Agency in Manhattan. Two weeks later I flew with Lee to Oberlin College, so he could become the fifth person in our immediate family to study there, and Seth flew out from New York to help launch Lee. We carried Lee's boxes into a brick dorm on the sweet, cool green North Quad, where Donny and I had met as freshmen, a ridiculous thirty-six years earlier. We left Lee there and returned in the rental car to the Cleveland airport. Seth flew back to New York, and I, bereft, sat alone at my gate.

It seemed especially unfair for these goodbyes to hurt so much, since the working THEORY was that Donny and I would AVOID the pain of empty nest by continuing to FILL the nest. I sadly phoned Donny from the waiting area. "I don't think our plan is working. We're getting all the pain of empty nest anyway . . ."

"I know," he said. "But we don't get to go to Paris."

The moment I clattered over the threshold with my small suitcase around six o'clock that evening, I found the family in chaos. Battles for supremacy among the four boys—ages ten, twelve, thirteen, and thirteen—which had started out of sight in the basement in July, had risen to the main floor of the house. The boys were hitting each other with loud smacks and punches right in front of us; Yosef was getting pounded the most and screamed the most piercingly. Donny and I yelled "Stop fighting!" and "Stop hitting!" so often that night, and with so little result, we might as well have been yelling *Hit him again! Hit him harder!* The nurturing older brother version of Daniel had disappeared overnight; he looked stern and exasperated. Yosef no longer brimmed with joie de vivre. He was a deflated Yosef, acting glum without reason, and acting glum with good reason, and he hated every American food except pancakes.

Helen whispered to me that Yosef hadn't spoken to her since I'd left on Monday, but she didn't know why, and that Sol was not speaking to Jesse, because Jesse had borrowed a pair of Sol's shoes without asking. At dinner, Sol pointedly took his plate and went to sit alone in the living room to avoid sitting at the same table with Jesse. "Get in here!" I yelled. "Sit with the family! I haven't seen you since Monday!"

"I'm finished," he muttered in reply, dumping his plate in the sink.

I believed the new boys had introduced the Silent Treatment into our family, because I knew Haregewoin had punished her children that way. I'd seen her pointedly ignoring this or that boy or girl until the child sank to a deep fathom of despair, after which Haregewoin would finally open her arms and forgive. Excommunication shrinks a child's spirit. It's the punishment I most hate in the world, having experienced it as a child. I have never used it with my children, but now this soundless weapon was passed hand to hand eagerly among the boys.

After dinner Lily shook her head ominously at me, helped clean up, and went upstairs. Helen vanished, too. "Doing homework," Lily said crisply when I looked in on her. She was not in a mood to talk. I peeked in on Helen in her bedroom, and she held out her arms to me and burst into tears. I held her as she cried. "I just . . . I just . . . I just don't feel close to anyone . . . in the family . . . anymore."

The next day, the sight of sweet potatoes in a kitchen drawer made my heart drop with longing because I'd bought those sweet potatoes for *Lee* and had forgotten to prepare them; and then my heart sank again when I saw that Daniel was strolling about in Seth's enormous neon green Crocs. Seth hated those shoes and had probably given them to Daniel, but they made me sad.

Daniel sat down at the kitchen table to peel and eat a mango. "I'm feeling so homesick for the big kids, for Lee and Seth and Molly," I admitted to him.

"Mom!" he barked. "You sick?!"

"No, not sick. Homesick—it's a feeling inside, when you miss your family."

"I know this! Me this! Family gone. Trip gone. Oh my God I say, this family." He was talking about his feelings after our spring break trip to Addis, when we'd left him and Yosef behind. After he finished his snack, he went into the living room and called Lee with his brand-new cell phone. I overheard him. "Lee!" he barked. "You sick?"

The white noise of overlapping Silent Treatments filled the house. Yosef wasn't speaking to Helen, Sol wasn't speaking to Jesse, and Daniel wasn't speaking to anyone. Wordlessly, the kids bumped into one another with sharp elbows and shoulders, like bullies in a school hallway. The static of I'm-not-talking-to-you was interrupted only by occasional outbursts of shouted insults and curses. *"Niftam!"* (the Amharic word for "snot") was flung; it was a fighting word. They came to blows over "snot."

I suddenly realized that since Yosef and Daniel's arrival in June, Lee and Seth had been home—until this week. The older guys had kept everything moving, made everything funny. They took the younger six bowling and swimming and to the movies. When Daniel asked, "Jump-o-leem? Jump-o-leem?" they went outside and hopped on the trampoline with him. They made cookies or ice cream sundaes in the kitchen at two in the morning. They watched the many-sequeled *Star Wars*, *Lord of the Rings*, and *Back to the Future* on long, hot summer nights, enjoying the fact that it was Daniel's and Yosef's first time to see these great films. Everything about our enlarged family seemed bright and possible while two affectionate clowning older brothers, with money and driver's licenses, lived at home.

When they left, it seemed that playfulness and camaraderie had departed, too.

The younger kids felt something was missing. Daniel sent Lee a text message at Oberlin at nearly one a.m. on a school night:

Daniel (12:58 a.m.): allolee
Lee (12:59 a.m.): How are you Daniel?

Daniel (1:00 a.m.): Iamfaynehawareyou

Lee (1:01 a.m.): Pretty good. I'm going to visit some friends tomorrow. Why are you not asleep now?

Daniel (1:03 a.m.): Okbay

Lee (1:04 a.m.): Hahaha. Ok. I was just asking though. I'll see you in 30 days.

Daniel (1:09 a.m.): Iseeyouto30DAYSOKBAY

Lee (1:10 a.m.): Bye Daniel. I miss you.

Daniel (1:12 a.m.): Imisstobye

Our family no longer generated happiness. Borrowed items of clothing were yanked back. No one liked dinner. No one took out the trash. The bikes were left out in the rain. No one would come to the library with me. Somebody took somebody else's sports drink out of the refrigerator and drank all but the last drop and put it back. Blockbuster videos were so overdue that we now *owned* them. Insatiable demands for iPods, computers, and cell phones rose clamorously from the group of boys. Donny, tired of hearing it all, trudged upstairs and went to bed early on many nights. Franny trudged up behind him and Theo trotted up behind Franny. They were fed up, too. I feared that this household sounded like, looked like, and felt like nothing so much as a group home.

47

Fighting Words

In an attempt to lift everyone's spirits in a way that Seth and Lee would have done, I drove the five youngest children to a park. We deposited our water bottles and snacks on a quilt and spread across the field until Daniel kicked a soccer ball smack into Jesse's face. Jesse, in pain and surprise, yelled, "What the fuck?" and then, feeling that he was getting a bloody nose and feeling that Daniel had attacked him on purpose, yelled "Motherfucker!" at Daniel. Daniel went berserk. He didn't understand many English words, but he understood this one. He flew at Jesse with a face twisted by hatred, took him down, and throttled him while I pounded on Daniel's back with a baseball glove and shouted at him to stop. Across the playground, a dozen younger mothers, cooing to gentle small children, fell silent and watched us. Embarrassed, and scared by the violence, I grabbed our things and herded everyone right back to the car. Jesse stopped his bloody nose with a paper towel. "Motherfucker" was a terrible word in Ethiopia. Daniel had taken it as a specific insult aimed at the memory of his late beloved mother. I had to shield Jesse from Daniel all evening.

I lost sight of what Donny and I were trying to do and why on earth we were doing it. I couldn't set things right. I went into my office and typed "HELP!!!" in the subject line of an e-mail. I sent it to my friend Andrea Sarvady, who lived in the house directly across the street.

When the Internet was young and Andy e-mailed me for the first time, I e-mailed back: "You know you could open your window and SHOUT and get the news here faster." But over time, we became regular e-mail correspondents, despite the fact that when I leaned back in my desk chair, I could see her house through my front window.

Rather than replying by e-mail, Andy—a black-haired, fast-talking, and sarcastic woman who had lived in hip locales like San Francisco and Park Slope—ran right over. I bounded up the stairs and she ran up behind me. I closed my door and we sat on my bed. "The older three," I wept, "Molly, Seth, Lee, so wonderful . . . amazing people . . . all far away . . . Lily, Helen, so loving, smart . . . nice to everyone—"

"Got it," said Andy, "and the four younger boys are a train wreck."

I covered my face with a Kleenex. Andy, in black leggings and a blue-jean dress, with a short and stylish haircut, was a nationally syndicated political columnist who had previously worked as a high school counselor and middle school teacher.

"Let me take this one," she said. "I'll meet with the boys tomorrow after school. Send me a list of the issues, get a poster board and a marker, and don't tell them I'm coming."

"But the emotions are so complicated!" I said. "Daniel used to be so protective of Yosef, but now it's like he's dropped him completely. Yosef cries all the time, Daniel's mad at everyone, Sol hates Yosef, Jesse hates Daniel, Yosef's not speaking to Helen, Lily probably feels *completely* displaced—she went from being the adored youngest of four to being the oldest of six kids at home in constant warfare. There's no family life; there's no fun anymore at all. Without Seth and Lee here, everything's crashing."

Andy laughed. "I'm not going anywhere near the touchy-feely stuff. I don't care about their feelings! They don't love each other—so what? They still have to *behave*. I'm going strictly behavioral on this one. Just send me your list."

I sent:

Unpleasant behaviors include:
- Getting mad at each other over small things.
- STAYING mad at each other, bearing grudges for days and days.
- Giving each other the silent treatment.
- Giving Mom or Dad the silent treatment, sulking.

- Eating dinner elsewhere to avoid someone in the family.
- Hitting; hurting each other in play accidentally; hurting each other deliberately.
- Acting annoyed when asked to help clean up, to take the garbage cans out, etc.
- Borrowing something from a sibling—or taking something from a sibling—without permission; refusing to give it back when it's asked for.
- Refusing to share something for no reason. This is a family; we should share.
- Acting entitled to all the good things—new clothes, bikes, cell phones, computers—without earning it in any way.

What we want is:
- A house where everyone feels safe and where everyone feels valued.
- A house with a happy and playful mood, not an angry, grudging mood.
- This is not a free-for-all everybody-for-himself; it is a family.

At five o'clock the next afternoon, Andy breezed back across the street. "Okay, guys!" she called without preface, peeking into many rooms to collect them all. "Come on! Let's go! Right now!" Bewildered (Yosef and Daniel had met her only once) and caught off guard, Sol, Jesse, Daniel, and Yosef followed Andy downstairs to the basement rec room.

"You gals run upstairs, we don't need you," she told Lily, Helen, and me. But she asked Azeb to come along and translate for Yosef and Daniel so there would be no misunderstanding.

Andy began (she later told me) bluntly: "Guys, if your family was a soccer team, you'd be losing. Team Samuel *sucks* right now. A team of *babies* could beat Team Samuel. You are not pulling together, you are not communicating, and you're going to lose.

"Your mom told me what's going on over here and I don't like it. I'm going to read you a list of what I think is happening here. You tell me if anything is not correct."

As she read my list, the boys slumped deeper and lower into the sofas. "I'm not saying it's YOU or it's YOU," Andy said. "I'm not interested in who is doing what. I'm just saying that this is all happening in YOUR FAMILY, RIGHT NOW, and it doesn't feel good."

Azeb, translating, was less tactful (I learned later). She didn't translate verbatim, she editorialized. When Andy said, "I'm not saying it's YOU or it's YOU," Azeb said, "Yosef, this is *you*."

When Andy said, "I'm not interested in who is doing what," Azeb said, "Yosef, listen to Andy."

When Andy read the list of problems, Azeb inserted comments like, "Yosef, you know you did this one."

Andy leaned the poster board against the Ping-Pong table, wrote "TEAM SAMUEL" across the top, and said, "Now: I want suggestions on how to make Team Samuel better. I want every one of you to give me at least one idea."

The boys raised their hands. Andy called on each one and then wrote down their proposals.

1. No fighting.
2. Don't do the things on Mom's list.
3. Talk—don't just act mad.
4. Don't be annoying.

I would have loved to see the boys raising their hands.

"I want you all to be GREAT tonight and tomorrow," Andy said. "I don't want to hear, 'But it wasn't on the list that I couldn't get up at four in the morning and watch TV.' Just be great—you know what great is. IF you're great, your mom will take you to the movies tomorrow night. Whoever is not great will stay home."

The boys ran up the basement stairs. Daniel found me first, hugged me, and said, "I'm sorry, Mom." Jesse hugged me and said, "I'm sorry, Mom." Sol hugged me and said, "I'm sorry, Mom." Yosef hugged me and said, "I hate Azeb."

Then they and Helen and Lily went outside and played basketball for an hour until dinner. They all came running in, sweaty and happy, and someone yelled, "Team Samuel!" After dinner, first Daniel, then Yosef, kissed me and thanked me for dinner. The following afternoon Donny and I took a few of the children to the Ethiopian community youth soccer scrimmage; Daniel, Sol, and Yosef were foolishly placed on the same team. Their team won 14 to 1, which reminded us that our boys were not terrific athletes *because* they were Ethiopians; they stood out even among Ethiopians. "Team Samuel!" they yelled as we drove home.

On Saturday night, as the reward for all this greatness, I took them to the stupidest movie ever made—*Balls of Fury*—and they loved it.

On Sunday evening I found Lily, Helen, and Yosef dancing in the kitchen: Lily and Helen performed the trotting, hand-clapping, knee-slapping country dance to the song "Cotton-Eye Joe," which was playing on a CD player; and Yosef performed a traditional Gurage dance, arms extended, hands clasped, legs galloping.

I left the kitchen to do some laundry.

When I returned, Lily and Helen were doing the Gurage dance and Yosef was dancing to "Cotton-Eye Joe."

Andy was delighted with my reports on our progress and continued greatness. "You know it won't last," she warned.

"It might last," I said.

"No." She laughed. "It won't."

"Oh. Will you come back when it all falls apart again?"

She promised that she would.

48

A Haunted Night

Halloween is always a tricky holiday to explain to recent American immigrants. Daniel formed the impression that it was necessary to badly scare the neighbors in order to abscond with their candy, so he changed his mind about the nice, puffy Spider-Man costume I pulled from the closet; he wanted something worse-looking. A friend took Daniel costume shopping for me, sparing me the dreaded pre-Halloween visit to Party City. Daniel returned from the weirdest shopping trip of his life, hurried into the bathroom, and emerged as the Undead from the Crypt: tattered clothes, protruding ribs, and thick dabs of blood everywhere. The mask was a bloody, half-skinless skull under wild, matted gray hair. I screamed. He was ecstatic! "I do Dad now!" he yelled, and tore upstairs. His earnest, long-legged, awkward gait was evident under the layers of ugliness. There was an enthusiastic shout of fear from upstairs. Then Daniel reappeared. "I do Dad. Now I do Lily," he cried, and dashed off again.

After these successes he spent a long time in front of the bathroom mirror. He came out with his costume neatly folded under his arm. Suppressing a smile, he predicted, "Many candy me."

———

Donny and I offered to walk with Daniel on Halloween night, and Lily offered to take him along with Helen and her friends, and Jesse invited him, and Daniel could have joined Yosef and his two new best friends, but Daniel said, "Go *my* friend," which meant he would tag along with Sol and a bunch of seventh-grade boys.

The night began badly because Sol strolled out of the house at sunset in jeans and a T-shirt while Daniel was dressed as Creature from the Grave. The seventh-graders weren't planning to trick-or-treat, they said; they just wanted to hang out, enjoy the scene, and visit the Haunted Trail in a nearby subdivision. Daniel discarded the costume shirt and mask and ran to catch up with Sol and the other guys. They walked to the most celebratory of Halloween-observing subdivisions, where families covered their yards, rooftops, and windows with Halloween decor: tremendous bats hovered over doorways, glow-in-the-dark skeletons dangled from balconies, and wavering airborne ghosts rose along hidden wires. Spiderwebs draped the bushes and mailboxes. Bloodcurdling screams were emitted by loudspeakers hidden within shrubbery. Witches' cauldrons steamed with smoke; severed heads rested on a picnic table; and middle school boys dressed as ghouls ambushed people from behind Styrofoam gravestones.

What happened next is a subject of dispute, but—either by accident or by design—Daniel got separated from Sol and the friends.

"He *losting* me," Daniel later said, feeling that Sol had ditched him.

Sol would shrug off the accusation. "I looked around and I didn't see him."

"Why didn't you just call Sol?" I would ask Daniel. He had a cell phone now.

"No my phone. Costume no pocket."

Daniel found himself alone amid hundreds of bizarrely dressed white people kindling fires and hanging witches from trees while manufactured fog leached into the streets and horrible screams blasted from hidden places and macabre scenes of torture and death materialized in front of him wherever he turned. Surely there were kids he knew all around him, but masks and makeup disguised them. He caught got in a spiderweb and his struggle roused a two-foot-wide glittery red-eyed spider just overhead. Thinking he saw his friends in the distance, he cut across a yard, and a wolf-headed monster dropped down from a tree and howled at him. With a creak, a nearby grave opened and a skeletal woman emerged with grasp-

ing fingers. He began to run, jumping over and dodging gruesome creatures and severed limbs. Somehow he escaped the subdivision and jogged
toward our neighborhood. Helen and Lily spotted him striding briskly
down the hill toward our house. "Daniel! Come trick-or-treat with Helen!"
called Lily. Head down and silent, he angrily waved them away. He loped
across the street and into our house, ran down the stairs to the bedroom
he shared with Sol, slammed and locked the door, and got into bed. Lily
reached me on my cell phone (I was following Jesse's group), and I ran
home and knocked on the basement bedroom door.

"No!" Daniel yelled in a strangled voice.

"Come out, Daniel, please. Come with us. Come with me and Dad."

"No!"

"Daniel, come trick-or-treat. Come on! Let's go get you some
candy!"

"No!"

"Daniel, let me in. I won't make you come out. I just want to talk
to you."

He unlocked the door and threw himself back into bed. He pulled
the blankets over his head and rolled over to face the wall.

"What's going on?"

"He losing me," he said ominously from under the blankets. "I *new*.
He know I can not."

"You got separated from Sol? You got lost?"

"No. He leave me. *He* losing *me*."

"You think Sol lost you on purpose? I don't think so."

"*Yes*, Mom."

"Will you come out with us?"

"No, Mom. Alone now."

More was at stake here than the disastrous Halloween night, I realized as I left him alone. I thought back over Daniel's attempts to make
friends these past four months and his eagerness to have friends, and I
suddenly felt sorry I hadn't helped him more. I'd relied too much on Sol,
as if it were a simple matter for a thirteen-year-old boy to instantly share
all the attachments and relationships of his three years in America with
the new guy.

I remembered the day we'd given Daniel a cell phone (because everyone else his age in the family had one), and he'd carefully copied all the
phone numbers in Sol's phone into his own. That night he sat down and

began to call them one by one. "You have to stop. Don't call them!" Sol had said.

Daniel was shocked, and hurt.

"Sol, why couldn't Daniel call your friends?" I asked him the next day.

"It was late. He was going to wake everybody up."

But Daniel didn't buy it. "He say no. His friend no my friend."

I remembered the day I'd asked a neighborhood friend whether her son—also named Daniel—might invite our Daniel to their house sometime. That afternoon the phone rang. It was her Daniel, for my Daniel. A moment later Daniel was flying out of the house. "Go my friend house!" he yelled, and sprinted up the hill.

Five minutes later the phone rang again. It was my friend. "Your Daniel is here."

"Your Daniel invited him."

"My Daniel invited him to come over on Saturday."

This was Wednesday. "Can he stay?" I asked.

"Yes, of course!"

I remembered the summer day that Daniel needed to go to the pool immediately for a gathering of friends. "Really? Are you sure?" I'd asked. I hadn't heard from other mothers that their sons and daughters were going, nor did Sol have any news of a get-together. But Daniel was emphatic, so I drove him. I waited with him . . . but no one arrived. He jumped in the water to play by himself. "I okay, Mom! I wait many friend!" he called happily, so I drove home. Two and a half hours later he phoned home. "Mom, come." No friends had arrived; he'd misunderstood.

The morning after Halloween, Daniel looked forlorn. Sol swore he hadn't "ditched" Daniel; he'd walked across the street to greet a couple of soccer teammates, and when he'd turned around, Daniel was gone. "Sol didn't lose you on purpose," I told Daniel. "Halloween is always crazy; people lose each other all the time."

"No, Mom. His friend no my friend. In Ethiopia I many friend. Here no friend. He saying no."

While the kids were at school, I bought a big bag of discounted Halloween candy. I greeted Daniel with it at the front door that afternoon. "Daniel, look! For you! Your Halloween candy!"

He refused it. Eyes averted, voice very low, he said, "No, Mom. No candy me."

49

The Silent Treatment

Lily ran to get me around 11:30 one night as I read my way toward sleep by dim lamplight. "Mom! Come FAST! RUN!!" she cried, and fled. I leaped out of bed, leaving Donny asleep behind me, and flew down two flights of stairs after Lily. In their basement bedroom Sol and Daniel were in a violent brawl—a snarling, bloody fistfight like something from a movie I wouldn't have seen, since I don't like to see fights. Punching and scratching, the two spun like a cyclone out of their bedroom and thwacked against the outside door, huffing and pummeling. They stripped off their shirts and attacked each other again and again in the semidarkness of the basement hallway. Jesse hovered nearby, amazed that something large and bad was happening in the family and he was innocent.

"STOP!" I cried, but they kept punching, hard. With little experience of this kind of thing, I stepped between them to break it up and instantly got nailed by a fist to the left cheek. "Oh, Mommy!" screamed Helen, and ran to me. In the momentary shocked cessation of hostilities, after the Hitting of the Mother, Lily dragged Sol backward out of the fray. Daniel slammed back into the bedroom. Sol was wild-eyed, red-eyed, and panting hard. "I'm going to kill him," he breathed. He had bloody lines on his neck from Daniel's long fingernails.

"GO TO BED!" I choked out. "ALL OF YOU, GO TO YOUR ROOMS *RIGHT NOW*!!" Yosef and Jesse evaporated. In the upstairs bathroom, Lily and Helen cleaned Sol's scratches and applied Neosporin while he sat on the closed toilet panting with adrenaline and fury. In the mirror, my left cheek glowed red from the punch. After Sol went to bed in Jesse's room, I descended to the basement, told Daniel good night, and trudged back up the two flights of stairs, exhausted in advance by the hard psychological and family-reconstruction work that lay ahead and wondering, *Am I still a mother, or have I become a social worker?*

The air was frigid between the two seventh-graders the next morning. They walked separately to the school bus stop and stood as far apart as possible. When the bus passed our house, I glimpsed Daniel sitting in the front row and Sol sitting in the back. I recalled Brother and Sister Bear doing the exact same thing in *The Berenstain Bears Get in a Fight*. So this was normal! This was the kind of thing that happened between Brother and Sister Bear! The boys came off the school bus that afternoon and found separate paths to our front door, along opposite sides of the street. Each came in, greeted me, got a snack, and acted as if the other didn't exist. *It's only the first day,* I reminded myself.

At bedtime, Daniel didn't know where to sleep, for Sol had reclaimed the bedroom that had been his first. Daniel took a blanket and lay down on a sofa in the living room.

I had to wake Daniel up the next morning for the first time, for Sol, who leaped up at dawn every day, had been in the habit of waking Daniel. Again the frigid air, the tense mood. Again the primly separate walks to the bus stop and sitting far apart. But this was only day 2.

"Guys, enough," I said on day 3. "Stop this. Let's get back to normal." They didn't.

"What were you even fighting about?" I asked Sol.

"I don't know! He went *crazy*!" he said.

"What were you fighting about?" I asked Daniel.

"I am sleep. Yosef come in. I wake. Sol come in, put CD on loud, Ethiopia CD. 'I sleep!' I tell them. Loud CD, no stop."

"You tried to kill Sol because he woke you up by putting on loud Ethiopian music?"

"I am *sleep*," he said.

On day 4, I sat beside Daniel in an upstairs bedroom to try to talk in simple terms about anger management. "It's a strong force inside you, your anger. You are a very strong young man. But if the anger controls *you*, that's no good, that doesn't make you strong. *You* have to be the boss of your anger. Anger is like a wild horse. You are the rider. You have to steer it and to pull it back." I'd used these words many years before with Lee, who'd had an explosive temper as a very small boy. One afternoon he chased Seth through the house waving a fireplace poker; that night I described anger to him as a wild horse he needed to bridle and steer. It had worked beautifully!

Now, as I finished my speech, Daniel stood up, approached me with stiff formality, hugged and kissed me, and said, "Thank you, Mom."

Day 5. Day 6. Day 7. The silence between the boys continued. Daniel withdrew from social life. When seventh-grade boys came over to hang out, shoot baskets, toss a football, Daniel stayed and asked to watch TV. When a friend invited both Sol and Daniel to come to the movies, Sol went and Daniel stayed home.

Day 8. Day 9. Day 10. "There's deep anger inside you," I now told Sol as he lounged on the basement sofa one afternoon, waiting for a soccer game to come on. I turned off the TV. "It's like this big thing you can't get around. You should be able to move beyond this fight, and you can't. What do you think has made this seem so important?"

He shrugged and asked to watch soccer.

Day 11. "It's because we did that wrong thing," I told Donny, "that thing in the adoption world you're supposed to avoid: 'virtual twinning.' We've got two strong thirteen-year-old boys and they're having a power struggle. I know Sol is the alpha of the younger kids. But Daniel comes from the same background. He won't defer to Sol. Maybe Sol's mad at having his supremacy challenged."

"Is it a bad thing for Sol to have his supremacy challenged? We should hold the power in the family, not one of the kids," Donny said.

Day 12. Day 13. Day 14. "They're still not talking to each other," I told Donny.

"At least they're not hitting each other."

On days 15, 16, and 17, I tried to be content with these insights: *They're not challenging our supremacy. They're not hitting each other.* And yet I still felt upset. The boys were tearing at the fabric of something delicate and lovely. I didn't expect them to *love* each other—it was too soon, maybe they'd never love each other—but I wanted them to *act* like brothers as a stage along the journey toward *feeling* like brothers. I wanted a basic level of kindness to prevail among my children; I didn't want one excommunicating another. I didn't want these hurtful stones of silence to be thrown hour after hour, day after day. If this were a holding facility, it would be adequate to know that none of the juveniles was actively stabbing, strangling, or poking the eyes out of a fellow detainee, but we were supposed to be—we were trying to become—a family.

We reached day 18 of the hostile silence that splintered family relations. Every gathering felt fragile, every dinner took place on a fault line, and every collective burst of laughter sounded false to me. Hanukkah was coming. Toward the end of the month, the older kids would fly home from San Francisco, New York, and Oberlin. How could we enjoy having everybody under one roof with a rift of fury cutting through the family like the 38th parallel?

I prepared for Hanukkah in the midst of glum and silent children. It was like rowing toward a bright, distant shore with their deadweights in the boat. I was able to present the historical context; it was the thread of family happiness that was lacking. Yosef and Daniel grasped the heroic story of tiny ancient Israel vanquishing the Hellenized Syrians something like this: In 1896, in the Battle of Adwa, against tremendous odds, Ethiopia defeated invading Italy. It was the first military victory of an African nation against a European one in modern times. Ethiopia, alone among African nations, remained uncolonized during the "Scramble for Africa."

Similarly, against tremendous odds, the ancient Israelites resisted the empire of the Syrian ruler Antiochus Epiphanes. In 164 B.C.E., after years of guerrilla warfare, they triumphed, reclaimed Jerusalem, and resanctified the Temple. In short: a small country fighting for freedom defeated a more heavily armed European colonizer. This was clearly something to celebrate! But why, in tribute to the Maccabean Revolt of two thousand years ago, I dropped off the kids at the Dollar Store in North DeKalb Mall to buy gifts for one another was beyond my—or anyone's—ability to explain. The morning after the group visit to the Dollar Store I glanced out the front window and beheld Jesse, Yosef, and Sol jamming new plastic rifles into the mud and shooting mud pellets at each other. I knew without asking: what they purchased at the Dollar Store, instead of Hanukkah gifts for siblings, were air rifles for themselves.

In case they were attacked.

By ancient Greece or Syria or Italy, or whoever the hell was coming after them next.

"Guys, listen, we *cannot* go on like this," I told Sol and Daniel. "It's not good for the family! It's not good for *me*. Hanukkah's coming. I'm *not* going to have this during Hanukkah. I cannot buy presents and make special foods and have us all sing songs and play games if you two are not speaking to each other. So stop it! Okay? Please! This is supposed to be a *happy* time!" I let them go, and they veered off in different directions without looking at each other.

I taped up two decades' worth of children's handmade decorations on the mantel and windows. We went to synagogue, wrapped gifts, and lit *Hanukkiahs*. Yosef and Daniel learned to chant the blessings. There were a few fun secrets and surprises. I broadcast my favorite Jewish cassette tapes from the kitchen tape recorder. We "saved" the last night to celebrate with Molly, Seth, and Lee later in the month. It was all very nice, perfectly pleasant. "It's boring this year," Lily and Helen told me. As soon as the candles burned down every night, the girls retreated upstairs to Lily's room. The family time disintegrated quickly.

Toward the end of the week I glanced out the kitchen window and happened to see Sol and Daniel step off the middle school bus and walk their very separate paths to our front door.

"What?" I cried to Lily. "Are they still not talking??"

"Duh," she said.

"This whole time? All through Hanukkah? They never made up??"

"No, Mom."

"How did I miss this? I'm an idiot! They tricked me! I'm such a sucker. I can't believe they weren't talking all through Hanukkah."

I ran upstairs to my bedroom, slammed the door, and got into bed. I leaned over and turned on the electric blanket. *THIS is why it hasn't been a sweet Hanukkah!* I thought. The days, the weeks, I'd wasted preparing for and launching the holiday, making sure everyone felt included and loved!

It was the shortest day of the year; night dropped down rapidly. I jumped up and lowered the window shades, then got back in bed. I couldn't believe I'd missed the ongoing boycott. I'd been blinded by the candle flames, the sizzling latkes, the shiny paper and ribbons, the gold-wrapped chocolate gelt. I'd been blinded by my own efforts to give everyone a happy time. I got up again, reached for the phone, got back under the covers, and called my friend Barbara McClure, who knew both Sol and Daniel very well, having tutored them in math for a year, for free, out of friendship.

"I'm *so mad*," I whispered to her. "I don't think I can do the last night of Hanukkah. I don't think I can leave my bedroom. I'm going to stay in bed. Hang on a minute." I went to the bedroom door, locked it, and returned to bed.

"Oh, I hope you won't punish everyone because of this!" said Barbara.

"It's pointless. There's no enjoyment anyway. It's amazing the effect that two people hating each other can have on a small group."

"I wonder if the boys *want* to start talking again, but they just can't do it," she said. "Remember how incredibly generous Sol was when Daniel came? He stayed home from sleepaway summer camp to be with him. He translated for him. He took him everywhere, introduced him to everyone. He even translated for me so I could teach Daniel math. Maybe he's feeling, *I did all that for him and what do I get? He punches me.* I don't think you should end your holiday early over this."

"Okay," I sighed. I saw that I was making the fight too large and important; I was erecting the theory of "this family is not working" or even "this has turned into a group home" upon the spongy ground of minor teenage hostilities. I washed my face, put on a sweater, and went downstairs. As Sol came through the kitchen, I asked him, "Did you give me a Hanukkah present?"

"Yes!" he said, startled. "The picture frame—you know? I painted it for you?"

"Oh, right, I love it! Will you give me another Hanukkah present?"

He looked concerned.

"This one is free," I prompted.

"Uh-oh."

"Just try, little by little, okay?"

"Okay," he said, and I kissed him.

But Hanukkah ended and they weren't speaking.

I'd missed the silence for most of the eight days of Hanukkah; now I was on the lookout for it. It was subtle. All the kids crowded together, kicking a soccer ball in the yard or standing in line with their dinner plates to reach the serving pots on the stove; you had to watch closely to see—in the tangle of relationships and joshing and voices—that one circuit had gone silent. I felt we were all scaling down to this lower, unhappier level of family life.

"Daniel, please," I said one night.

"*Mom!*" he exploded, the first time he'd ever shown anger at me. "Not me! You want to see? Look!" He stormed downstairs to the bedroom he used to share with Sol, but no longer did. Sol was getting into bed.

"Sol: *good night*," said Daniel.

Sol said nothing.

Daniel turned and stomped back upstairs.

"Sol!" I cried. "Daniel just told you good night."

"I didn't hear him," said Sol.

"I know why Sol's not talking to Daniel," Jesse told me one morning.

"You DO? WHY?"

"It's like . . . after he gets in a fight with somebody, it's hard to start talking again."

"How do you know?"

"I just know. Me and him used to fight a lot and we couldn't just start talking again even when we weren't mad anymore."

"Do you think you can help them sort it out?"

"Yeah, I'll help them. I'll talk to Sol."

Jesse attended the Friends School of Atlanta. The Quaker values of simplicity, peace, integrity, community, equality, and stewardship (SPICE) made sense to him, calmed him, helped bring him into maturity. He was handsome, athletic, and charismatic, brimming with musical and artistic gifts. He hadn't wanted to go to Friends for middle school. "Friends??" he'd cried as his classmates and his brothers headed off to Shamrock Middle School. "What kind of a stupid name is the *Friends* School? It sounds like the Fun School or the Happy School. I want to go to a school with a real name!"

Now, though he joked about the Friends ethos, he absorbed it. He sat in the passenger seat beside me in the car one day, with Helen in the seat behind him. She began to playfully annoy him, poking him with the tip of an umbrella on the back, on the neck, on the head. "Stop it, Helen." "Stop it, Helen." Even half a year earlier, it might have quickly enraged him. "Stop it, Helen." He used to be easily triggered, which had once made him a target for bored kids in the mood to see an explosion. Now she poked him again.

"*HELEN!!*" he yelled. He turned around in the seat, grabbed the umbrella, and . . . didn't hit her with it. Looking her straight in the eyes, with a level voice, only semi-spoofing, he said, "Helen. Violence is *not* the way."

He performed in the annual school talent show; he was a "beatboxer"—a young master of the art of verbal percussion. He was such a good beatboxer that he'd been invited to audition by the producer of the fabulously popular Grammy-winning hip-hop duo Outkast. He wore his colorful T-shirt, baggy jeans, and baseball cap. After his performance at Outkast's studio, the producer—a tall and big man, a powerful African American music industry grandee and millionaire—said to his assistant: "Send in the mama."

"Mama, your boy has a big talent, a *big* talent," he told me. "It's a *strange* talent, but it's a big one."

"*You* think it's strange? I thought it came from jazz and hip-hop! I'm a middle-aged Jewish woman! *I* think it's strange!"

"Where's your boy from?"

"Bulgaria."

"Look at that. And yet he is *urban*, urban as he can be, urban as he can *be*."

Though he didn't need Jesse for the upcoming album, he liked him very much and invited him back to the studio several times to rehearse with other artists.

Now, before his beatboxing act in the Friends School talent show, Jesse was asked by a Morehouse College friend Sean Maloney, "Jess, you going to win?"

"Sean," said Jesse with that mock-patient tone he used to conceal an authentically new and less frazzled approach to life, "these are *Quakers*. This is the *Friends* School. *Every* child is a winner at Friends." Then he ascended the stage and brought down the house.

So now, when Jesse said he'd talk to Sol, I realized that he was the only one who could realistically do it. They confided in one another. And Jesse knew about rage, about fighting, and about peacemaking.

This time I tried to stay out of it. I said nothing more to either Sol or Daniel. I did try to demonstrate how pleasant and delightful it is to live happily together with others rather than to drag through life surly, heavy with grudges and complaints. A lot of family fun was nearly within reach—Molly, Seth, and Lee were about to arrive. Big games of Risk, Scrabble, basketball, and Ultimate Frisbee would start, and late-night kids-only cooking parties and movie watching, along with the ubiquitous top-to-bottom trashing of the house that would be discovered by me early in the cold, dark winter mornings while all of them slept pell-mell, crossways on one another's beds, or stretched out, with feet stuck into each other's faces, along the sofas, as if they'd been overcome by sleep potions and had collapsed just before dawn. All Sol and Daniel had to do was release the anger and let the wild rumpus start.

Later I would wonder whether this silent fury was the last hurrah of two separate units: the small independent corporation of Yosef-and-Daniel, and the seven-child-and-two-parent family that was proving to have less-than-porous boundaries.

Over the next few days—perhaps helped along by Jesse's friendly, casual invitations to both of them to hang out, maybe given impetus by my dewy-eyed hopefulness, or possibly swept along in the hoopla of the older siblings' arrivals—Sol and Daniel began to communicate. I noticed they were not only jumping on the trampoline but passing a soccer ball back and forth to each other while they jumped. In the house, the once-dead circuit between them was dimly lit by a current of syllables.

By the end of winter break, they were amiably conversant. On the first school morning of 2008, they walked together to the bus stop. It was, truly, the beginning of a wonderful friendship.

What turned the tide? Had they resolved something? Had there been a power struggle? Had someone won, or had they fought to a draw? Did they determine at what volume, if any, post-bedtime Ethiopian CDs should be played in a bedroom in which someone was trying to fall asleep? I had no idea.

When it happened again—and it *would* happen again between varying sets of younger children over the years (though not between Sol and Daniel) because the Silent Treatment is a difficult weapon to eradicate—

I would blunder ahead along the same lines. Each fight, each glitch, each mini-tragedy offered a moment for family introspection, discovery, and repair. Each offered a chance to emerge at a slightly better, closer level. I tried to relay the same news to my unhappy children every time: that a life guided by friendliness, patience, and forgiveness is happier than one warped by old resentments, a sense of victimization, and a desire for revenge; AND that each child is free to choose which mood to share, which memories to dwell upon, what kind of person to be.

From that time, we began to lurch and scrabble ahead as a new entity, not residents of a group home, but a many-armed, multi-legged, lavishly eyed crab-walking creature, like something in a sack race—with abundant hair, umpteen ribs and toes and fingers, a cornucopia of brains, and plenty of heart—a family.

Daniel turned out to be a writer. That December, six months after arriving in America speaking no English, he wrote, in English, this poem:

> Water and ice friends one day
> the water said I am good you
> are not good because you
> don't move but I can move.
> The ice said oh you are not
> strong I am better than you.
> The water said I can go
> anywhere but you can't go. I
> can help people if they are
> thirsty. The ice said I can help
> people for skating games. The
> water said all life think they
> need me but they don't need
> you. The water said you can't
> hot but I can cold and hot.
> The ice said I can make a
> snowman. They can hold me
> but they can't hold you. The
> water said we are very good

friends we don't have to talk
about bad things lets go play
games.

Not only was it a beautiful poem in its own right, it was a story of conflict between two powerful opposing forces, about reconciliation, and about moving beyond reconciliation to play.

50

Everything You Always Wanted to Know About Sex, but Couldn't Spell

On a fine spring day in 2008, surprising words cropped up on my computer. I had logged on to Google to pick up some biographical information about the United Nations special envoy for HIV/AIDS in Africa, Ambassador Stephen Lewis, of Toronto. I typed the letter *S*, then paused to recall whether he spelled his name as Steven or Stephen, when, helpfully, a drop-down menu offered recent *S* searches, including "sax," "saxing," "saxing boys and girls," and "saxing Brintnte sprs."

But no one in the family plays *saxophone.* I chuckled to myself. *They must have meant "trombone" or "trumpet."*

Then I thought: *I wonder if one of the boys is thinking about switching instruments.*

Then I thought, *They can't spell.*

I returned to the Google search bar and hit a few random letters. Every key I touched produced a little spurt and cascade of misspelled dirty words and phrases. I went back to the beginning of the alphabet and did this in alphabetical order. You had your male body parts, your female body parts, and—in the *C*s and *F*s—a few correctly spelled popular four-letter words. I cheered up momentarily in the *V*s with the appearance of the word "Virginia." *All right, so sometimes they actually do use my computer to do their homework!* I thought with relief, glancing down the list for hints of Jamestown, the Royal Colony, and Thomas Jefferson.

But then I recalled, not for the first time: *They can't spell.*

At Amazon.com, new products were presented for my approval, based on my "recent searches." Just for me, they were saving a video version of the *Kama Sutra. Wow, that's some good spelling!* I thought. *I thought it was spelled* Karma *Sutra.*

Perhaps Seth and Lee, now twenty-three and twenty, had looked into erotica, but they'd come of age in an epoch closer to the lifetimes of Thomas Edison and the Wright brothers. When they were young teenagers, computers were old, slow, and black-and-white, more toaster or window fan than science fiction portal into every crevice of the known universe. In their youth, sexy images were reproduced in magazines and also arrived in the mail in the *Sports Illustrated* swimsuit issue or the Victoria's Secret catalog. To conceal testosterone-fueled research from his mother, a twentieth-century boy shoved his magazines deep under his bed, in the moldering twilight company of old socks, chewed gum, and misplaced homework. No electronic trail lingered. Twenty-first-century boys were unlucky in this way.

I felt confident in my ability to protect my twenty-first-century boys from pornography on the Internet. Only a few months earlier it was television I was concerned about. Not pornography on television: just too much television. My greatest maneuver had involved the household electrical system. I wondered if a single switch in the breaker box might control the big-screen basement TV. One afternoon I stood before the open breaker box and experimented. All over the house, up and down the stairs, in halls and bathrooms, in the kitchen and on the porch, lights flashed off and on. The squawks of protesting children—momentarily divorced from a computer screen or the microwave—also beeped on and off. Then I found it! A single switch! I flipped it, and the big basement television went black. It took the VCR and the DVD player with it. No more scolding necessary! I could walk through the basement without snarling "Can't you kids ever pick up a *book*??"

That was the end of the summer of 2007. Yosef and Daniel's arrival two months earlier had pushed television watching in our house to record levels. They were getting up in the night to watch; they were racing home from school to watch. Yosef was especially thrilled with Disney Channel comedies like *That's So Raven* and *The Suite Life of Zack and Cody*. I hid the television cord from the boys, but they found it. One day when I trotted downstairs to remove and hide the cord, it was missing. Later, Yosef pulled the cord from its hiding spot, plugged it in, turned the volume low, and settled in to watch *The Fresh Prince of Bel-Air*. I had to admire his ingenuity, and did, before ripping the cord out of the back of the TV with my bare hands.

The breaker switch was a different story. Yosef and Daniel, Jesse and Sol did not know about the breaker box. They did not know about electricity. They were too busy watching TV to hear about it.

So the TV went dead and stayed dead for a month, until Lee came home from college. Every fall Lee has to watch the World Series, college football, and NFL football, and then he has to watch ESPN updates and highlights about the games he just watched. I wanted Lee to enjoy coming home, so I flipped up the breaker and allowed the juice to flow back to the basement television components.

"Lee very smart!" Daniel remarked to me. "When Lee come, everything fix!"

A week later, when Lee went back to school, the TV mysteriously died again. I was boundlessly pleased with myself, although the TV-diminished environment didn't actually lead to more reading by the four boys. It was not like anyone said, *Well, I can't watch TV; maybe I'll catch up on some poetry.* They mostly passed the time by punching one another. Then one evening Helen and Lily decided to watch a movie on the basement TV. As the brothers watched, Lily strolled over to the breaker box, opened it, and flipped up the switch. The TV hummed to life! So did the VCR! And the DVD! "Lily, how did you know?" I said.

"Oh! Why, was that a secret? The day the lights were going off and on all over the house, I figured you were trying to find the breaker to turn this TV back on."

"No, I was looking for the breaker to turn this TV *off*."

"Lily *very* smart," Daniel was already offering. "When Lily downstair, everything fix."

By sundown on the day I discovered the new research interest, "saxing," I had purchased and downloaded a software product called Net Nanny. Any attempt to visit a website featuring a female other than Cinderella, Indira Gandhi, Julia Child, or Prime Minister Margaret Thatcher was blocked by the sudden appearance, in profile, of a British housekeeper in a white apron, starched collar, and little peaked hat. In her hand she held up, victoriously, a computer mouse that she'd evidently just cheerfully yet violently yanked out of the back of somebody's hard drive.

I was really smug about Net Nanny for two months.

The four younger boys—ages twelve, thirteen, fourteen, and fourteen—were stymied by Net Nanny for a day and a half. A clever friend of theirs secretly taught them how to turn off my computer, turn it back on, and quickly create a "guest" account other than mine. My computer "guest" was named Franny. On Franny's account, there was no Net Nanny and there was no Mom; there were, however, plenty of fleshy, top-heavy, rouged, and evidently outgoing young women.

I may not be of the Internet generation, but even I knew that a rat terrier would have no interest in a computer guest account. Wordlessly I retaliated with stricter software than Net Nanny. The new protective software was called Safe Eyes. Safe Eyes stopped young teenage boys from accessing any website other than one entitled www.Funwithfractions.com.

So the boys downshifted to other media.

One day a $467 bill arrived from our cell phone carrier. Close scrutiny revealed that the excess charges arose from the boys' cell phone numbers: hard-core sex scenes had been downloaded from the Internet onto the tiny screens.

"I didn't know they *had* Internet access on their phones," I protested to Customer Service (not wanting to say, *I didn't know you could even get two female breasts on such tiny screens*). "They told me they needed cell phones so they could call when soccer practice was over!" Hadn't each portrayed himself as at risk of abandonment, alone and fearful on a darkening and vast soccer field as night closed in, long after the parents of boys with cell phones had come and gone? Customer Service waived the charges because the boys were not supposed to have Internet access on their mobile phones.

So that portal was closed. But the boys journeyed on.

A cable TV bill arrived from Comcast, charging us for a pay-per-view purchase of an X-rated movie about pole dancing.

Pole dancing is *not*, I recently learned, the festive springtime event of

European folk culture in which young girls hold ribbons and weave in and out around a central post, wrapping it in a rainbow of pretty colors while adult males in short pants and kneesocks whistle into wooden flutes. That is "Maypole dancing." Pole dancing is another thing entirely. I am learning so much!

When I checked the date on the Comcast bill, I realized I'd had a middle school son home sick on that very day. At the precise hour of the movie screening, he'd been "napping" on the basement sofa in front of the rec-room TV, upon which non-Maypole dancing was being anthropologically examined.

Furious with the twenty-dollar fee for that movie, I pounded down the stairs, found this son, and held out the bill to him. "This was the day you were home sick. That was your movie, and it cost us twenty dollars! What are you going to do about it?"

"Oh, okay," he said mildly. He slipped into his bedroom, removed his wallet from a drawer, took out a twenty, and handed it to me.

Mollified, I couldn't think of anything to say other than "Hey, thanks!"

Back upstairs in the kitchen, I had misgivings, which I shared with Donny. "I'm not positive, but I think that I just sold our fourteen-year-old son pornography."

"*That's* not good," said Donny.

To which I replied, "I feel like his *pimp*."

Of course we tried "parental controls" on the television!

Parental controls should have the subtitle "Ask Your Kids to Show You How to Install These Things." The only parental controls we ever successfully set up on a television blocked nothing the children wanted to view, but resulted in our being unable to watch the Jim Lehrer *NewsHour* on that set ever again.

Thus it should not have been an enormous surprise when, on a Saturday afternoon in August, another cable TV bill arrived, this one charging $120 for unsanctioned pay-per-view purchases, through the cable box in the basement, of XXX-rated movies involving, variously, lingerie, lesbians, Las Vegas, and—no doubt—the *Kama Sutra* and perhaps even Virginia.

This time I was really mad. We'd *had* the excruciating and one-sided discussions about relationships, true intimacy, and respect for women. I'd held these conversations (or "monologues") with our daughters and I'd held them with our sons, because my husband (defender of the criminally charged) is incapable of allowing such delicate topics to cross his pure lips. I explained how demeaning it is to women to be perceived as sex objects; I touched upon the importance of respect in the approach to intimacy and marital happiness. The night I sat on the edge of Sol's bed to broach the subject, he fell straight backward onto his pillow, as if he'd been shot, and then reached out and pulled the bedspread up and over his face, refusing to reappear.

On the afternoon that the pay-per-view bill arrived, the four younger boys and friends were lounging around the kitchen table eating cold cereal and Popsicles.

"I need to talk to the Samuel boys RIGHT NOW," I announced, the bill shaking in my grip as if I'd just grabbed a live duck out of the air.

The boys' friends evacuated.

Helen peeked in, wondering if she was needed.

"I said the Samuel BOYS!" I roared. Helen fled.

I smashed the fluttering bill flat onto the table. "One hundred twenty dollars!" I shouted. "Who is going to pay for this?"

Daniel and Yosef instantly lost all English-speaking ability.

Sol put up both hands in self-defense and shook his head no. He glanced around with a shocked and concerned expression, as if startled to find himself in such low company.

Jesse, sighing, coolly raised one finger, as if signaling a waiter to bring the check. "It was me," he said.

"Really?" I asked, stunned at the rapidity of the confession. "All the movies? You?"

He sighed again. "Yep."

"Jesse, that is a *ton* of money."

He *tsk*ed sadly in regret at his own behavior and said, "I know." He shook his head, as if to say, *What am I going to do with myself?*

"Go get your allowance book," I snapped. He handed over the account register while his three brothers watched expressionlessly. "This will take you till . . . December to pay back," I said. "You've got no spending money till then."

"Okay, Mom."

"Can *we* go?" asked Sol, eager to put distance between himself and this distasteful subject.

"Go." I waved the others away.

In a minute, Sol was back. For the second time in a three-month period, he was removing a twenty-dollar bill from his wallet and handing it to me.

"What's this for?" I asked.

"To help Jesse."

"Really?" I asked, startled. I was touched.

"Here, Mom," said Daniel, having regained a few words of English. "Help Jesse." He gave me a ten.

Yosef then produced forty dollars. "Yosef, sweetie! You don't have to do this."

He shrugged modestly as I kissed him.

"Jess, sheesh! You've got nice brothers," I said. "You'll be able to pay off the rest of the bill easily."

With a lump in my throat and tears in my eyes from these fraternal kindnesses, I made my way to the front room, where Donny reclined in his overstuffed chair reading his law books. "You will not *believe* what just happened. We have incredibly sweet boys!" I told him about the money they'd donated to Jesse's case without anyone asking for it.

Donny glanced up from the *Eleventh Circuit Criminal Handbook,* said, "They watched the movies, too," and returned to his reading.

Why? Why am I such an idiot? I've been raising children for decades and this insight would never have occurred to me.

The next day, I found Jesse eating a bowl of Froot Loops alone in the kitchen. "Jess," I said, "those movies . . . Did any of the other boys watch them with you?"

"Mom! Are you kidding me? I didn't watch any of them! Did you see the times those movies were ordered?? Five in the morning! They watch them before school. I don't get up that early!"

It was true. The former goatherds were up at dawn every day.

I sputtered to reply. "Well . . . why did you say it was you?"

"Did you see their faces? They were terrified," he said, and returned to his Froot Loops.

When I relayed this news to Donny, he laughed and said, "They must have been thinking, *Jesse's always in trouble. Jesse can take the heat.*"

I'm a sucker for sibling solidarity. To celebrate Jesse's having paid off his bill and the spirit of fraternity that helped him do it, I took the kids to a movie. I took the six youngest males and females to the Disney/Pixar animated movie *WALL-E*. "Thanks, Mom!" "That was really fun, Mom!" everyone said when we got home from our big night out. Lily and Helen headed upstairs to their bedrooms, and the four boys ran for the basement stairs.

51

Songs of a Summer Night

Spring 2008, Atlanta: Daniel, fourteen; Fisseha, fifteen;
Helen, twelve; Jesse, thirteen

The Ethiopian kids were homesick for the spicy food of their homeland—and Jesse loved it, too—so I took them all out to a neighborhood Ethiopian restaurant called Moya. Lee's friend Sam, who'd come to Ethiopia with us and was now an Emory student, came, too. At Moya, we were guided through the air-cooled darkness of the main dining room to the outside patio, which was separated from the parking lot by a black ornamental fence. It was a sweltering night under a pink sky heaped with clouds. The waiter, besieged by the excited children's voices in English and Amharic and the exuberant flapping of menus, quickly lost track of the order. He asked me in English, "Are you ordering the whole menu?"

"Yes," I said, "it seems we are.

"Wait," I continued. "Maybe not the *kitfo*." (*Kitfo* is raw meat.)

"*Kitfo*, please, please!" cried Sol.

"The whole menu," I said.

Everything should be prepared with the maximum red-hot chili pepper heat of the Ethiopian spice *berbere*, the children specified. They bounced in their seats with eagerness and blew spitballs through their straws as we waited for a fiery hot meal on a sunlit evening I'd thought was hot enough already.

Platters and bright woven covered baskets began to arrive. The children dug in with both hands. This was as it should be, as Ethiopian food is eaten with the fingers: you tear off a bit of *injera* and scoop up a morsel of *wat* with it. When you've eaten everything else, you eat the final layer of *injera* that covers the platter like a doily under all the stews; thus cleanup involves merely the whisking away of a few clean plates and baskets. (I live in envy of the Ethiopian mother.)

There was *doro key wat* (chicken stewed in *berbere* and served with hard-boiled eggs), *sik sik wat* (beef stewed in *berbere*), *yemiser selatta* (lentils with jalapeño peppers), *timatim fitfit* (diced tomatoes, onions, garlic, jalapeño peppers), *tibs wat* (cubed beef simmered in *berbere*), *gomen* (fresh collard greens simmered in spices), *miser wat* (hot, spicy lentil stew), *shiro* (spicy pureed split peas), and three orders of *kitfo* (beef tartare, served raw).

I couldn't eat most of it. I loved the *kikwat* (corn stew) and *lab*, a cool, crumbly white cheese. But everything else was too peppery. I hid behind my glass of mango juice. "Mom, try this!" the children offered. "Not hot, Mom." They weren't trying to trick me, but even the salad of diced tomatoes had been seasoned with chili peppers. I accepted a rolled-up bite of something from Sol's fingers. Tears rolled down my cheeks in regret that a blowtorch had just burned off both my lips.

The kids ate until they could eat no more.

Then they ate more.

Then they pushed back from the table with their hands over their stomachs and groaned.

Then they pulled back to the table and ate more.

Then they got up and ran to the bathroom.

Then they came back and ate everything left on the table.

Exuberant, fueled by *injera*, supercharged by jalapeños, the children excused themselves, thanked the waiter, hurried through the air-conditioned restaurant, shook the owner's hand, and exited. Sam and I waited on the patio for the bill. We watched through the patio fence as the kids pounced on one another's backs. They played piggyback tag up and down the sidewalk and ran piggyback races across the parking lot. They staged walking races. They ran backward races. They ran bend-over-like-this-with-your-arms-hanging-down-like-a-monkey races. They ran let's-slam-full-tilt-into-Mom's-parked-car races. They ran stick-out-your-butt-and-waddle-like-this-while-farting races. I sat quietly, thinking,

Anyone who objects to the behavior of four Ethiopian children and one Bulgarian Romani child will never think they're mine.

As I exited through the restaurant, every diner in the restaurant glanced up at me and said something like, "Your children are having a lot of fun."

On the car ride home, it began: first a gigantic, long-drawn-out belch from Jesse in the far backseat. It sounded like the roar of a lion and impressed everyone. "Jesse! Say 'Excuse me,'" I called from the front seat.

Yosef replied with a series of high-pitched, gurgling burps. Daniel and Sol swallowed hard and responded with enormous guttural bellows, like the greeting of surfacing hippos. "Stop!" I cried. "This is gross! Say, 'Excuse me!'" Then Helen—petite and stylish, with her manicure and her cute capri jeans and her gold sandals—outdid them all with a volcanic bellow that seemed to erupt from the center of the earth.

After a moment of awed and admiring silence, the boys cheered.

I kept my eyes on the road and away from Sam, as, really, what could one say? The belches were constant now, overlapping and obscene, high-pitched and low. Toots and muffled detonations were coming from their nether ends as well, and some whimpering tunes—like the whines of incoming missiles—the origins of which were impossible to identify. The sputtering pops and kabooms sounded like the night sky on the Fourth of July.

I lowered all four windows and opened the sunroof. I breathed through my mouth, trying to take in only the wind off the dark streets. The nonstop yawp and yurk and the fetid air reminded me of a pond I once visited in Vermont. I had slopped up close in muddy ground through high grasses in a haze of mosquitoes as a variety of frogs and toads performed a guttural symphony. Spring peepers made soft, whistly toots, the perfect score for the firefly light show. Green frogs were calling *goink goink*, like the plucking of banjo strings. An American toad screeched a dry, high-C vibration, like the sound of the unoiled wheel of a car in a sharp turn. Periodically, an American bullfrog pumped its low foghorn.

Now, in the car, a spring peeper (Yosef) squeaked, and the green frogs and American toads (Sol, Daniel, and Jesse) provided a brass section; and, most thrilling, the American bullfrog (Helen) sounded its deep and commanding *moo*. Helpless to stop the chorus in my car, I tried to appreciate the rough song and gassiness as something of a natural phenomenon rather than willful misbehavior.

As we drew closer to home, explosions flared all around me, as if I were steering a jeep through a minefield in a World War II movie. I held on to the steering wheel with both hands. Sam allowed himself just one comment: "You wouldn't want to light a match in this car."

As I pulled into the driveway at home, I ordered the children to stay in the front yard to finish. "You don't need to come into the house like this," I said.

"We'll stop, we'll stop!" they cried.

"Oh, no. I'm quite sure if you were capable of stopping, you'd have stopped in the car when I asked you."

"No. We can stop!" they said with big smiles.

"Really?"

"Oh yes!" they said, standing at silent attention to prove it. Skeptically, I opened the front door to them. *Big* mistake! For the rest of the night, there were small lapses, peeps, whistles, and rippling blasts all around me, but—no matter how quickly I whirled around—I couldn't catch the transgressors. The children somehow stayed out of my sight line yet within earshot. The last cheery trumpet calls faded only after everyone, with their full tummies, had fallen asleep.

Recently we returned to the same restaurant, now called Selam, to celebrate Azeb's niece's graduation from high school. An Ethiopian disc jockey blasted popular Ethiopian music—a mix of contemporary artists and traditional melodies from various regions and tribal groups. A newly arrived older woman sat at our table, her skin drawn up smoothly by her crisply wrapped headscarf. She knew no English, but chatted with Sol in Amharic and with Daniel in Gurage. When her plate of *kitfo* arrived, she sliced off red hunks and shared them with Sol. An unmarked glass bottle sat on each table, looking like apple juice. Yosef poured most of it into his glass and gulped it down, after which we learned it was *t'ej*, honey wine. The older woman found this hilarious. Upon hearing that he was now drunk, Yosef staggered to the dance floor alone and invented a few whirling steps while the boys at our table whistled and clapped for him; then he wandered around the dining hall and introduced himself to every person at every table with a handshake and a big hug. He was thirteen, five foot eight, a beautiful athlete and natural comedian with a radiant smile. Adults looked across the dining room to learn to whom this charismatic young man belonged. I felt prouder than on the night here two years earlier, when my children cavorted in the parking lot, powered by digestive expulsions.

Music from the Gurage region blasted from the loudspeakers. The spry older lady at our table was Gurage, like Yosef and Daniel. She hastened to the dance floor. Everyone urged Yosef and Daniel to join her. Yosef jumped up to be her partner, joining in the dances from his region: arms extended in front of him, hands clasped, feet running. It took a bit more urging to get sober Daniel up there, but finally he, too, performed the long strides of the running Gurage dance.

At Big Atetegeb, Mrs. Haregewoin had occasionally thrown parties like this for the children from both houses. The children sat in a big circle on the cool cement floor of their dining room; the caregivers began clapping and singing and called the children up by tribal affiliation. They knew who was Gurage, who Amhara, who Tigrean, who Oromo, who Somali, who Sidamo, who Wolayta (to name only the most populous of Ethiopia's seventy-plus ethnic groups). Mrs. Haregewoin expected even the toddlers to be able to perform the dances of their people. It was, to me, always a moving demonstration of the fact that these orphans had once belonged to somebody, to families, villages, tight-knit communities. Someone had taught them their language, their faith, their music, and their dances.

The songs all sounded exactly alike to Donny and me, a kind of driving, monotonous rhythmic line accompanied by nasal singing. Yet some songs instantly inspired scores of people to push back from their tables, dash to the dance floor, and crowd together in festive performance.

"*This* is a popular song!" yelled Donny into my ear as dozens of Ethiopians sprinted past us to the dance floor.

"For all we know, this is the 'Hava Nagila' of all Ethiopia," I yelled back.

The song changed: now it was the music of the Amhara people—Sol's turn to show what, if anything, he retained. Handsome, slim, wild-haired, bright-eyed, in a button-down black shirt rolled to the elbows, he demurred, but then he allowed himself to be pulled into the crowd. We hadn't seen him do his traditional dance since the week he arrived in Atlanta at age ten, six years ago. The Amhara dance is an impossible-looking feat of shoulder shaking and neck extending and almost birdlike preening and strutting. If you didn't grow up doing it, you'll never master it. Sol is an artist of the soccer field; now he showed himself to be a dancer, too. He put his hands on his hips and danced gracefully, beautifully vibrating his back and shoulders, his long ringlets bouncing against his shoulders. He beamed with sweat and exertion and pleasure. Amhara adults, men and women, danced with him. It seemed to me that time dropped away, as if the intervening American years were but an overlay, while the gold of his Ethiopian village childhood shone through him.

Later I learned that the forty or more Ethiopian teenagers at the party had all been born in America; they spoke Amharic and knew the traditional dances, but only my sons—along with all the adults in the room—were from the Old Country.

Her brothers all tried to lure Lily to the dance floor, but she, lovely in a white summer blouse, rosy-cheeked from the sun, merrily enjoying the music and food, tossed back her curly hair, laughed, and declined. She had been to Ethiopia and felt perfectly relaxed in the restaurant, but she knew you had to grow up with these dances in order to execute them correctly.

Three of our sons' best friends—Grace (grahs) from Congo, Josiah from Liberia, and Kafu from Somalia—were with us. Of course they knew that Sol, Daniel, and Yosef were Africans, but—in the context of our American, English-speaking household with its white parents and white siblings—our guys often may have appeared African in theory rather than in practice. Now Kafu, Josiah, and Grace looked on as their friends chatted in Amharic, ate raw meat, and performed impossible tribal dances. Josiah and Grace tried to move like the Ethiopians, but gave up and jitterbugged instead with some cute Ethiopian girls. When Sol speared into the red chunks of *kitfo*, Grace, a refugee from Congo, looked across the table at me in horror and mouthed the words *Oh my God.*

"Where's Helen?" our hosts asked. She, too, was from the Amhara people. She, too, should be dancing.

Helen had gone to the pool with her girlfriends. "Please," I texted her. "Please. I'll come get you. Everyone's asking for you."

"I'm at the pool," she replied.

"Please," I wrote. "Yosef's dancing."

"Really?"

"Daniel's dancing."

"WHAT?"

"Sol is dancing."

An amazed delay, then her reply: "Can I wear Lily's new blue dress?"

I passed the phone across the table to Lily, who rolled her eyes and texted back: "Yes."

I zoomed home to retrieve Helen and her friend. The crowd welcomed Helen and guided her to her table. She happily accepted the platters of food prepared for her and for her white American friend. Helen loves to dance and takes dance lessons in jazz and tap, but we'd not seen her perform an Ethiopian dance movement since 2002. From her seat, she gazed admiringly at the dancers, especially at a tall, slender girl with upswept hair and earrings sparkling from the top of her earlobes. "I want my ears pierced like that!" Helen yelled to me above the music.

"Yeah, right," I yelled back.

The restaurant throbbed with music as one ethnic group succeeded another on the dance floor.

Sol, Daniel, and Yosef were dancing hip to hip, shoulder to shoulder in the flamboyant, leaping crowd. "Helen, go!" I scolded, giving her a poke.

She leaned over to shout a question: "Can I get my ears pierced like that girl?"

"You know what? *Dance*, then yes."

"REALLY?" And just like that, she was up, hands on hips and shoulders bouncing. She remembered! She laughed hard while dancing, throwing back her head, but her body knew the shaking, vibrating movements. I was so moved I nearly cried.

Our kids spend most of their time and energy being American teenagers, and American-Jewish teenagers, with the accoutrements of computers, iPods, cell phones, car pools, gym memberships, and summer camps; they sing in choral groups, learn trumpet or flute, study French and Hebrew, rent movies at Blockbuster, and get driver's licenses. Recently Donny asked Sol, regarding his thick, long tangle of curls, "What do you call that hairstyle?" and Sol wittily replied: "A Jew-fro."

But on this night on the dance floor they stood revealed as their original selves, radiating the truth that they are first and always children of the Ethiopian people. Donny and I earned the respect of the adults in the room that night, too, for treasuring and preserving that within our children that is Ethiopian.

52

Another Mother

But what of Jesse? The Ethiopian children had regular contact with others in the Ethiopian American diaspora, but Jesse had not laid eyes on another Bulgarian Romani since leaving Bulgaria. The other children all remembered their first parents—Sol had *visited* his—but Jesse, placed in an orphanage as a toddler, arrived here without such precious memories.

Knowing that he was a Romani gave us something to hold on to, something with which to bind him to the planet. Together we plotted the journey of the Romani people out of northern India into Eastern Europe a thousand years ago. But he longed for more knowledge. He was entitled to more knowledge. He always wondered if he looked like anyone. He was always the one at the dinner table to announce things like "Mom, Lee has your eyes, and Seth has your smile" or "Uncle Bobby looks like Daddy." We could never return the favor with any comments of similar sweetness.

Before Helen's arrival in 2004, he overheard a conversation about the new sister and grasped that her parents had died. He took this to be an important clue about his own history. One morning that winter, he and I were hurrying to school, late, on foot, the first bell ringing in the distance, about to cross the last intersection, our right feet in the air above the macadam, when the six-year-old suddenly announced, "My birth parents are dead."

"Whoa . . . *what?*"

"Like Helen's. My birth parents are dead."

"Well, Jess . . . actually, they're . . . they're not; they're not dead."

I'd feared this moment; I'd feared the archetypal question: *Why didn't my parents keep me?*

Now? I thought. *We have to do this now, while racing to school? Am I really going to say, "I don't know why they couldn't keep you, buddy. Have a nice day"?*

"Really?" he said. "My birth parents are *alive*???"

"Yeah, Jess, as far as I know, they are."

We crossed the intersection in silence. I took his small hand. We stepped onto the school lawn. Late arrivals were scurrying toward the front door. I couldn't think what to say, so I waited for his next question.

"Wait," he said, and stopped. "But I know . . . I know the *dinosaurs* are dead."

"The dinosaurs? Well, yes . . . yes, the dinosaurs *are* dead!"

"The dinosaurs are really *really* dead!" he said happily.

"They are, like, SO dead!" I agreed. "We are never going to see those dinosaurs again!"

"Okay, bye, Mommy!" he said, and dashed to class.

This was my greatest-ever example of: Make sure you understand what the child is asking before trying to answer the question. Jesse didn't want to know more about birth parents that morning; he wanted to know more about *death*.

But he also wanted to know more about life, about *his* life. "Do you think my birth mother looks like me? Do you think my birth father looks like me?" he'd ask. "Do you think I'll ever meet them?" I looked into buying one of the new do-it-yourself DNA kits so that we could swab Jesse's cheek and receive a map plotting the journey out of antiquity of his genetic family. Meanwhile, Donny and I quietly hired an investigator in Bulgaria. I'd heard good things about this man. I sent him a copy of Jesse's birth certificate, on which his birth mother's national identification number appeared.

Within the month, the investigator found Jesse's birth mother! She lived in a village near his birthplace. The young woman was gracious and warm toward the investigator, and she easily established the truth of the connection through documentation. She was delighted to receive photographs and news of Jesse and happily shared family pictures with the investigator to be sent to America.

We were lucky! I knew of other families whose searches yielded no results, and others who reached a birth mother who told them, "No one knows about that child. Never contact me again."

As Donny and I opened the digital images e-mailed by the investigator, the fact leaped out at us: Jesse was a clone of his birth mother. He had her coloring, her kind eyes, her smile. She squinted into the sun beside a cement building; she was slender, freckled, curly-haired. (*Boingy hair!* I thought.)

"Oh my God, he's going to be over the moon," I said. "She looks like him! And she's *so pretty!*"

Lee strolled into my office. He knew nothing of our investigation. I enlarged the picture and said, "Guess who this is."

"Who is that?" he asked.

"Who is that?" I repeated.

"Oh my God. Is that Jesse's birth mother?"

I wanted Jesse to control the velocity of these discoveries, so I waited until the next time he asked; I sat on the information until Jesse seemed ready for it again. Sure enough, he asked, "Do you think I'll ever meet my birth mother?"

"You know what?" I said. "Dad and I hired a nice man in Bulgaria to find her for us. I sent him beautiful pictures of you and I wrote a letter telling all about you. He's going to find your birth mother and give everything to her, and maybe she'll write back."

"Okay."

I waited again. About ten days later he asked, "Did that man find my birth mother?"

"Great news! He did! We're going to get pictures of her tonight!"

We couldn't be there in person for this meeting, as we had been with Sol, but we all accompanied Jesse to the computer that night. We seated him in the desk chair and told him to get ready. I opened the first file. And there she was: the woman of his dreams. Still young, lovely, brown-skinned, slender in blue jeans and a sweater, smiling into the bright sun and looking exactly like him.

"Is that my mother?" he gasped.

"Yes!" we all cried.

After a long moment Jesse murmured, "I'm not a mystery anymore."

We clicked slowly and admiringly through all the photos, including one in which a tiny great-grandmother was bent double, evidently in joy, for she held in her hand a photograph of Jesse I'd sent the investigator.

That night Jesse asked me, "Are you worried that I love her more than you?"

"No, Jess, of course not!" I said, thinking, *I was the one who found you in the lonely, impoverished orphanage; I brought you home, made you our son, helped you become an all-American boy . . .*

Before I could get any further with this self-satisfied rumination, Jesse offered, as if reassuringly, "Because I love you both the same."

I laughed and hugged him. It didn't hurt my feelings! I wanted him to feel loved and connected. I wanted him to know that he was also someone's "biological" child.

I interpreted his words—that he loved me (*I gave him the best years of my life,* etc.) the same as he loved a woman he glimpsed briefly in infancy—to mean something like this: *I love my life as a child of our family, and I love my history and my people and my first family. I love both aspects of myself.*

That was the path to wholeness.

53

The Jewish Guide to Raising Star Athletes

All right, we admit it: we had to adopt to get athletes.

For many years, Donny and I drove onto the gravel parking lots of baseball or soccer complexes without creating a stir. Lee, of course, was our baseball player. By age four, he was aiming for the major leagues. A year later he became the first kindergartner to protest to his coach the fact that in official T-ball baseball regulations, the infield fly rule was not in effect. But around age twelve or thirteen, Lee sensed that he was not headed for the majors. Heartbroken, he quit baseball. When he returned a year later, it was out of pure love of the game. He would make his career plans separately.

In soccer, our son or daughter was the player put in toward the end (if our team was ahead). Have I mentioned that Seth has a gift for spotting four-leaf clovers? He can be strolling down a sidewalk with friends when he suddenly stops, reaches back into some greenery, and plucks out a four-leaf clover, almost without breaking stride. We've got four-leaf clovers all over the house. Seth brought this valuable expertise to the soccer field. In the midst of play—two teams darting and feigning and moving the ball up and down the field—the ball was kicked toward Seth according to the theory that he would take it to the goal. Seth ran toward the ball, ran toward it, and then he . . . slowed down, glanced back . . .

While everyone else was yelling, "GO SETH!" Donny and I were yelling, "NO, SETH!" "He's going for it," Donny said. Seth spun away from the likely path of intersection with the speeding soccer ball, turned around, and plucked a four-leaf clover from the soccer field! For Mommy! The play collapsed while the skinny fellow with the sparkly eyes galloped across the field to toss me the limp little plant. He dashed away in high spirits, no doubt feeling he'd performed a valuable service. "He brings our team so much good luck!" I called to the other parents.

If I ran into a coach off the field, he never knew my name.

NOW if we pull up late to a soccer game, the parents, teammates, and coaches are standing on the parking lot, shading their eyes against the sun and looking for the Samuels. Soccer coaches from around the Atlanta region call us, trying to recruit our children. One offered to waive the fees; another (when I pointed out that his field was a two-hour drive from our house) volunteered a team mother to drive my son to and from practice all year. He offered this without checking with the woman. One coach, from the Republic of Georgia, held a U.S. Olympic gold medal in soccer from the 1988 Seoul games. "With your son," he promised, "no one will get past me. No one."

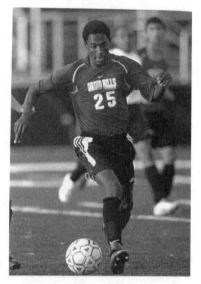

Daniel playing Druid Hills High School varsity soccer, 2010
(Photograph by Nill Toulme)

I, despite being obliged to sit on the sidelines of between four and twelve soccer games every weekend, still do not recognize offsides when I see them. I huddle in my folding chair with gloves, sunglasses, and a coffee mug, *The New York Times* open on my lap, glancing up from the Op-Ed page to applaud only when I sense that one of my children has just scored or made an assist. This happens so often that it's hard to concentrate on an article.

My first hint that we had stepped onto new parenting ground was this: I took newly arrived four-and-a-half-year-old Jesse to a neighborhood playground. He shimmied up the fireman's pole to the monkey bars and swung hand over hand across the cold horizontal bars. He did this without falling and crumpling into the wood chips. He did this without hanging helplessly and screaming for rescue. He did this without needing to be hoisted by me from one crossbar to the next. He traversed the monkey bars, turned around in midair, and swung back from the other direction. "Look at Jesse! Just look at him!" I yelled to my friend Alice Barger, mother of two sons.

"That's terrific," she replied.

"Jesse! Wow! Jesse, you're amazing!" I cheered. I glanced over at Alice to see if she was going to cheer, too, but she was looking at her watch or something. I squinted at her, trying to interpret her attitude. "Wait," I said suspiciously. "Your kids can do this, can't they?"

"Yes, Melissa," she laughed.

Sol playing Druid Hills High School varsity soccer, 2010 (Photograph by Nill Toulme)

One of the great traditions of Fernbank Elementary School is the Fun Run. On a cold fall weekend morning, barricades go up to block a few neighborhood streets; blue-jeaned parents in hoodies, holding travel mugs and video cameras, gather along the sidewalks. A police officer on a motorcycle leads the way, and a high school runner jogs at the head of the line to pace the children. The kindergartners and first-graders run a block and a half to a dead end, circle around, and then run back, some weeping, some tripping and falling down, all cheered by the crowd. The middle-graders travel a notch farther. And the fourth- and fifth-graders run a half mile. Then everyone enjoys glazed doughnuts and hot apple cider while somewhere in the distance, medals are distributed.

We always went for the good company, the crisp fall weather, and the doughnuts.

We didn't know from medals.

Then we adopted Helen.

As a kindergartner she reached the dead end, circled around, and was on her way back before most of her age-mates had turned the first corner. A gold medal!

As a first-grader, she was alone at the front of the returning hordes when she crumpled and dove into the grass along the side of the finish line. We thought she was confused about where the finish line was, but she was gasping deeply for breath. We learned she had exercise-induced asthma. We got her an inhaler.

When Helen was in second grade, we overslept! We leaped out of bed and ran to the car, but I couldn't get anywhere near the school. "Run! Your race is going to start any second!" I told her. She took off. She was too late, and beheld the disappearing backs and heels of her age group. Shyly she approached a teacher and asked, "Are you still allowed to run if you're late?" "Sure, honey," said the teacher. So Helen dashed to catch up with the race, caught the race, and won the gold medal for second-grade girls.

By that year, Sol had joined the family and was in fourth grade. When the PE teacher dropped her arm, the herd of fourth- and fifth-graders thundered down the block, turned left, and disappeared from sight. We parents mingled, chitchatted, reviewed the highlights of our summer vacations, and then a man to my left said "Oh my God" and looked at his watch. I glanced up and saw, all alone on the horizon, Sol! He wasn't sprinting; he was just loping along. Not knowing he wasn't supposed to pass the high school runner, he had passed him. Not knowing he wasn't supposed to pass the police-man on the motorcycle, he had passed him. He hit the finish line without breaking a sweat, turned on his heel, and came to find Donny and me.

We got two gold medals that year.

We *owned* the Fernbank Fun Run. It was around then that someone asked us for the first time, "Do you *scout* these kids?"

Yosef playing GSA club soccer (Photograph by Douglas Smith)

Sol graduated from Fernbank, Helen was in her fifth and final year, and Yosef arrived from Ethiopia and started fourth grade. Our children knew that the great Ethiopian distance runners raced as a team. They paced one another or designated a team member to wear out the competition, clearing the way for Ethiopians to take gold, or gold and silver, or gold and bronze, or gold and silver and bronze in 10,000- and 50,000-meter races. We had recorded some of the great Ethiopian Olympic finishes. That year at the Fun Run, I didn't make chitchat and I didn't refill my coffee mug. Donny was out of town and was listening to the race live on my cell phone. I watched the empty street before most parents sensed that the race could be nearing an end. When two little figures appeared in the misty morning, it took only a moment to identify them as Helen and Yosef. They were holding hands. They released their hands at the last second and Yosef finished first overall and Helen first among girls. Two gold medals.

The following year, our last, Yosef competed as a fifth-grader. That was the year people said, "The only competition is for second place."

One afternoon at recess, fifth-grade Sol was engaged in a pickup football game on the school playground. The PE teacher, Peggy Sutton, a middle-aged blond woman in Bermuda shorts and a clean white polo shirt, got on her walkie-talkie and beeped the principal. "Mr. Marshall, can you come out to the playground right away?"

"I'm on my way," came the voice through the static, and Jason Marshall, a onetime athlete, now in his early thirties, a graduate of Morehouse College and Harvard University, exited his office. In his suit and tie, he hurried to the fields. "What's going on?"

"I'll bet you five dollars," said Ms. Sutton, "that Sol can throw a football from the monkey bars to the baseball backstop."

"What are you talking about? That's got to be . . . what? . . . fifty yards. And he's ten years old? No way."

"Five dollars?" repeated Ms. Sutton.

"You're on."

"SOL!" she yelled across the field. "THROW THE FOOTBALL! Did I mention," she added to the principal, "that it will have a perfect spiral?"

Sol launched the football in a soaring arc. It quivered eagerly, nosing through a flight pattern that would have been the pride of a Division I college quarterback.

Mr. Marshall reached into his pocket, removed his billfold, and drew out a five-dollar bill.

"Thank you, Mr. Marshall," said Ms. Sutton crisply.

"You're very welcome, and thank *you* for your involvement in the well-being of our students," said the principal, returning to his office.

When Daniel was in eighth grade in middle school, he was persuaded by friends to run cross-country with the high school JV team. He went to a couple of practices and hated it. "Mom, my legs they are break," he complained. Reluctantly he rode the bus with the team to the first 5-K DeKalb County meet. His long legs swiftly carried him to the front of the pack and beyond. He followed the trail into the woods but reached a fork in the path and didn't know where to go. He jogged in circles for a minute until the high school boys racing for second place caught him. "Where am I go?" he asked. They were Ethiopians, from schools all over DeKalb County. He recognized them as countrymen, but they did not recognize him. "They think I am Sudan," he told me later. They nicely pointed out the route. He thanked them politely, picked up his pace, and won. The following week he came back and won the county meet again. Then he quit cross-country. "Mom," he complained. "My legs they are break."

It's not like the biological kids didn't notice.

Lily, in ninth grade, tried track. Lily is beautiful, ebullient, smart, and funny; she gave track her all. "Runner on the track. CAUTION: runner on the track," came the amplified voice through the loudspeaker. Lily was alone on the track, pounding around her final lap, finishing the mile after all other milers had finished, winners had been announced, and the next race was starting. Helen, a fourth-grader, had come to cheer for her big sister. Now she felt confused. "WHY?" she began in a high-pitched voice, then paused to think how to frame her question to capture the current situation (Lily rounding the last curve, bands of fresh runners passing her by). "Why do you *enter* a race if you're not going to *win* it?"

"Do me a favor, Helen," I said. "Do not ask Lily."

Lee ran with the Druid Hills High School cross-country team a few years before Daniel got there. Lee wrote about his running career in his college admissions essay:

When I made the varsity cross-country team, I knew (and the coach knew) that I would never finish a county meet better than 27th. No *fe-range* [white person, Amharic] ever does. No, those top spots are strictly reserved for my friends, Abdighani, Abdifata, Abbukar, and Abdi (Somalian, Eritrean, Ethiopian, and Sudanese) and their countrymen. At my urban public high school, where students come from 60 different countries and where white American-born students are in the minority, the best I can do—other than finish 45th—is, as newspaper editor and sportswriter, to cover their phenomenal performances.

Though I never won a race, I did have the good fortune to pick up some key phrases from my teammates. I can compliment a girl from East Africa on her hairstyle. I can say "Wow, Ethiopians sure are faster than white Americans" in four different languages; and I can, of course, since we are teenage males, say "Screw you," which I would never sincerely say to an East African except to draw a laugh . . .

Other friends, the stars of the school soccer team, come from Japan, Mexico, Afghanistan, South Africa, Somalia, Ghana, and Ethiopia; statewide sportswriters nicknamed the team "The United Nations." The rest of our crowd of friends—black and white Americans—rode around the state cheering them on and waving the flags of their respective homelands all the way to the state semifinals.

My home life is not much different . . . My Ethiopian brother Fisseha, a former goat-herd, can throw a spear (that he carved with a kitchen knife) a full 200 feet and pierce a Frisbee mid-air, a useful skill when you are a hunter-gatherer of the African savannas, less useful when you live in Georgia, unless you have a personal vendetta against squirrels. Recently, Fisseha taught me a great new phrase that I am sure will be useful: *Ante Ahiya Keet Timaslaleh. You look like a donkey's ass.*

In my last career cross-country meet last month, I ran my three-year personal best: 5K in 19:30. Stunningly, my time was good enough for 23rd place! Exuberant, I hobbled around looking for my African teammates. "I finished 23rd! I finished 23rd!" I yelled between fits of panting.

They're always so polite. Mattieu Gebreselassie, the seventh-ranked runner in Georgia, who had run six miles TO the meet, completed the 5K three minutes ahead of me, and had already run his one-mile cool-down, shyly said, "Ehhhh, Lee . . . um . . . none of the Somalians are here. It is Ramadan and they are not eating."

What could I say other than "Yeah? Well *Ante Ahiya Keet Timaslale!*" and then run for my life, knowing full well I wouldn't get very far?

Seth, in San Francisco, where he works as a sound engineer and producer at NPR affiliate radio station KALW, plays Ping-Pong daily against fellow sound engineer Chris Hoff; so far, Chris has won 222 games and Seth has won once. They keep their score on a public whiteboard; the 222 appearing as hatch marks and crossbars, while Seth's ONE, his *1*, is a One beyond all ordinary ones—tall, broad, handsome, ornately decorated, covered with loving curlicues and other embellishments. After every game, while his colleague adds another hatch mark or slash, Seth tenderly attends to his One.

Lily, in eleventh grade, tried out for her high school varsity volleyball team. She loved volleyball; she loved leaping and hitting; she loved having teammates. "I'm worried," she said, preparing to drive herself to school for the tryouts.

"Really? You've been playing for two years. You'll make it, won't you?" I said.

"I don't know. It's going to really suck if my teammates all move up and I don't. I'm happy to stay with JV if they stay, but if I'm the only eleventh-grader left behind, that will be awful."

That's what happened. One by one her JV teammates were summoned to the other side of the gym while Lily sat on the gym floor leaning against the wall with unchosen ninth- and tenth-graders.

She came home and ran up the stairs to her room, yelling only "NO!" in a choked voice when I called, "How did you do?" I ran up behind her.

She'd thrown herself facedown on her bed. I couldn't tell if she was crying.

"I'm so sorry, sweetheart," I offered.

She lifted a teary face from the pillow and demanded: "Why'd you have to adopt all the Ethiopians? It just makes it *worse!*"

"Oh, Lily . . ." I began, not knowing if she was serious.

She raised her head again. "Why couldn't you have adopted overweight white children from *Texas*? Then I could have been better than someone at a sport!" I burst out laughing, and she did, too, and we went downstairs so she could be cheered up by her siblings.

54

Gurage

I drove Yosef to soccer practice on a spring evening in 2010. Because he was gifted at this game—as fast as a panther, flashing the smile of a young carnivore—he practiced on fields on the far side of Stone Mountain with a highly competitive team. I pulled onto the highway while he leaned back to enjoy his iPod. "Talk to me," I said, poking him in the arm. "Be with me."

"What?" He pushed a button to pause a rapper's voice mid-obscenity. Green land flowed away from the highway on both sides; fuzzy-headed weeds blew back in the wind from the car. Small ranch houses and soft-looking old farmhouses appeared at half-mile intervals. "Does this ever remind you of Ethiopia?" I asked. I opened the sunroof and lowered all the windows; twilight, dust, and heat enveloped us.

"Yes," he said, and then moved to replace his earphones.

"Tell me," I said. "What do you remember?"

I tried to picture his village, Gafaht, in the Gurage region. His and Daniel's oldest brother, Wogene (wo-gen-ay) and their grandmother, Awude (ah-wood-ie) still lived there. It was beyond the reach of paved roads and electricity; people lived there the old way—farming, raising animals, carrying water from a well, horseback riding from one place to another—in a land of hyenas and cheetahs. I imagined the midnight sky brilliantly suspended above the mud-and-thatch huts, like tremendous electronic Times Square billboards advertising dazzling stars and constellations.

"We had a cow," Yosef now told me in the car. "When the cow died, it was terrible. Everyone had horses. We didn't see many cars, maybe one car a year. When you want to go, you ride a horse." It was his job to take the goats or sheep up into the hills every morning to forage on wild grasses. He was about five or six, he thought.

"You did that alone?" I asked.

"No! With my friends!"

They hollered to each other when they were ready to go, something between a scream and a yodel that traveled across the landscape to the next *tukul*. In suburban Dayton, Ohio, in the 1960s, my brother Garry and I and our friends had a yell like that: "*Ah-eh-ah!*" meaning, *Meet at the fort!* Yosef and his friends and their dogs and grazing animals hiked up the dry, rocky hills. The boys lolled in the weeds, climbed trees, drank from streams, ate berries and wild nuts, made up games, built temporary huts as shelter against the midday African sun, napped, and headed home at day's end toward the scent of cook-fires.

The evening sky was streaked with green as we neared the soccer fields, the trees awash in new leaves, rustling their skirts. "You played soccer in the village?" I asked.

"Yes, but we didn't know it was named soccer or *futball*. I thought we made up the game."

Barefoot, on hard ground, they kicked a ball made of cloth rags, with dried grasses wrapped around it. Later, after the deaths of their parents untethered them from the village, Yosef and Daniel were delighted to see that the kids at Haregewoin's foster home played the kicking-ball game—probably they knew it from *their* villages. The first time they saw professional soccer on a black-and-white television was a moment of amazement. So many villages around the world!

In Atlanta, it had felt very strange to play "soccer" with inflated synthetic-leather balls while wearing cleats on green fields under the guidance of adult coaches. Then they excelled. Yosef consistently ranks first or second-highest scorer for his age group in the state. Like everything else from Gafaht, the old barefoot kicking-the-ragbag ball game seemed more quaint, distant, and forgettable with every passing year. Daniel and Yosef hadn't seen their grandmother and brother since the deaths of their parents and younger brothers four or five years earlier. Did Awude and Wogene even know the boys had gone to America?

Spring break 2009: Donny and I drove with Sol, Daniel, Jesse, Helen, Yosef, and friends to a rental beach house in Grayton Beach, Florida. The kids swam and fished in the ocean, rode bikes up and down the beach, and were invited to cookouts and sleepovers at friends' beach houses.

It was also Lee's spring break from his Israeli college, Ha'mercaz Ha'Beintchomi Herzliya, the Interdisciplinary Center of Herzliya. He and his closest friend, Maya Selber, flew to Ethiopia. Of Jewish-Moroccan-Israeli descent, born in Philadelphia, Maya was beautiful, fine-boned, large-eyed, and brimming with laughter. Lee wanted her to meet the Atetegeb and AHOPE kids, and Sol's grandmother Tschai. He wondered if it would be possible to travel to the Gurage region to search for Wogene and Grandmother.

Lee phoned Yosef and Daniel's uncle and asked about traveling to Gurage, escorted by the uncle if possible.

"How long you will stay in Ethiopia?"

"Ten days."

"No, there is not time for trip to Gurage. If spring rains come, rivers flood. You will not return for two months."

Lee sounded so disappointed that the uncle offered to try to send a message. "I don't know if they will receive it. I will invite them to come meet you in Addis." He promised to call if he heard anything. His message traveled in a southwesterly direction from the capital by cell phone and then by pony express. Four days later the uncle phoned Lee to say that the pair had arrived safely for their first-ever visit to Addis Ababa. They had ridden on horseback to a city, and then they got on a bus.

The moment Lee got out of the taxi at the uncle's house, he recognized them: the handsome, serious country widow and the humble boy of sixteen, both looked like Daniel. Wogene, though older, was shorter and slighter than Daniel.

"He looked tired and worn," says Maya.

"He looked malnourished," says Lee. "He was wearing his best clothes, I could tell: jeans and a T-shirt. He'd probably just gotten them, to meet us."

After polite bows and handshakes, all were seated on kitchen chairs inside, in a room with whitewashed brick walls and a cement floor. The dignified grandmother wore a snug black wrap around her head and a cotton shawl across her wide shoulders. She seated herself cautiously and slowly, as if she wanted to avoid the possibility of committing an error, or maybe she wanted to go easy on her knees after a day and a half of rough travel. Or maybe she wanted time to prepare for whatever it was she was going to hear from these young people. This was not a woman often blessed by good news. She looked with cautious concern at the white Americans; she had no idea what message was about to fall from their lips, or why she had been summoned to the capital to hear it.

"I'm Lee, Yosef and Daniel's brother," Lee began, and our family friend Abebe (ah-*beh*-beh) translated; but as an opening conversational gambit, Lee's introducing himself as Yosef and Daniel's brother fell flat. Awude blinked slowly at Lee and again, slowly, at Abebe, and showed no emotion. Wogene, fidgeting in his excitement at arriving in the big city, also had no reaction to this news.

"You know Yosef and Daniel are in America, right?" Lee tried again. No, they had not known this.

"You didn't know they were in America?"

No.

"My parents adopted them."

Cognitive dissonance.

"You know what it means to be adopted?"

Not sure.

Abebe stroked his spare mustache in thought, then leaned forward, clasping his hands between his knees, and gently explained the basic principles.

Awude riveted a pair of powerful coal-black eyes on Lee. She sat erect and sternly listened to every word he spoke. Then she spoke at length to Abebe, a minor-key melody in her husky voice. Meanwhile, Wogene was trying to make sense of his surroundings. He was extraordinarily stimulated, growing more animated or agitated by the moment. "A car in the street honked," says Maya, "and Wogene *jumped*. I started taping him on my little Flip video camera, and then I showed him, and when he saw himself on the video—oh my God, I never saw such shock on anyone's face in my life!—he was like, *How is that possible?! Wow, what is that?!* He took the camera and was examining it from every direction.

He was really shy and timid and bewildered, but at the same time he was excited and curious."

Now Abebe spoke to Lee, translating for Awude. She and Wogene had never known what became of the boys. They had not understood what the boys' uncle had done with them. Perhaps he had tried to explain, but the idea of adoption to America sounded far-fetched, inconceivable. They thought the boys had become foreign workers or servants, perhaps against their will. They had not felt confident that the boys were still alive. It was their central grief, almost too painful to speak of, that after losing the boys' parents and two younger brothers, they had lost Daniel and Yosef.

She sighed heavily, looked levelly at Lee, blinked once again, skeptically.

He reached for his backpack and pulled out an envelope of photographs. Here were Daniel and Yosef in bright soccer uniforms, posing with their teams; here they were in swimsuits on the beach; here they were in the midst of friends, blowing out birthday candles; here they were at a bowling alley. Beaches, bowling balls, birthday candles, Grandmother recognized nothing but this: her grandsons were alive, cared for, and happy. They'd grown tall! She covered her mouth with one broad hand and then covered that hand with her other hand.

"They are great boys," Lee told Abebe, who translated. "They go to school. They study math and English and science. When they are older, they will go to the university. They miss you both very much. They asked me to find you."

Grandmother covered her face entirely with her shawl.

Lee looked at his watch and opened his cell phone. "Now," he told them, "we're going to call Yosef and Daniel."

On Grayton Beach, Yosef and Daniel biked along the blacktopped sandy streets wearing sunglasses, swim trunks, and flip-flops. At night they sat around a campfire while one of their friends strummed a guitar. Yosef tormented Daniel endlessly. One night on the beach, he dumped fistfuls of sand into Daniel's swim trunks from behind. Daniel shrieked and gave chase. Ecstatic, Yosef flew down the beach in the dark. As he passed a large group of white beachgoers, he screamed, "HELP ME! HELP ME!! THERE'S A BLACK MAN AFTER ME!"

The vacationers registered his words in time to turn and behold wild-eyed Daniel huffing at top speed across the sand straight at them. They got out of his way.

Back at the house, Yosef shrugged and said, "No good. I forget it is the two thousands. In the 1950s those people will stop Daniel." He shook his head, as if lamenting the decline of civilization. "No one cares anymore."

"Both of you be here at the house at ten-thirty tomorrow morning," I told them. "We're going to try to make phone contact with your grandmother and Wogene. It will be five-thirty in the evening in Ethiopia and Lee and Maya will be with them."

We had trouble establishing the connection. Every squawked syllable and dropped call was more painful than the last, as if it really might not be possible to bridge such a tremendous distance. But finally I heard Lee's voice, and he heard mine. I passed my phone to Daniel, and Lee gave his phone to Wogene.

Wogene had never held a phone before. He couldn't hear anything. Maya rotated the phone around to Wogene's ear, and a noise flew out of the speaker.

"Hello?? Hello?" Daniel was yelling, walking around barefoot in a storklike way in the sandy front yard, wearing plaid Bermuda shorts and a sleeveless T-shirt, picking his feet up fast after stepping on prickly seeds. "Mom, there's no one there. Hello? Hello? There's no one."

In Ethiopia, a double miracle unfolded in the life of Wogene Gizaw: first, the miracle of the telephone. *Watson, come here, I want you.* And then the miracle of hearing his brother's voice again in this lifetime.

"Allo? Allo? Dan-ee-el? *Anta? Anta?* [Is it you? Is it you?] Allo? Dan-ee-el?"

Maya says, "Wogene was ecstatic. He was chirping and screaming in excitement. He was holding the phone in front of his face and yelling at the phone, grinning from ear to ear. He thought he had to face the phone and yell to be heard, and then mash the phone halfway into his ear to hear something."

In Grayton Beach, Daniel handed the phone to Yosef so that Wogene could yell, "Allo?? Allo, Yosef? *Anta? Anta?* Yosef?" and then Awude took the phone and wept and spoke at great length to her lost boys, relaying bottled-up years of concern and advice. Then she gestured to Lee that she wanted to speak to *me*. Lee told her, through Abebe, that I didn't speak Amharic or Gurage, but she waved that report away as nonsense and insisted that we talk. "Allo? Allo? Awude?" I said, and she ran away with the conversation, sharing grandmotherly murmurs of gratitude and relief and recommendations and hope and boundless love.

"We needed no translator," I told Lee when he took back the phone.

"Wogene needs money to go to school," he said.

"Of course, yes, let's help him."

"He walks eight miles every day to school, and eight miles home. But there's a nearby school he could go to if he had tuition money."

"How much?"

He covered the phone and there was a muffled discussion while I thought, *Oh my God, have we just taken on another private school tuition?*

Lee returned. "Ten dollars a semester."

Lee then bestowed enough money on Wogene to pay for every semester of schooling for the rest of his life, and other funds for Grandmother.

We all said goodbye and hung up. Yosef, Daniel, and I stood teary-eyed on the sand yard on the Florida Panhandle. Then they hopped on their bikes and rode back to the beach.

Several hours later, around midnight in Ethiopia, Lee called back. "What's the matter?" I cried, hearing his breaking voice.

"I feel so terrible for Wogene," he said, and sobbed. "He has such a hard life. He spends his life walking to and from school and to and from the well. He has nothing. And he was incredibly happy. This one-hour encounter was like the greatest thing that ever happened to him. He was ecstatic just to hear Daniel's and Yosef's voices. And he's going back now to nothing."

"It's not nothing. He has his grandmother, his village, his friends."

"They're dirt-poor. They've lost the rest of their family. When will we ever see him again? And our lives compared to Wogene's . . ."

Lee was crying, and I could hear Maya crying behind him.

He wasn't asking us to adopt Wogene—Wogene was too old to be adopted and he couldn't leave Grandmother anyway. Lee was just crying.

55

Ten Things I Love About You

It's September again: time to meet the Explorers! Schoolchildren open the glossy pages of their social studies textbooks to Henry the Navigator, Vasco da Gama, Amerigo Vespucci, Ferdinand Magellan, and Vasco Núñez de Balboa, the names redolent of saltwater, candle wax, and whale oil. The feather-capped men appear in profile in black-and-white etchings, their arched eyebrows and sharp little beards already pointing west. Children believe that the misshapen medieval maps and lunatic histories are important keys to the grown-up world. They assume that adults sit around at dinner parties saying things like, "Were you aware that the English explorer John Cabot (1450–1499) was born in Italy and his name was originally Giovanni Caboto?" To which a guest will reply, "I personally always found it remarkable that Prince Henry the Navigator of Portugal (1394–1460) was a patron of voyages but never actually sailed on any!"

No one reveals to the children that once they leave elementary school, they will never hear the names Cortés or Vasco da Gama again (or not until they become parents). Like Peter Pan, Babar, and Curious George, Balboa and Magellan belong to the world of childhood.

———

This fall, our African fertility statue once again reclines on a high closet shelf behind Donny's torn wool sweaters. He/she worked hard for our family. He/she brought us four African children, and a Bulgarian Romani.

We gained more than the five children: we gained Tsehai and Waganesh and Fisseha's extended family; Jesse's birth family; and now Daniel and Yosef's brother and grandmother. We acknowledge these deep relationships and our responsibility to help the children stay in touch.

"Things You Never Thought You'd Hear Yourself Say as a Parent" was the name of a list maintained by our friends Dr. Steven and Linda Bell of Rome, Georgia. It included two items from my long-ago parental repertoire: (1) "I want you to hit each other outside." And (2) "Please don't wrestle with the scissors near the baby." Now the Bells are grandparents, but I still have children in the house to whom I am forced to say ludicrous things.

Sol, now sixteen, spotted a tiny two-wheeler in a neighbor's garbage can up the hill from our house. By moonlight, he jogged up to retrieve it, then rocketed down the steep hill, legs akimbo, long Afro blown back, screaming at the top of his voice. He staggered in the front door carrying the bike and gasping, "I found out why they threw it away: it doesn't have *brakes!*"

"That's the kind of bike you brake by stepping backward on the pedal," I said, heading toward the den. "Little-kid bikes don't have hand brakes."

"Oh," said Sol. Having been a goatherd during the years that American children learned to ride sixteen-inch bikes, he wasn't acquainted with their brake system. Now he sat on the little seat, bent forward, and propelled himself across the dining room. His legs rotated the crank arms of the pedals with the speed of a cartoon cyclist. His densely curly hair remained in the blown-back position, making him appear even speedier. As he whirred through the den, I looked up from the newspaper and pleaded, "*Don't* make me say 'No bike riding in the house.'"

He turned right, coasted down the front hall, and banked right again. In the dining room, he picked up six-foot-tall Daniel, who put his feet against the frame, clung to Sol's shoulders, and leaned back. Sol came huffing with him into the den. I peered over the top of the newspaper and said only, "Sol. *Fisseha.*"

On the next lap, fourteen-year-old Helen was wrapped around Daniel's neck, screaming in mock terror while Sol pedaled hard, working up a sweat. "Are you really going to make me say this?" I said as they turned right and headed down the hallway. When the tottering threesome crossed the kitchen threshold into the den *again*, I yelled, "NO BIKING IN THE HOUSE!"

With instant obedience, Sol made a sharp right turn just outside the door to the basement stairs, throwing off Daniel and Helen and plunging headlong down the steps, bucking and shrieking. "You're not wearing a helmet! Don't ride your bike down the stairs without a helmet!"

Downstairs, Sol parked the bike outside the bathroom and went inside to take a shower. Later that night I found it parked next to his bed. He'd ridden it the seventeen feet from the bathroom to his bedroom. *Now all the kids will want indoor bicycles!* I thought with vexation. To avoid a referendum on the subject, which Donny and I would be bound to lose, I quietly wheeled the small bike outside.

In the evenings, Helen and Lily escape upstairs to Lily's bedroom, to a girl's realm of warmth and congeniality. They read and study by the fragrant curl of smoke rising from a stick of incense on the dresser. Helen takes charge of iTunes on Lily's computer, inflicting Rihanna and Justin Bieber on the older sister who would, at least sometimes, prefer Gershwin or Saint-Saëns. They paint their nails. They pick out each other's outfits for the next day. They reread all of *Harry Potter*, in order. They read Jane Austen. They lean back on the pillows and watch movies on Lily's computer, choosing from among longtime favorites like *She's the Man, A Cinderella Story, 10 Things I Hate About You, Anastasia, The Lion King*, or reruns of *Glee*. "After we watch a movie, we stay up till all hours talking about it and catching up on other gossip," Lily says. "We update the List. We have a HUGE list (I'm talking over two hundred names) of hot actors/movie characters/cartoon characters that we 'call.' As soon as we spot a new actor in a movie, we race to 'call' him. If we ever *meet* one of the guys on *my* list, I get first dibs. If he's on *her* list, she gets first dibs. She thinks her list is better, but I'd say it's a close call.

"For a while we tried to create our own Jazzercise class in my room. We often have dance parties. Sometimes we invite Jesse, who's a really good dancer. One night we listened to classical music and wrote out little stories that could correspond to each piece. When Helen goes to the bathroom, I'll sit out in the hall and write messages to her, sliding them under the door, and she will write back. The policy, unless otherwise stated, is that she sleeps in my bed. On the nights she sleeps in her own room, we have code knocks on our mutual wall that communicate different things. Whoever wakes up first wakes the other one in some really annoying way."

Getting dressed up is challenging for me, made more so by the fact that I must run the gauntlet of stepping into Lily's room and presenting myself to teenage girls before I can be released into the outside world. I apprehensively knock, and enter. The girls stop what they're doing and stare for long moments, often with expressions of shock or disbelief. Lily will be the first to speak: "Oh, for the love of God."

Helen goes next: "Mommy, I love you so much!"

The worse I look, the more compassion I inspire in Helen. She gets the same look on her face when I try to shoot baskets with the kids in the driveway, or when I approach the dinner table with something new I've cooked. If she gets up, races across the bedroom, and throws her arms around me, I know we'll be starting over from scratch. Working from both my closet and Lily's, the girls pull together a new outfit for me. They confiscate the scuffed Earth shoe–looking things I'm wearing, hide them, and authoritatively point at a pair of Lily's heels instead. Lily loosely knots a scarf around my neck, Helen tugs downward on my skirt, Lily lends me a pair of her earrings, Helen runs to find lip gloss; then the two of them stand back, confer with each other, and give me permission to leave the house.

They share their clothes and jewelry with each other, too. Helen goes further: she allows her *friends* to borrow Lily's clothes. Before Lily graduated, she and Helen both attended the Paideia School. Lily grew accustomed to spotting her T-shirt or jacket coming across campus toward her on Helen; when she began spotting missing items coming and going on Helen's friends, that got a tiny bit irritating. (One day, at the movies, Lily saw a favorite shirt headed her way on a friend of Sol and Daniel's—on Josiah, from Liberia. Lily and Josiah came face-to-face, both wearing Lily's shirts, and both burst out laughing.)

Molly reaches out to her younger sisters. Lily spent spring break in San Francisco last year and her first Oberlin winter term there in January 2011. The two girls hiked, cooked, biked, and ate out with Molly's friends. "You two must have had so much fun and been so close growing up," a friend said over dinner.

"Hmmm, not really," said Molly. "When I left home at eighteen, Lily was seven."

Now Lily has left home at eighteen, and Helen is fourteen. The hole it has left in Helen's daily life is unspeakable, irreparable. They text, talk, e-mail, Skype . . . but it's not the same as the daily intimacy they have treasured since the moment Helen stepped foot in the house in 2002. "Helen, you *have* to come visit me; all my friends are dying to meet you. You're all I ever talk about," Lily tells her.

"Mom, can I go to boarding school?" Helen asked me recently. "Can I go to boarding school in Ohio, near Oberlin?"

They plan to share an apartment someday, when Helen's an undergraduate and Lily's in graduate school; they're considering New York City, on their own, or San Francisco, near Seth and Molly.

In 2009, as Lily packed for two months of study in Israel, Helen approached with a bon voyage gift. She had made a scrapbook for Lily, with pages labeled "Your Favorite Ethiopians," "Your Favorite Bulgarian," "Your Whole Family," and so forth. And she'd made a list. She reduced the movie poster from *10 Things I Hate About You*, crossed out "Hate," wrote in "Love," and offered:

10 Things I Love About You
1. Even after you yell at me one hundred times, I still eat and sleep in your room and wear your clothes.
2. I don't how it's possible but we wear the exact same size.
3. I tell you everything and you tell me everything.

4. Even though you hate it when people copy you, I follow your very steps in life (Paideia, volleyball, tap . . .).
5. You like to pick on Jesse as much as I do.
6. We have the exact same taste in EVERYTHING!!
7. You're not too tall so we can go anywhere and pretend to be the same age!
8. You don't treat me like a little kid (like our brothers do).
9. When I wake up in my room, you're in here playing SIMS because you have nothing else to do.
10. Out of everyone at the orphanage YOU CHOSE ME!

56

DNA

Four of our children are our genetic descendants, five are not. But Donny and I have been no less surprised over the years by the personalities, habits, passions, and talents of our "bio" kids than of our adopted kids. The throw of the dice of 3.4 billion DNA base pairs—collected and sifted out of the two hundred thousand years of human evolution—can land as look-alike knockoffs of Mom or Dad, or with strong resemblances to a distant ancestor from Lithuania or to an even more distant ancestor from the Afar Depression in Ethiopia's Great Rift Valley. Of course all nine of our children, like all humanity, descended from Great Rift Valley; some just took a more direct flight to Atlanta than others.

Our four oldest kids' introduction to the shuffling of the chromosomal deck used to be recited like this:

Molly was a finger-sucking straight-haired cover lover (as a baby and small child, she liked to suck two fingers; in the night she burrowed deep under her blankets).

Seth was a non-finger-sucking curly-haired cover lover.

And that might have been that, if we'd stopped at two. What two very different human beings we had produced!

Then Lee came along: a thumb-sucking straight-haired cover kicker.

And Lily: a finger-sucking curly-haired cover kicker.

Genetics 101.

With Jesse's arrival, we could see that he was a straight-haired cover lover. But had he ever sucked his fingers? It seemed unfair to recite our litany without him, so we let it slide. Then, somewhere down the line, with the addition of more children, we picked up the theme of genetic categories again. They'd multiplied exponentially. And strong resemblances existed in-house—family traits—perhaps the result of what Joe Kayes called "airborne genes."

The family shorthand now looks like this:

Night owls: Seth (bio), Jesse (Bulgaria), Helen (Ethiopia). Up at dawn (former goatherds): Sol (Ethiopia), Daniel (Ethiopia).

Shiny hair blows in the wind: Molly (bio), Lily (bio), Helen (Ethiopia). Brillo-like hair remains unmoved by wind, water, hail, or ice: Seth (bio), Sol (Ethiopia), Daniel (Ethiopia), Yosef (Ethiopia). Twiddles own hair while reading a book: Molly (bio), Seth (bio), Sol (Ethiopia).

Allergic to cats: Seth (bio), Lee (bio), Daniel (Ethiopia), Jesse (Bulgaria). Horseback riders: Molly (bio), Daniel (Ethiopia).

Trombonists and attempted trombonists: Seth (bio), Lily (bio), Jesse (Bulgaria). Trumpet: Sol (Ethiopia), Yosef (Ethiopia). Double bass: Molly (bio). Flute: Helen (Ethiopia). Dancers: Lily (bio), Jesse (Bulgaria), Helen (Ethiopia). Beatboxer: Jesse (Bulgaria). Composer: Seth (bio).

First to leave the house for an outing, ready to roll: Lee (bio), Yosef "I-Was-Born-Ready" (Ethiopia).

Even with a two-hour warning that he has soccer practice this afternoon, will be jogging around the house looking for his shin guards while

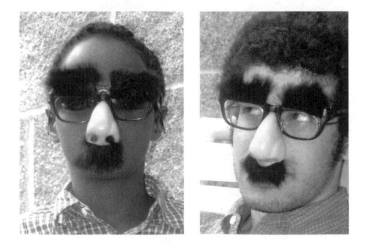

everyone waits in the idling car in the driveway: Daniel (Ethiopia, biological brother of Born-Ready Yosef).

Amharic speakers: Sol (Ethiopia), Daniel (Ethiopia), Yosef (Ethiopia), Lee (bio). Reads Hebrew: Molly (bio), Seth (bio), Lee (bio), Lily (bio), Helen (Ethiopia). Hebrew speaker: Lee (bio). Reads Ancient Greek: Molly (bio). Can kind of sing the French national anthem in French: Seth (bio), Lily (bio), Helen (Ethiopia).

Cannot swallow a pill, ever, in any circumstance: Seth (bio).

Appears downstairs seeming a little wobbly and announces: "I think I may have eaten too many baby Tylenols": Seth (bio).

Soon after arrival, spotted walking across the front yard on his hands: Jesse (Bulgaria).

Loves to cook: Molly (bio), Sol (Ethiopia), Helen (Ethiopia). Adds blueberries to scrambled eggs: Sol (Ethiopia).

Enjoys a plate of raw meat in Ethiopia: Lee (bio), Sol (Ethiopia), Daniel (Ethiopia), Jesse (Bulgaria), Helen (Ethiopia), Yosef (Ethiopia).

Helen with her grandmother, Mrs. Ruth Samuel

Gets a tapeworm from eating raw meat in Ethiopia: Lee (bio).

Stylish dressers: Molly (bio), Lee (bio), Lily (bio), Jesse (Bulgaria), Helen (Ethiopia).

"Let's play Risk!": Molly (bio), Lee (bio), Lily (bio), Sol (Ethiopia), Helen (Ethiopia). Most likely to win Risk: Molly (bio). "Let's play Scrabble!": Molly (bio), Seth (bio), Lily (bio), Helen (Ethiopia). Most likely to win Scrabble: Seth (bio), Helen (Ethiopia). "Let's play Monopoly!": Molly (bio), Lee (bio), Lily (bio), Sol (Ethiopia), Helen (Ethiopia). Most likely to be tricked by smiling brothers entering her bedroom with Monopoly, offering to play when in fact they have trapped a flying cockroach under the lid to make her scream: Lily (bio).

Overturns upholstered living-room chairs for use as soccer goals: Sol (Ethiopia), Daniel (Ethiopia), Yosef (Ethiopia).

Broken lamps, to date: two. Broken picture frames: two.

Elementary school president: Lee (bio), Lily (bio), Helen (Ethiopia).

First-place winner in science fair or social studies fair: Molly (bio), Seth (bio), Lee (bio), Helen (Ethiopia).

If entering a footrace, will win: Sol (Ethiopia), Daniel (Ethiopia), Yosef (Ethiopia), Helen (Ethiopia). Bikers: Molly (bio), Seth (bio), Jesse (Bulgaria). When shooting one hundred basketball free throws in a row, will sink eighty-seven: Jesse (Bulgaria). Bowling team members: Seth (bio), Lily (bio).

Attended Oberlin College or Oberlin Conservatory: Molly, OC '04 (bio), Seth, OCC '07 (bio), Lee, OC '07–'08 (bio), Lily, OC '10–'14 (bio).

Protested, "I don't want to go to a school that has to take me! I want to go to a school that really wants me! Can I do a 'legacy-blind' application?": Lily (bio).

Accepted at other schools, chose Oberlin anyway: Lily (bio).

Helped carry soccer team to State Cup trophy: Sol (Ethiopia), Daniel (Ethiopia). Led basketball team to middle school championship: Jesse (Bulgaria). Won national gold medal for photography: Lily (bio). Won trophy for Bowling, Most Improved: Seth (bio).

Uncanny sense of direction, in any city on any continent: Sol (Ethiopia).

Zero sense of direction, even if three blocks from home: Seth (bio).

When riding home with friends, once looked out the window and said, "Hey, now *this* looks familiar!" and his friends shouted, "This is your street!": Seth (bio). Whenever he holds a compass, the needle points toward his chest rather than toward North, causing him to walk in increasingly small circles: Seth (bio). Can't buy him an iPhone with a GPS app because the last time he got a new phone he drove straight to the neighborhood pool, happily announced, "I got a new phone!" and leaped into the water to join the family, destroying the new phone instantly: Seth (bio.)

Favorite soccer teams: Manchester United (Daniel, Ethiopia), Barcelona (Sol, Ethiopia), Tottenham (Lee, bio), Arsenal (Yosef, Ethiopia). Favorite basketball team: L.A. Lakers (Jesse, Bulgaria). Favorite baseball team: Atlanta Braves (Lee, bio).

Missed Game 7 of the 1992 National League Championship Series in which Francisco Cabrera drove in Sid Bream from second base, defeating the Pirates and sending the Braves to the World Series as announcer Skip Carey screamed, "Braves win! Braves win! Braves win!" because he was upstairs reading a biography of Miles Davis: Seth (bio).

Provided details for prior category: Lee (bio).

Runs screaming and averting the eyes from the sight of a dead squirrel on the sidewalk: everyone but Helen.

Holds up semi-decomposed dead squirrel by the tail and asks in high-pitched squeak of a voice: "May I dissect this?": Helen (Ethiopia).

Only possible future candidate for medical school: Helen (Ethiopia).

Has professional website: Molly, www.californiasislands.com (bio); Seth, www.sethgsamuel.com (bio).

Has Facebook page: everybody.

Facebook friends with Mom: Molly (bio), Seth (bio), Lee (bio), Lily (bio), Daniel (Ethiopia), Helen (Ethiopia).

Danced together joyously, arms around each other's necks, faster and faster, closer and closer, in an Israeli circle dance to celebrate Yosef's bar mitzvah last spring, laughing until they cried, faces streaming with sweat and tears, whirling until the shorter ones were nearly lifted off the ground, their legs flying out beyond the circle: everyone.

Started life in a family: Molly (bio), Seth (bio), Lee (bio), Lily (bio), Sol (Ethiopia), Daniel (Ethiopia), Jesse (Bulgaria), Helen (Ethiopia), Yosef (Ethiopia).

Through conditions far beyond the child's control, original family was lost: Sol (Ethiopia), Daniel (Ethiopia), Jesse (Bulgaria), Helen (Ethiopia), Yosef (Ethiopia).

By joining this family, through birth or adoption, family life was regained or enlarged, enlivened, and enriched: all of the above.

(Photograph by Patrick Riordan)

Acknowledgments

Yes, my children know I'm doing this.

Yes, my children have had veto power.

Yes, there are incidents that never saw print, having been throttled in the infancy of their composition.

No, I'm not going to talk about those incidents in public; that would defeat the purpose of the children having had the last word.

Note: Yosef thinks that the book is essentially a biography of his heroic life thus far, with eight siblings filling in the background through minor and supportive roles. "I'm the star of your book, right?" he asks me to confirm every week. Please try not to disabuse him of this notion.

Note: Jesse *did* grant permission for me to quote his childhood semi-Bulgarian statement regarding a swimsuit/bathroom mishap: "Penis *ne* stuck." He prefers, however, that this quotation never be repeated in polite company.

Note: The No Biking in the House Without a Helmet rule is hereby extended to outlaw Rollerblading and skateboarding in the house, even with helmets.

Thank you to: Farrar, Straus and Giroux, especially Sarah Crichton, publisher of Sarah Crichton Books, with whom it has been a joy to work;

Acknowledgments

and to Daniel Piepenbring, Kathy Daneman, Jennifer Carrow, Jeff Seroy, and Amanda Schoonmaker, who wittily sped the process along.

Thanks to: Donny, Molly, Seth, Lee, Lily, and Helen for proofreading, fact-checking, copyediting, and editing, all work provided free of charge and in great good humor. Thanks to Sol, Daniel, and Jesse, and to Garry Greene, for sharing history and memories. Thanks to Yosef for being the hero of this important sports biography. (See note above.)

Thanks to: my readers Kathryn Legan, Andrea Sarvady, Alex Kotlowitz, John Baskin, Judith Augustine, and Tema Silk for their literary sensibility, criticisms, laughter, and encouraging words.

Thanks to: the David Black Literary Agency: David, Dave Larabell, Susan Raihofer, Leigh Ann Eliseo, Joy Tutela, Antonella Iannarino, and Allie Hemphill. David, this one's for you.

A Note About the Author

Melissa Fay Greene is the author of four books of non-fiction on civil rights and on the African HIV/AIDS pandemic, a two-time National Book Award finalist, and winner of the Robert F. Kennedy Book Award, the Salon Book Prize, the Chicago Tribune Heartland Prize, and the ACLU National Civil Liberties Award, among others. Her books have been translated into fifteen languages. She and her husband, Don Samuel, live in Atlanta and (obviously) are the parents of three daughters and six sons.

Please visit her online at www.melissafaygreene.com.